Solaris 2.X

Internals and Architecture

John R. Graham

McGraw-Hill, Inc.

New York San Francisco Washington, D.C. Auckland Bogotá
Caracas Lisbon London Madrid Mexico City Milan
Montreal New Delhi San Juan Singapore
Sydney Tokyo Toronto

Library of Congress Cataloging-in-Publication Data

Graham, John R.
    Solaris 2.x : internals and architecture / by John R. Graham.
       p. cm.
    Includes index.
    ISBN 0-07-911876-3
    1. Operating systems (Computers)   2. Solaris (Computer file)
  I. Title.
  QA76.76.O63G72 1995
  005.4'469—dc20   95-10087
                                                             CIP

pbk 1 2 3 4 5 6 7 8 9 0 DOC/DOC 9 9 8 7 6 5

ISBN 0-07-911876-3

*The sponsoring editor for this book was Gerald Papke. The book editor
was Jim Gallant, and the managing editor was Susan W. Kagey. The di-
rector of production was Katherine G. Brown. This book was set in ITC
Century Light. It was composed by TAB Books.*

*Printed and bound by R. R. Donnelley & Sons Company of
Crawfordsville, Indiana.*

MH95
9118763

Contents

Acknowledgments   xi
Introduction   xiii
List of Abbreviations   xvi

Part 1   Kernel Overview

Chapter 1. The Kernel as Resource Manager   3

Process Virtual Address Space   4
The Text Segment   6
The Data Segment   6
The User Stack   7
The Kernel Stack   8
User Mode   8
Kernel Mode   9
Synchronous vs. Asynchronous Kernel Functions   10
An Example   12
Summary   13

Chapter 2. Solaris Kernel Architecture   15

Kernel Structure   15
/kernel Directory   18
Kernel Tuning Concepts   21
The /etc/system File   21
Other Entries in /etc/system   22
Summary   23

Chapter 3. System Calls and Hardware Considerations   25

The System Call Interface   25
System Call Number   26
Hardware Considerations   27
Interrupt Levels   27

The Clock Handler   28
Summary   29

Part 2 Thread Architecture

Chapter 4. Concepts and Theory of Operation   33

What Is a Multithreaded Program?   33
Why Use Threads? Or Why Not?   34
Basic Thread Concepts   35
The Threaded Model Using fork( )   35
Threaded Process Model   36
Operation of Threads   37
Lightweight Processes   39
Managing the Lightweight Process Pool   40
A Note about Threads and LWPs   41
Synchronization   41
Solaris Synchronization Primitives   42
Mutex—Mutual Exclusion Lock   43
Semaphores   43
Reader/Writer Locks   44
Condition Variables   44
Summary   46

Chapter 5. Implementation of Thread Architecture   47

The LWP Data Structure   47
The Thread Data Structure   48
The CPU Structure   50
The "Big Picture"   51
Synchronization Structures   52
Summary   54

Chapter 6. Using Multithreaded Architecture   55

Deadlock   55
Strategies for Writing Threaded Code   56
Properties of Signals in Threaded Processes   57
Signal Handling Strategies   58
The Threaded Kernel and Multiprocessors   58
Summary   59

Part 3 Memory Management

Chapter 7. Hardware Architecture   63

Definitions and Terms   63
   Virtual Memory   63
   Address Space   64
   Page   64
   Segment   66

Context   66
Cache   66
System Architecture   67
Multiprocessor Architecture and Cache Snooping   68
Performance   69
Summary   70

Chapter 8. Implementation of Virtual Memory   73

Concepts, Terms and Definitions   73
Implementation   75
The Address Space   76
Kernel Address Space   76
Segment Descriptions   77
Segment Types   78
Anonymous Memory   79
Copy-on-write (COW)   80
Pages   80
The Virtual Memory Roadmap   81
Summary   83

Chapter 9. Global Memory Management   85

Global Paging Concepts   85
System Paging Strategy   86
Swapping Control   88
Summary   90

Part 4   Process Management

Chapter 10. Scheduling Concepts   93

Definitions   93
Tightly Coupled vs. Loosely Coupled OS   93
Symmetric vs. Asymmetric Multiprocessing   94
Preempts and Interrupts   95
Real-Time vs. Bounded Dispatch Latency   97
Fundamental Scheduling Concepts   97
Scheduling Implementation   98
Priority   99
Scheduling Classes   100
Process States   101
Scheduling   102
Summary   103
Addendum for Solaris 2.4   103

Chapter 11. Scheduling Class and Process Lifetime Implementation 105

Scheduling Class Implementation   105
The Proc Structure   107
The User Area   108
The "Big Picture" Revisited   108

Process Creation with the fork( ) System Call   108
Steps in Process Creation   110
Process Termination   112
Process Cleanup with wait( )   113
Creating a New Process   114
Summary   115

Chapter 12. Process Scheduling   117

The Dispatch Queues   117
The Turnstiles   118
Thread Scheduling   119
Preemptive Scheduling   120
CPU Selection in an MP Architecture   121
The Final Scheduling Pieces   121
Interrupt Handling   122
Priority Inversion   123
Use of dispadmin(1M) to Control Scheduling   124
Summary   127

Chapter 13. Real-Time Programming   129

Components of Dispatch Latency   129
Basic Guidelines for Running Real-Time Applications   130
Runaway Real-Time Processes   131

Part 5   File System Management

Chapter 14. File System Architecture   135

The Vnode (Virtual Node) Structure   135
Virtual File System (VFS) Structures   137
Looking Up Files   139
Local Structures and Links   140
File Descriptors   140
The open( ) System Call   141
Summary   142

Chapter 15. File Systems   143

File System Types   143
The BSD Disk-Based File System   145
System V Enhancements and EFT   148
Pseudo File Systems   149
   /proc File System   149
   Virtual Swap Implementation   152
Performance and Swap Partition Size   153
Summary   154

Chapter 16. File System Operations   155

Data Structures for File Systems   155
     Superblocks   155
     Cylinder Group Structures   156
     Directories   156
     Inodes   158
Filename Lookup   160
Read and Write System Calls   161
Tuning Read Ahead with maxcontig   164
Summary   165

Part 6   Solaris Network Architecture

Chapter 17. Network Implementation   169

Networking Technology   169
Network Driver Implementation   170
What Is a Stream?   171
Streams and the Network Interface   172
Transport Independent RPC   172
Transport Layer Interface (TLI) Programming   174
IP Multicasting   174
Kerberos Authentication   175
Network Parameter Tuning   175
Summary   177

Appendices

A. Tutorial for Using adb   179

B. Code and Shell Script Examples   189

C. Data Structure Summary   207

Glossary   209
Bibliography   213
Index   215
About the Author   223
Disk Instructions   223

Acknowledgments

There is new science emerging these days known as *chaos*. Chaos has been made popular by the movie *Jurassic Park* and the books *Complexity* by Mitchell Waldrop and *Chaos* by James Gleick. Chaos is not really new, it is a new way to look at some traditional problems. Chaos study dictates that no problem stands alone. You cannot examine a local weather phenomenon without looking globally; physics is not possible without mathematics, or for that matter economics. The same is true with operating systems. You cannot examine the scheduling subsystem without examining the virtual memory mechanisms or file I/O operations. What I have tried to present with this version of an internals and architecture book is a broader view of the interaction of the subsystems. This presentation has been made at the sacrifice of some of the details of the various data structures and algorithms, but what has been added are pictures and explanations that help to show the bigger picture. This approach has been tested over the past five years as I have taught this subject and other related subjects to many different audiences. To that end, I would like to dedicate this book to all of those students who have taught me more than I have ever taught them. I hope you will find this book interesting and enjoyable.

On a more personal note, I would like to thank my inspiration and support staff: my daughter, Sarah, my wife-to-be (or wife depending on when this is published), Dian, my friend Priscilla, and my dog, Wyatt, whose greatest joy in life is to sit in my lap while I sit at the keyboard.

Introduction

Since its beginning in 1969 as a project of AT&T, the UNIX operating system has grown to a very large established base of over a million sites at universities, businesses, scientific research sites, and made some inroads into the home computing base. The attraction of the system is its ability to span all of these architectures, from PC to mainframe, and provide to the user a consistent interface and predictable results.

The various shells (Bourne, Korn, C...), electronic mail, connectivity through **uucp**, text formatting programs (**nroff, troff**...), in short, the user interface and utilities are the things attractive to a user. A person can sit down at any UNIX based machine and reasonably expect the same interface and response to a given sequence of commands. With the advent of POSIX (Portable Operating System Interface), COSE (Common Operating System Environment), SVID (System V Interface Description), and other standards, the expectation of commonality is even greater.

The other part of the operating system that the user does not see is commonly referred to as the *internals* of the operating system. What are the programs and support routines in place that perform the user tasks and how do they work? Those programs and subroutines are the subject of this book. The book will concentrate on the implementation of the System V Release 4 (SVR4) of UNIX as implemented by Sun Microsystems in their release of SunOS 5.x. There will be a detailed examination of the data structures and algorithms that activate the user tasks. The difficult part of writing a book of this nature is attempting to find the appropriate target audience. This book has been reviewed by a representative group of people and there seems to be three basic categories of readers for a book of this type.

1. An experienced programmer (probably a C programmer, maybe C++), who has been using UNIX or SunOS for a while and wants to know the new features provided by SunOS 5.x, Threads, real-time programming, and process scheduling to name a few.

2. Someone who has a familiarity with SunOS or other version of UNIX internals and wishes to compare that knowledge with current Sun technology.

3. An experienced applications programmer who wants to know how the internals work and how to write programs to take advantage of the architecture.

I think each group will find something of value in this text. The first chapter starts with some basic concepts, such as how system calls work and the function of the kernel, which more experienced readers may want to pass over. For those interested in specific examples and performance comparisons, there is an appendix and a companion disk of code sample that will demonstrate most of the essential points made in the chapters.

It is important to note that it is not essential to have access to Sun source code to understand the details of what is happening. The data structure descriptions come from the header files found in the standard distribution and the algorithms come from white papers, conference proceedings, the AnswerBook, and other publicly available resources. The target of this book is to provide a common reference where all of the pieces are tied together.

Structure of this Book

The overall objectives of this book, then, are twofold: to provide understanding of the inner workings of the operating system and to provide useful programming tips, where possible, to take advantage of that understanding. To that end, the book is organized in six major parts, each examining a major subsystem of the kernel. These are followed by three appendices.

Part 1—Kernel Overview

Part 2—Multithreaded Architecture

Part 3—Virtual Memory Architecture

Part 4—Process Management

Part 5—File I/O Management

Part 6—Network Architecture

Appendix A—Tutorial for using **adb**

Appendix B—Code and Shell Script Examples

Appendix C—Data Structure Summary

Ideally, each part of this book would stand on its own, without relying on the other parts, so a reader could choose the topic of interest. Unfortunately, with a topic such as internals this is very difficult. For example, since the basic scheduling entity is a thread and not a process, it would be difficult to grasp scheduling concepts without understanding threaded architecture.

Therefore, each part is further broken down into several sections. This first chapter within each part will describe the basic "theory of operation," while subsequent chapters will examine the actual implementation of that theory. The theory of operation chapter will describe basic concepts, definitions, and flow of information without too much concern for specific data structures. If you are interested in process management only, you could read the theory of how threads work and get a good enough idea of the concept of threads to understand the scheduling. If you do decide to read a section thinking that you know *most* of the ideas that will be presented, a helpful reference section will be the Glossary. By using the Glossary, you will be able to gather a quick understanding of a term without reading an entire section.

There are three appendices that provide what I believe to be the real reason you may use this book. Appendix A contains a tutorial/introduction to the uses of **adb** in crash dump analysis. After having read about all of the data structures and algorithms, **adb** can help you actually read the kernel road map and see what has happened. Appendix B will provide some code examples that actually take advantage of the knowledge that has been gained, including threaded code, access to the /proc file system, and the **mmap( )** call. Each of the programs shown are complete and have been compiled and tested on a SPARCstation 2. Timing and benchmarks, when shown, are also from an SS2.

Why Do I Care?

A question that comes up often when discussing internals of an operating system is: "What good is this to me as a user or a programmer?" The feeling is that the operating system has been in use by programmers for a very long time and they are content to let the OS do its magic. Unless you have access to operating system source code and intend to modify the code, the answer to this question is not intuitively obvious. A parallel objective of this book is, whenever possible, to provide examples where the particular feature being examined is being utilized to the best advantage. This may be a piece of code that runs faster or is simply easier to code and understand. By understanding how the system works and seeing an example of the principle in action, programmers can better ply their craft. For example, there will be a description of the virtual memory subsystem as implemented by Sun. This is an excellent example where a programmer can improve performance by using the **mmap( )** routine to utilize the VM architecture directly and speed things up.

This approach is very useful, but there will be times when understanding will have to be enough. For example, the interface to device drivers will be explained, but unless you intend to write a device driver, the techniques used will not be of a lot of use to the application programmer. A close examination of the path from a user program to a device driver routine (a stack trace, for example) would show a series of function calls that do not appear to be the most obvious or direct path. Yet, this is a portion of the kernel operation that must be accepted as is and there is little a programmer can do to take advantage. In the end, I think there is something for everyone interested in a better understanding and more efficient implementation of systems programming techniques and hopefully, it is presented in a way that is direct and enjoyable to read.

Finally, I would like to add that although this is a technical book, writing is an intensely personal endeavor. I understand there will be reactions to this book concerning both style and content. I have tried to write in the style that I teach, a style that has served me well over the last several years—that is brief, to the point, and at times entertaining. I hope that is an opinion shared by my readers.

List of Abbreviations

ANSI	American National Standards Institute
COSE	common operating system environment
COW	copy-on-write (see Glossary)
CPU	central processing unit
Gb	gigabytes (1,024*1,024*1,024)
GID	group identification
K&R	Kernigan and Ritchie
K	kilobyte (1,024)
LWP	lightweight process
Mb	megabytes (1,024*1,024)
MMU	memory management unit
MP	multiprocessor or multiprocessing
MT	multithreaded or multithreading
nfs	network file system
OOP	object oriented programming
OW3	Open Windows Release 3
PID	process identification
POSIX	Portable Operating System Interface
PPID	parent PID
rfs	remote file system
RPC	remote procedure call
SVR4	System V Release 4
TCP	transmission control protocol
TI-RPC	transport independent RPC
UDP	user datagram protocol
ufs	UNIX file system
UID	user identification
VAC	virtual address cache
VM	virtual memory

Kernel Overview

1

The Kernel as Resource Manager

The traditional UNIX operating system supports the notion that a file has a *place to live* and a process has a *life* [1]. These two notions and the two entities involved, a file and a process, are still central concepts to the SunOS operating system. The purpose of the kernel is to act as a resource manager to control the needs of these two items.

The kernel is needed to manage these resources primarily for two reasons:

- The resource is in limited supply and multiple requests for access must be controlled (one disk drive, one serial interface, one network interface,...)

- The resource is critical or shared and user access to the resource must be controlled (shared memory, message queues, process data structures,...)

Some other examples of resource that must be protected by the kernel include the following:

- CPU
- Memory
- Disk drives
- Network
- Profiling timers
- Time-of-day-clock
- Interprocess-communication
- Other processes

In short, the function of the kernel is to make critical or protected resources available to the user process in a *safe* manner. This idea of resource management leads to

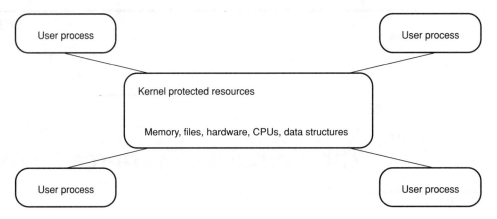

Figure 1.1 Kernel as resource manager

the first approach at a block diagram for kernel functionality. Figure 1.1 will be refined as more concepts about kernel operation are added.

Here are some examples of a process requesting a system resource or service:

- A process will need a file (**open( )** system call) and access to the data that is stored there (**read( )** system call).
- A process will communicate with another process or machine via the network. (**socket( )** or **t_open( )** system calls).
- A process desires to communicate with another process via shared memory (**shm_at( )** system call).
- A process needs to start another process (via **fork( )**) and communicate with open files.

Notice that any request for system services is made through a system call. The function of system calls is to request system services. Anytime a process needs a system service or resource, a system call must be made and the kernel will run on behalf of that process to acquire the service or resource. This leads to an important concept: the distinction between kernel mode operation and system mode operation.

While the kernel is running on behalf of a user process to acquire a resource, the process is running in *kernel* or *system* mode. All processes run in either kernel mode (also known as *system mode*) or in user mode. The transition from user mode to kernel mode is made via the system call and the transition from kernel to user mode is made when the system call returns.

Process Virtual Address Space

Since the kernel's function is to make a protected resource available to a user process, it is useful to understand what resources are available at any given moment, i.e. in user mode or kernel mode. To do that, we will examine the process address space of typical process. Figure 1.2 shows the virtual address space layout of a process. In other words, what does the program look like while it is in execution?

This first thing to note is that this is a *virtual* address layout. This means that the addresses shown do not have any relationship to the underlying physical memory locations. For a given invocation of the process, a virtual address will remain the same, for example the virtual address of a variable, but the physical address (page frame number in RAM) will be different. At this point we, are concerned with what the virtual address map looks like. The concept of mapping virtual memory to physical memory is covered in Part 3.

The next thing to notice is the size of the virtual address space. The addresses range from 0 to 0xffffffff. This number was not random, it is 32 bits, which is the largest size of all addresses in current Sun hardware. This was not always true nor will it continue to be true. Older hardware (Sun-3) had only 28 bits for the largest address and in the future, 64-bit addresses will be the standard. Thirty-two bits translates to four gigabytes (4Gb) of virtual address space.

Also, note the order of the various pieces of the address space, labeled in Figure 1.2 as text, data, and stack. Each of these pieces is known as a *segment* and all Solaris processes will have these segments laid out in exactly the same order. A segment is a range of contiguous virtual addresses. A *process address space* is a collection of such segments. The actual layout of the segments is a well-known format called *ELF* (extensible linking format). For readers familiar with older versions

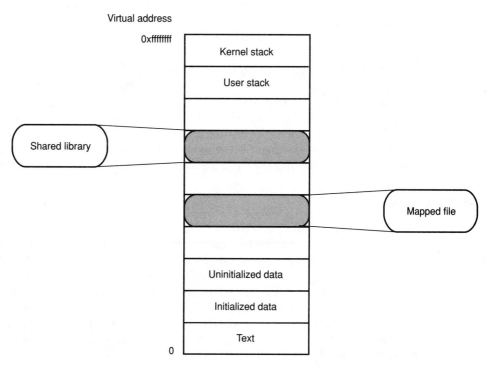

Figure 1.2 Virtual address space of a process

of UNIX, ELF is slightly different in implementation than older formats such as *coff* or *a. out*, but the concept is the same.

At this point, it is important to note that each segment has a specific purpose and set of characteristics. The usefulness of these characteristics will be made clear as the book progresses. For now, we will look at the contents of each segment that will be the same regardless of virtual address format.

The Text Segment

The first segment, the one with the smallest virtual address is known as the *text* segment. The text segment contains the actual executable instructions as they were assembled from assembly source code. The assembly source code probably came from the compiler that translated the C (or FORTRAN, or COBOL, or ...) code into assembly source. No matter where the instruction came from, the assembly language instruction was then translated into 0s and 1s and found their way into the text segment. The important properties of the text segment are: it is read-only, it is shareable, and it is backed up by the file system. Read-only simply means code cannot be executed that writes to the addresses that define this segment. When this happens, normally the program will receive the **SIGSEGV** (segmentation violation) signal and the process will terminate.

The idea of shareable means that this segment may be reused by another process. For example, if one user starts the **vi** editor, and then another user starts the **vi** editor again, there is no need to create a new text segment for the second invocation, the original segment will be reused. This is accomplished by mapping the same piece of physical memory (which contains the text segment) into more than one virtual address space.

The last property mentioned, the segment being backed up by the file system is important when we start discussing paging and swapping. When system resources get low and it becomes necessary to make room in memory for other activities, the kernel will move certain pieces of segments out of main memory. Since the text segment has not been changed since it was first used (it is read-only), and we know where to find a copy of the original (in the file system), it will not be necessary to save a copy of this segment, in other words, it does not require a copy to the swap area.

The Data Segment

The contents of the data segment seem reasonably obvious from the name. If you guessed that the data segment contained data, you would not be far off. To be precise, the data segment is divided into two sections: initialized data and uninitialized data. The *initialized* data is global variables that have been assigned an initial value at the time the program was compiled. The initialized data segment is writable, private (non-shareable), and is initially backed up by the file system.

Private means that each invocation of a process will get its own data segment. This should make sense, since in the above example using **vi**, the data segment is the file being edited. It is not very useful to have two different invocations of **vi** editing the same file. The initial contents of the initialized data segment will come from the compiled (**a.out**) file. As the data changes and the system requires room in main memory, the updated segment will be copied to the swap area.

Uninitialized data has all of the same properties of initialized data except that its initial content will be zero. If this is a C language program, all global and static variables that are not given initial values will appear in this segment. Other languages will also store the global variables in the uninitialized data segment. Since the content is all zeros, there is no need to store that information in the compiled file and a block allocation of zeros will be made when the program starts rather than when the code is compiled.

In the virtual addressing scheme, the pieces of the data segment start at the next appropriate address after the text segment ends and grow as needed. This portion of the process image is also known as the *heap*. The heap can grow and shrink as the process continues toward completion. For example, when a shared library is linked in, the run-time loader will allocate a piece of virtual address space starting at the top of the heap. Any time the program encounters the **malloc( )** call, the library routine will allocate a piece of virtual address space starting at the top of the heap. Similarly, when a piece of memory is **free( )'d** , the top of the heap may be moved to make room for new allocations.

The User Stack

If the text segment has all of the instructions and the data segment has all of the data for the instructions to work on, what is left for the stack? Basically, the stack contains the *user context*. The context is all of the information needed to keep a process running. Such information includes:

- Contents of the hardware registers
- Program counter
- Arguments to the current function or system calls
- Local data for the current function
- Return values for the system call

Swapping out a process is like removing a car from the road while it is running to relieve a traffic jam. The problem is that we want to restore the car to the same state it was running in when it was removed. In the case of a process, the definition of the state, or context, is stored in the stack.

The stack is writable, private, and built entirely from (virtual) memory allocated as needed. In other words, no portion of the stack can be found in the original file that was used to start this process. A typical scenario for stack allocation may go like this:

- When a process is started, the arguments passed to the **main( )** function with the C language; **argc, argv,** and **envp**; are pushed onto the stack.
- Any local declarations for variables in **main( )** are pushed onto the stack.
- If a function is called from **main( )**, arguments to the function are pushed onto the stack and any local variables used by the function are pushed onto the stack.

- On return from the function, the arguments and the local variables are popped from the stack and any return value from the function is pushed onto the stack.

- When **main( )** exits, any value passed to the **exit( )** function is pushed onto the stack for the shell to read using **echo $status** (C shell) or **echo $?** (Bourne shell).

Just as the heap starts at the low address and grows toward the higher addresses during execution, the stack starts at the high address and grows toward the lower addresses during execution. The addresses between the top of the heap and the bottom of the stack are known as the *hole*. Any allocation of stack or heap must come from the hole.[1] If the top of the heap and the bottom of the stack should ever meet, meaning the size of the hole is zero, then no new allocations can be made. This may be the case when the error messages such as "Stack overflow" or "Malloc failed" appear.

The Kernel Stack

As Figure 1.3 shows, the user stack does not start at the highest address (0xffffffff). Rather, it starts at a slightly lower address (typically 0xE0000000) and there is some other information in the higher addresses. This highest address portion of the virtual address space is known as the *kernel stack*. The name kernel stack is a slight misnomer because all of the kernel program (text, data, stack, and other kernel segments) is mapped into this area. The kernel program, stored in **/kernel/unix**, is a program just like any other program, with its own text, data, and stack segments. The function of the kernel segments is the same as the segments for a user process except the stack must keep track of system-wide activities rather than individual processes. This means there is code for the scheduler, device drivers, system calls, interrupt handlers, DVMA (direct virtual memory access), and various tables needed to assist the kernel in its job.

Mapped into every process virtual address space is a copy of the various kernel segments. The use of this portion of the address space comes into play when a process enters kernel mode. The distinctions between kernel mode and user mode are examined next.

User Mode

When a process is running in user mode, it will use local data, locally mapped files, and a local stack. In short, the process will have all of the resources it needs to continue stored in the addresses below where the user stack starts. This is important because if all of the resources are available in user address space, they can be accessed very quickly compared to accessing kernel resources.

For example, a local memory mapped file can be accessed up to 100 times faster than executing read or write system call on the same file. The actual performance

---

[1]As it turns out, the virtual address space will have some *holes* in it because allocations may not be released in the same order they were allocated. This means new allocations may succeed even when the size of the hole is zero. In reality, a message such as "Stack Overflow" would occur from a runaway recursive function and the swap space would be used up before all of the 4Gb of virtual memory space.

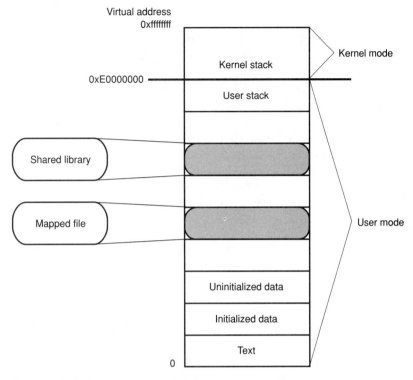

Figure 1.3 Virtual address space revisited

gain depends on many factors, such as architecture and network performance, but the comparison is still valid. Later, when threads are discussed, we will discover that a local thread context switch executes three to five times faster than a kernel context switch and faster than the traditional **fork** and **execv** system calls. This is because threads are a local resource, not a kernel resource and no kernel intervention is required.

Kernel Mode

When a process is running in kernel mode, it is running using a shared image of the kernel. All other processes running in kernel mode are also using this shared image and therefore things do not happen as quickly. A common example is a group of processes all requesting access to the same disk drive or even the same file. All of these processes will be operating in kernel mode, but since there is only one shared kernel and one disk drive, each process will have to wait its turn for access to the file.

This example is similar in nature to the previous examples where separate instances of a process such as **vi** are using the same text segment. The difference is that in the case of **vi**, a *user* segment is shared and therefore no kernel-managed resources are affected. Since each set of user resources is unique to that invocation of the process, there is no conflict. When two processes share a kernel-protected resource, the kernel must arbitrate access.

The kernel also controls access to software data structures as well as hardware. System V IPC (interprocess communication) shared memory segments, sockets or TLI endpoints, and process data structure are all examples of kernel resources that will be very slow compared to locally accessed resources.

When a process is running in kernel mode, all of the information the kernel needs to continue on behalf of your process must be contained in the kernel stack segment of the address space. This means that before a system call can make the transition from user mode to kernel the arguments to the system call must be transferred from the user portion of the address space to the kernel stack. Also, when the system call returns, the results of the system call are stored in kernel space and must be copied back to the user stack or, in the case of an error, the error status must be copied back. Figure 1.3 revisits the virtual address space diagram (Figure 1.2) and summarizes the ideas of kernel context and user context.

Notice that there is an additional item in the diagram, the address of the boundary between kernel space and user space. In Figure 1.3, it has been shown to be 0xE0000000. There is a document, called the *ABI* (Application Binary Interface) that specifies how the actual address space layout will look. The objective is to define the way a binary image looks so it can be portable at the executable or binary level. The ABI specifies that for SPARC architecture the kernel address space will start at an address no less than 0xE000000. This means that in the 4Gb address space, no more than 512Mb will be allocated to the kernel map. The actual starting address of the kernel map will vary according to architecture and for a particular kernel the boundary can be found by examining the kernel variable **KERNEL-BASE_DEBUG**. The primary usefulness of this value is to determine if a particular address is in user space or kernel space.

Synchronous vs. Asynchronous Kernel Functions

Generically, the kernel is divided into two portions, one which deals with *synchronous* activities and the other to deal with *asynchronous* activities. A synchronous activity is one that was caused by a direct request from a process. Such requests come in the form of system calls. An asynchronous activity is one that occurs without a user context. Normally, an asynchronous activity is some form of interrupt. Responding to system calls (or service requests) is one major function of the kernel and is an example of a *synchronous* activity. It is synchronous because the kernel acts directly as a result of a system call made by a process.[2]

The kernel must also respond to interrupts from devices. These interrupts occurred because a process requested a service from a particular device and when the interrupt occurs, the process must be notified that the service is ready. However, the interrupts do not have any knowledge of the source of the request. The request was started by a process and the kernel is simply notified when the device access is complete. This is an example of an *asynchronous* activity. Asynchronous activities are those caused from outside a particular process. Other asynchronous events include

---

[2]The number of system calls can also be used as a measure of how much work the kernel is doing or helping to determine if the system is being slowed down by too much kernel work. Using the **vmstat** command you can determine how many system calls were made during a certain time period.

some signals such as **SIGKILL** and **SIGINT**. Figure 1.4 summarizes the synchronous and asynchronous event handling of the kernel.

The picture of the kernel as a resource manager is now complete. There are three major modes of operation that must be regulated by the kernel: processes in user mode, processes in kernel mode requesting access to kernel services and devices, and responses to asynchronous events that typically (but not always) come from hardware devices. Each of these types of activities uses a different part of the process address space and each has different run-time characteristics.

A process in user mode is scheduled by the kernel and assigned a priority. Associated with that priority is a period of time that the process will be allowed to run before it must give up the CPU to another process. This period is known as a *time-slice*. Generically, the scheduler will select the highest priority process, assign it to a CPU and let it run. However, at any time, a higher priority process may enter the picture and take over the CPU, or *preempt* the currently running process. While in user mode, all of the resources a process needs are in the user portion of the address space.

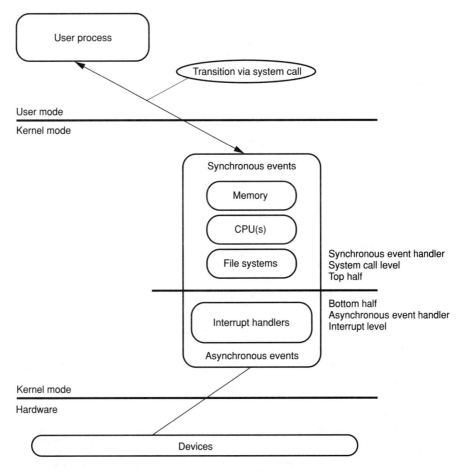

Figure 1.4 Asynchronous vs. synchronous kernel activities

A process in kernel mode runs exactly the same way, except that it is not given a time-slice. Kernel mode processes are still assigned a priority and may also be preempted by higher priority processes.[3] Kernel mode processes will run using the kernel stack portion of the virtual address space or kernel context.

The third category of tasks, response to asynchronous events, is handled in much the same way as a kernel task. An asynchronous event, such as an interrupt from a device, will be assigned to a thread and run at a very high priority. This is a major change from previous version of SunOS (see Footnote 3). In the past the ability to schedule an asynchronous task was not possible because there was no context with which to operate. The interrupt happened outside the context of the currently running task and outside the context of the task that started the device request, so there was no way to schedule such an event. The handler would stop the current task for a moment, handle the event, and then current task would return to its job. With SunOS 5.x, the asynchronous event will be assigned to a context (within a thread) and then run. Now, the interrupt handler can do all of the things an ordinary process can do.

There are exceptions to this scheme that will be examined in the process management section, but the model is basically complete. All of the user mode tasks, kernel mode tasks, and asynchronous events handlers are assigned priorities and the highest priority task will run first. If another task becomes runable and has a higher priority than the current task, a preemption will occur and the new task will continue.

An Example

We have introduced a great many concepts at this point and it may not be obvious when these actions occur. The following is a typical example of the use of the concepts described.

1. A process, running in user mode, makes a **read( )** system call. This would happen, for example, if the **cat <file>** command were executed. A request is made to the kernel to fetch the data from a file. Making the read system call puts the process into kernel mode because it is asking for access to a controlled resource (the disk drive). One of the arguments to the **read( )** call is a buffer where the results of the read will be stored on return from the system call (return to user mode). This buffer is a local resource that can be used when control is returned by the kernel.

2. The kernel must then execute the internal calls to find where the data for the file is located and go to the device where the data is stored.

   The kernel will then call the appropriate device specific routines (inside the device drivers) to initiate the hardware activities to retrieve the data. The time

---

[3]For those familiar with previous release of UNIX or SunOS, this is a major change. Historically, UNIX kernels are not non-preemptible. Processes desiring access to the kernel normally would have to wait until the currently running process returned to user mode before preempting. This became the primary reason a process could not run *real-time* on a SunOS/UNIX based system; *immediate* (or reasonably fast) access to a CPU could not be guaranteed. Now any process of higher priority that becomes runable will be able to preempt any other process, regardless of user mode or kernel mode status.

spent doing actual device access is fairly long in relative terms. Typical device access time (disk for example) is on the order of 15 milliseconds. In that amount of time, a CPU running at 40 MHz can run about 600,000 instructions ($40 \times 10^6 \times 15 \times 10^{-3} = 600 \times 10^3 = 600{,}000$)!

Rather than have the kernel simply spin CPU cycles and wait for the device to complete its work, the kernel will suspend operation of that process and work on something else. This is known as putting the process to *sleep*. At this point, the kernel will give up use of the CPU and any other (user or kernel mode) tasks may run.

3. When the device has completed its task, the kernel will be notified via an *interrupt* and the kernel will then wake the sleeping process so it can continue. The interrupt routine will run at a very high priority that can preempt any other lower priority tasks currently executing. The function of the interrupt routine is to place the sleeping process back into execution for completion of its original request. In this case, the request is a read so the data fetched from the disk will be copied back into user space and the return from the system call will take place.

Summary

This chapter has provided some insight to the basic structure of a process and kernel operations. At this point, the reader should have an understanding of:

- The differences between user mode and kernel mode operation
- The differences between preemption and interruption
- The differences between synchronous and asynchronous events
- The structure and function of the segments in a process virtual address space
- The types of resources managed by the kernel
- The function of system calls

The general operation of the kernel is described well in [1] and [2]. Both of these references, however, are based on different versions of UNIX. More insight on the interrupt handling can be found in [4], [5], and [9].

2

Solaris Kernel Architecture

The previous chapter has provided a very high-level view of what the kernel does and introduced some terms and concepts that are important for future understanding. In this chapter, we will look at the overall architecture of the kernel itself, the major subsystems involved, the directory structure for kernel modules, how to change behavior of the kernel by changing system parameters, and some general debugging techniques for examining the kernel.

Kernel Structure

For the most part, this book will not be looking at the past methods for kernel operation except where the change is dramatic and pointing out the differences is helpful to the understanding of the new operations. The structure of the kernel is such a case. Under SunOS 4.x, the kernel program was a large statically linked program stored by default in a file named **/vmunix.** As Sun continued its various releases from 4.0 to the latest in the series 4.1.3, this program grew progressively larger as the functionality of the kernel grew. The kernel (with a generic configuration) at release 4.1.3 is about 1.9Mb! As the file grew larger, the amount of memory required to run the kernel operations, and thus memory not available for non-kernel processes, also grew.

The other problem with the large kernel program was that it included support for many features that a given installation may never use. In this case, the system administrator was faced with the task of configuring, recompiling, and relinking the kernel. While this was not an overwhelming task, it was non-trivial and time consuming, and also required that the system be stopped and rebooted for the changes to take effect. These steps also had to be followed *every time* a kernel change was needed.

Under SunOS 5.x, the large kernel program has been replaced with a much smaller static core kernel program and a directory of loadable modules. With this model, the static core, stored in the file **/kernel/unix**, is much smaller, about 900K.

This means at boot time only the 900K of memory is allocated and locked down. These pages are used more efficiently also, since the core kernel in **/kernel/unix** contains only the pages required to run the kernel and no more. In other words, the static core does not contain support for any devices.

The model that is used now is very similar to the shared library model introduced in SunOS 4.1. In the shared or dynamic library model for processes, a process does not link libraries into its virtual address space when the program is compiled. Rather, a reference to the library and the specific library call is put into the program. When a particular library call is encountered the library is mapped into the process by the run-time loader (**ld.so**) and the process will continue using the mapped library. In other words, the process of linking a library to a program happens when the program runs rather than when the program is compiled. This technique is known as *dynamic linking*.[4]

There are several benefits to using dynamic linking. First, the actual compiled program is smaller because the library is not part of the program. It becomes another mapped segment at run-time. Next, overall system memory needs are smaller because libraries not used are never called into memory. Also, since the library will be shared by any process using that library, there only needs to be one copy of the library in memory, which is then used by any and all processes needing it. These improvements save disk space because the compiled image (the **a.out** or **elf** file) is smaller and saves memory usage. Figure 2.1 shows an example of how the shared library model maps files into more than one process.

The disadvantage of this model is that when a call is encountered for a function that is part of a library not currently loaded into memory there will be a delay while the library is fetched and loaded into memory and then mapped into the process. This performance hit is absorbed only by the first process to load a particular library, since other processes using the same library will share the original copy. For those processes not wishing to take this performance penalty, libraries can still be linked in a *static* fashion as they previously were. Due to the saving of using dynamically linked libraries, dynamic linking is the default.

A model very similar to the shared library model for processes was used to build the kernel process. When the system boots, the only thing that is loaded is the static core, which is stored in the file **/kernel/unix** (by default), or the kernel file specified during the boot process.

/kernel/unix contains only that part of the kernel needed to get started. Parts not included are device drivers, streams modules, scheduling modules, and file system modules. As each of these modules is needed, it will be loaded into the kernel address space much as the shared library is loaded into a process address space. Figure 2.2 shows an example of the kernel stack with several loaded modules.

---

[4]The other method for linking libraries is known as *static linking*. With static linking, the libraries are linked at compile time.

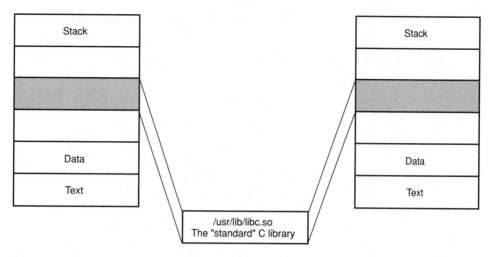

Figure 2.1 Shared library model

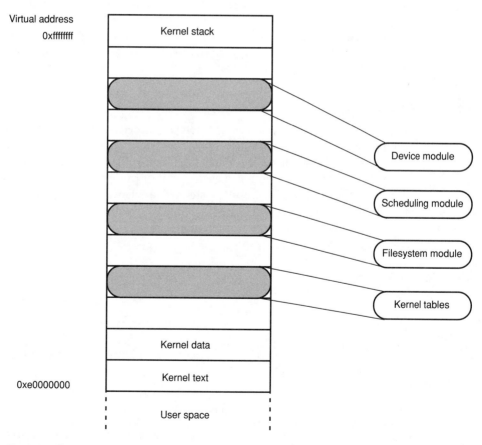

Figure 2.2 Static core and loadable modules

This model for kernel loading has the same advantages as the shared library model does for individual processes:

- Memory will be saved because the kernel itself is smaller and modules not needed will not be loaded.
- Disk space is saved because the kernel is smaller.

Since this is the kernel, there are some additional savings to be realized using this model.

- Booting is faster because a smaller file (**/kernel/unix**) is being loaded.
- Kernel configuration is not needed because **/kernel/unix** is already minimum configuration. New device driver or software modules are loaded into the directory and the system is rebooted. Modules will then be available as needed.[5]

The disadvantages of this model for kernel building are the same as the shared library model. The first time a kernel module is loaded, the process initiating the load will have to wait for the kernel to load that module. This penalty is the same as the penalty paid by the first process that loads a shared library. This penalty can be avoided by making an appropriate entry in the system configuration file **/etc/system** (using the **forceload** keyword). We will take a look at the **/etc/system** file later in this chapter.

/kernel directory

Looking in the **/kernel** directory will give you a very good idea of the overall kernel architecture and its various subsystems. The list of modules available for loading is listed in the **/kernel** directory. Each subdirectory has a collection of similar type modules. A complete description of each module is too lengthy to list here and changes with each release of the operating system. The following lists the /kernel directory and a brief description of the types of modules in each listing (as of release 5.3).

```
listing of /kernel directory
drv        - device drivers
exec       - executable file formats
fs         - file system types
sched      - scheduling classes
strmod     - streams modules
sys        - system calls
misc       - miscellaneous modules (DES, ipc, virtual swap..)
```

This directory listing is further explained by Figure 2.3, a block diagram of the SunOS kernel architecture.

---

[5] SunOS 5.x currently supports several different types of loadable modules; device drivers, scheduling classes, streams drivers and modules, and system calls. The most common type of module to be added is the device driver that can be added *without* rebooting the system by using the **add_drv(1M)** and the **modload(1M)** command. The other may require rebooting.

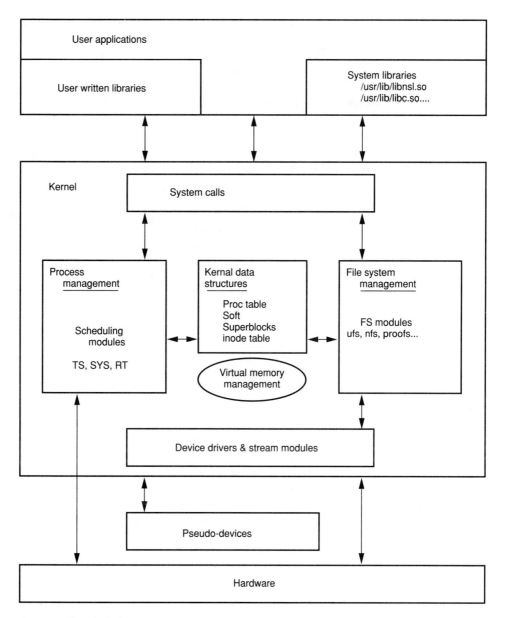

Figure 2.3 Kernel block structure

There are some things to note about Figure 2.3. First, the transition from user mode to kernel mode, as noted earlier, is made via system calls. Note that system calls are part of kernel code, not user code. All user written libraries, as well as libraries provided with the system, such as the network services library (**/usr/lib/libnsl.so**) and the standard C library (**/usr/lib/libc.so**), are part of user code. It is true that code provided in these system libraries may make system calls, but the code is still part of the user portion of the address space.

Next, note that there are still the two major components of the kernel: modules that relate to process management (a process has a *life*) and modules that relate to file system management (files have a place to *live*). Process management functions include scheduling (**/kernel/sched/***), System V type IPC (**/kernel/sys/semsys, /kernel/sys/shmsys**), signal handling, and process creation. Normally, the only hardware directly accessed via the process subsystem are the CPUs through the scheduler. Not every kernel function has a separate module in the **/kernel** directory. This means that the code for that function is part of the static kernel core (**/kernel/unix**) and does not need to be loaded.

File system management is responsible for access to various hardware through device drivers. It is important to note that although device drivers are actually linked into the kernel, and in that sense part of the kernel code, the kernel itself has no real idea about device specifics except how to access an appropriate entry point in the driver. This means the kernel does not have code in the static core that understands a SCSI tape drive, for instance, but the kernel does know how to access that tape drive via the driver entry points.

Not all device drivers manage real hardware. Although they have been around for a while, *pseudo-filesystems* and *pseudo-devices* are used more extensively in SunOS 5.x. A pseudo-device is simply a device that does not have real hardware backing it up. An example would be a device driver that accessed a piece of software such as a device emulator. The driver appears to the system as a normal hardware access and only the driver knows that a piece of software is being *driven*.

There is one other part of the block diagram for the SunOS kernel that is not found in traditional UNIX block diagrams, the Virtual Memory (VM) subsystem. Virtual memory is the ability to address more memory than exists in the physical memory (RAM). In other words, it *appears* to the process that there is more memory than there actually is. In the case of SunOS, it appears that there is 4Gb of addressable memory. The idea of virtual memory is not new and Sun is not the first vendor to implement use of virtual memory. However, Sun does provide the unique ability to use virtual memory to link the file system, devices, and processes into one manageable piece. This is done via the **mmap( )** library call.[6] In this way a file, even a device file such as **/dev/fb** (the frame buffer) can be mapped into the user address space and appear as a local resource to the process rather than a protected kernel resource. Since the resource is local and access through the kernel is not required, access is much faster. As it turns out, this mapping scheme is used everywhere by both users and the kernel itself to speed up operations. Since this is such an important part of the operating system, an entire section is devoted to it later.

The last major piece of the architecture to be discussed is the box labeled "Kernel data structures." These are items that are used by both the file system and the

---

[6]Although the idea of *mapping* objects, such as shared libraries and kernel modules has been discussed, this is the first mention of the actual call **mmap( )** that performs this operation. **Mmap( )** is the fundamental operation in Sun's virtual memory scheme and will be discussed at great length in the Virtual memory discussion.

process control modules to do their jobs. Kernel data structures include proc structures, inodes, superblocks, vnodes, address space structures, segment structures, and
many more. One of the main objectives of this book is to describe the most important
data structures that the kernel will access. For reference, all of the data structures
that will be described are defined in one of the header files in **/usr/include** and
usr/include/sys.

Kernel Tuning Concepts

One of the purposes of rebuilding the generic kernel supplied with the SunOS 4.x
systems was to change kernel variables to make system tables larger, to allow a
greater number of files, or more of a certain type of data structure such as semaphores or other System V IPC (Interprocess Communication) types.

One issue with changing kernel variables is understanding the effect of making
such changes. For instance, under SunOS 4.x there is a maximum number of
processes that the system may have running at any given time. This number was
stored in a kernel variable named **nprocs**. The number stored in the variable was
used to size an array of type **struct proc**. Every new process needs to allocate a proc
structure in order to begin its execution and the array is used as a pool from which
new processes could draw that particular resource. In SunOS 4.x, this array was
sized and statically allocated at boot time and added to the kernel heap in much the
same way a user program allocates space using the **malloc( )** library call.

If at any time all of the proc structures were in use, a message would appear saying "Proc table full". If this problem continued to happen, the solution was to have
the system administrator build a new kernel in which the variable **nprocs** would be
set to a higher value. This was done by looking in a file named **param.c** and making
the correct C code adjustment. This method worked fine, but there were some draw-
backs. First, the question comes up concerning how large you make the table. You
did not want to pick an arbitrarily large number because that would make a very
large table that added to an already large kernel. Remember, a larger kernel takes
away memory which then cannot be used by user processes. Additionally, the administrator adjusting the value had to understand C code. In this example the
change is easy, but not all changes were as trivial, nor were the consequences of all
changes so obvious.

The last issue with changing or tuning kernel parameters under SunOS 4.x was
that the list of available parameters to change was very small. There are a great many
values that could improve performance if adjusted properly, but are not so easily
changed. Such changes may require knowledge of the not-so-friendly debugger, **adb**.

Expanding on the model of allocating resources only when needed, SunOS 5.x has
introduced a new way to tune kernel parameters (via the **/etc/system** file) and a
new way to allocate system tables such as the proc table described above.

The /etc/system file

Under SunOS 5.x, the concepts for tuning the kernel are exactly the same. There is
still a list of variables, such as **max_nprocs, ufs_ninode, maxusers**, and others

that can be changed to help the performance of the system. However, there are some important differences. First, kernel variables that used to control the sizes of static tables no longer have the same function. For example, **max_nprocs** (same function as the old **nprocs**) no longer controls the size of the process table. **max_nprocs** is now used as a *high water mark* to indicate that no more processes can be started. The use of a high water mark means that initially there is a very small table or perhaps no table at all. During the operation of the system, the table will grow dynamically, as needed, up to the size of the high water mark. Attempts to grow the table larger than the high water mark will result in the familiar error messages, such as "Proc table full" in the case of **max_nprocs**.

The philosophy for this is the same as for loadable kernel modules and shared libraries: resources, in this case a table, are created only as needed. The other advantage, is that since there are no static tables created as part of the kernel, these sizes or high water marks can be changed using **adb** and the system will not have to be rebooted.

The **adb** method[7] for setting the system variables is the same as under 4.x. Use **adb** to change any kernel variable you need, except now when you change a variable that affects a high water mark and not the size of a table, you will not have to reboot the system.

SunOS 5.x provides an easier way to change variables if you can accept the requirement of rebooting. Values may be set in a configuration file that will be read when the system is rebooted. The default file in which to make these changes is **/etc/system**. By default, the file that comes with the system is empty (not really empty, but containing only comments). To change a value using the **/etc/system** file, you need to put a line very similar to Bourne shell syntax for setting a variable. The following shows some sample entries for an **/etc/system** file (without the comments).

```
forceload: rfs
exclude: rt
moddir: /kernel /usr/kernel
set max_nprocs=500
set maxusers=64
set ip:ip_forwarding=0
```

In this sample, **/etc/system** file, the variable **max_nprocs** is set to 500. This means that up to 500 process may be started at one time, but there will *not* be an array of 500 proc structures allocated for that purpose. Also note the setting of other variables in the **/etc/system** file. In theory, all variables in SunOS 5.x can be changed using the file. This is a double edged sword, since changing values without sufficient knowledge of the consequences can be very dangerous in terms of system performance.

Other Entries in /etc/system

The **/etc/system** file can also be used to improve performance for other system activities. As noted before, the various kernel modules are loaded on demand as they

---

[7]**adb** is a general purpose debugger that is shipped with all releases of SunOS and is the only method available for patching and debugging the kernel. Techniques for use of **adb** and examples for crash analysis and kernel tuning are provided in Appendix A.

are used by the system. This load will result in a performance penalty for the first process that uses the module. This performance penalty can be avoided by forcing the module to be loaded at boot time regardless of its ultimate usage. The **/etc/system** file is the place to take care of that.

When the *forceload* line is encountered, the named module will be loaded. The exclude line will prevent the named module from being loaded. The **/etc/system** file is read exactly once when the system is booted. Any changes made in the **/etc/system** file will require that the system be rebooted. The only way to make changes to kernel values without a reboot is to use **adb**. Changes made using **adb** should also be made in **/etc/system** so they will remain in effect when the system is rebooted.

The line *moddirs: /kernel /usr/kernel* is very similar to using a PATH environment variable in your shell. It will direct the kernel to search an alternate directory location when searching for a module to load.

Module loading is accomplished using the **modload**, **modunload**, and **modinfo** commands. If you want to force a particular module to be loaded without rebooting the system, you will need to issue a command such as:

```
#modload rfs
```

If you are making major changes to the default **/etc/system** file, you should make a copy of it and modify the copy. You can then ask the kernel to read the modified file at boot time instead of the original. This is done using the $-a$ option on boot. The $-a$ stands for *ask*. When booting with the $-a$ option, the loader will ask you which configuration file you wish to read to set up the system.

Summary

This chapter has introduced the overall architecture of the Solaris kernel and how the idea of shared libraries has been used to make the kernel more efficient and easy to reconfigure. We also took a look at how to adjust system parameters and what the effects of changing some of the parameters can have. As the book progresses, many system variables will be defined that can be used to tune the system as your particular site needs dictate.

3

System Calls and
Hardware Considerations

On the surface, at least from the programmers view of the world, making a system call is no different than calling any other function. Clearly, though, an ordinary function call does not initiate a trap to the kernel, change the mode of the CPU, or any of the other things that must occur to gain access to a kernel resource. This chapter examines the details of what happens when a system call is made.

Although this book is not about hardware or how SPARCstations work, there are some basic hardware concepts and considerations that need to be introduced so the remaining chapters have more meaning. We will take a look at hardware interrupt levels, the time-of-day clock, virtual address cache, and the role of the MMU.

The System Call Interface

When a process makes a system call, which is any function detailed in section 2 of the SunOS Reference manual, the first step is to invoke a *wrapper* that is found in the standard C library. The purpose of this wrapper is twofold. First, it hides the implementation details from the programmer, and second, it is an aid to portability across releases.

Unlike ordinary user written library routines, system calls are kernel code, either statically linked to the kernel program or loaded as needed when called. This means that an ordinary user function does not have access to the kernel code implementing the system request. To make this request transparently, a wrapper has been written which, when called by the user, will begin the transition to kernel mode, coordinate the return, and set up the return values. The wrapper executes the following steps:

- It places the system call number into one of the global registers.

- Executes the SPARC **trap** instruction. The trap instruction will change the execution mode from user mode to kernel mode. The trap instruction will invoke the kernel trap handler routine.

- The trap handler will invoke the routine **syscall( )** to handle the system call.

- When the system call returns, the wrapper examines the registers for return values and returns to the user.

The real work of the system call is done in the internal routine **syscall( )**. **Syscall** is called with two arguments: the trap type and a copy of the registers. For system calls, the trap type should be type 0 (**ST_OSYSCALL**) or type 8 (**ST_SYSCALL**). These trap types are defined in **/usr/include/sys/trap.h**. The only time type 0 will be used is when trying to run an old SunOS 4.x (BSD) type program. Trap 0 is used to indicate that the system call number is old and will have to be remapped to the new system call number. Trap type 8 is the usual way SunOS 5.x calls **syscall( )**.

System Call Number

The system call number is an index into the system call entry table, the sysent array, for short. The actual table is stored at the kernel symbol **sysent[ ]**. The table is an array of struct sysent. The declaration of a struct sysent can be found in **/usr/include/sys/systm.h**

```
struct sysent {
        char sy_narg;          /* number of arguments *
        char sy_flags;         /* flags */
        int (*sy_call)();      /* the actual function address */
        krwlock_t sy_lock;     /* lock for loadable calls */
}
```

The system call number assigned to a particular system call can be found in **/usr/include/sys/syscall.h**.[8] When the wrapper for a system call is entered, the system call number, or index into the sysent array, is placed in one of the registers and extracted by the **syscall( )** routine to fetch the arguments and invoke the code for the system call. The pseudo-code for the **syscall( )** routine follows.

```
syscall ( type,rp) {
    fetch the address of the code from the sysent[] entry;
    fetch the number of arguments from the sysent[] entry;
    copy the correct number of arguments from the user stack frame;
    make the actual call;
    Check for errors;
    if error was due to interrupt or signal {
            check restart flag to restart call;
                - OR -
            return error (EINTR);
    else /* some other error */
            set return value and error;
    }
    check for signals and process (ISSIG);
    check for preempts (cpu_runrun);
}
```

---

[8]There is also a file, **/etc/name_to_sysnum**, that is used to map system calls to system call numbers. Code for a sample system call module and the modifications needed for this file are shown in Appendix B.

From a user perspective the system call number is useful because system call may be made directly, bypassing the wrapper, by using the system call number. There is a library call **sycall(3B)** that takes as an argument the system call number of the system call you are interested in. (This will not be confused with the internal routine **syscall** whose entry point is **_syscall**.) Notice this is in the library (3B), the BSD Compatibility library functions. This means that this interface may not be supported in future releases and probably should not be used. This is certainly a sound idea because bypassing the wrapper and trapping directly to the kernel is not a good idea. What would happen if the next release changed the system call numbers?

Hardware Considerations

One of the things that must happen each time a trap or an interrupt occurs is that the machine context must be saved. The machine context or state includes the values of the registers, the program counter (PC), and the *processor status register (PSR)*. The PSR is a 32-bit word that contains, among other things, the state of the CPU (supervisor[kernel] mode or non-supervisor[user] mode), the current interrupt level, the carry bit, the overflow bit, the zero bit, whether traps are enabled, and whether there is a floating point unit (FPU). For a detailed description of the PSR, look in the file **usr/include/sys/psw.h**. Of these fields, the one we are most interested in now is the processor interrupt level (PIL). The PIL is very important because it will dictate exactly what can occur on a particular processor at any given instant.

Interrupt Levels

The interrupt level is a number ranging from 0 to 15 (on a SPARC CPU). The interrupt level is a machine(CPU) dependent feature and is used to synchronize processes wishing to access common critical resources. The interrupt level is used to block routines below a certain level. For instance, if the interrupt level is set at level 7, any other task wishing to operate at level seven or lower will be blocked until the interrupt level is lowered.

Typically, this situation occurs when dealing with device interrupts. For example, the tape drive may interrupt at level 5, which means that while the interrupt is being serviced any subsequent interrupt at level 5 or less will be blocked until the interrupt service request (ISR) is complete. Figure 3.1 shows the typical interrupt levels on a SPARCstation.

Although the specific interrupt levels are machine dependent, for example the range is from 0–7 on a Motorola 680X0 and 0-31 on most Digital Equipment Corporation (DEC) hardware, the principles are the same. There are some things to note about Figure 3.1. First, the level 10 interrupt, labeled "clock" is the basic timer on the SunOS system. This interrupt will occur 100 times per second, also known as a "tick." Note that the serial communications interrupt is at level 12. Serial communications interrupts typically come from modems and other serial devices connected to the tty ports. What will happen if a clock interrupt (level 10) occurs when a level 12 ISR is being serviced? The answer is that the clock interrupt may be lost!

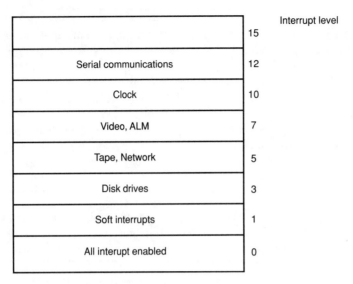

	Interrupt level
	15
Serial communications	12
Clock	10
Video, ALM	7
Tape, Network	5
Disk drives	3
Soft interrupts	1
All interupt enabled	0

Figure 3.1 Interrupt priority levels on a SPARC CPU

The Clock Handler

Since so many things key off of the clock ticks, it is useful to examine in some detail what happens when the clock ticks occur. The function **clock( )** gets called from the clock interrupt handler and performs the following steps:

- Updates the CPU time for active (currently running) threads
- Updates system, user and idle time for the CPU
- Updates the time-of-day
- Checks the callout queue for work to do
- Updates system statistics (used mainly by routines like **vmstat, iostat, swap**…)
- Notifies scheduler
- If a clock interrupt came in while doing all of this, starts again

These tasks seem straightforward and the only new concept is the *callout queue*. The callout queue is a linked list of functions that are scheduled to be run sometime in the near future, where *near* is defined as a number of ticks. The functions that are on the callout queue are those that need to be run in a timely fashion, but not necessarily at the high interrupt priority level of the clock. Typically, things that are on the callout queue are functions like watchdog timers, pager activities, and other device driver utilities. Functions are placed on the callout queue by calling a kernel support routine **timeout(9S)** and removed from the callout queue by calling **untimeout(9S)**.

The callout queue is actually a linked list of **callout_t** structures (see **/usr/include/sys/callo.h**). Generically, the structure contains the function to run, arguments to pass to the function, a time to run, and a pointer to the next member of the list. Also, the number of elements on the callout queue must be managed. In the past, a fixed size table of size **ncallout** was allocated and if too many functions were placed on the callout queue a panic could result. Under the current implementation, the callout queue is increased as needed when more functions are placed on the queue. As the callout queue entries are used up, a chunk of additional **callout_t** structures are allocated, where a chunk is 1K/(size of **callout_t**), roughly 36 structures. This leads to the configuration shown in Figure 3.2.

At this point, we are trying only to introduce the concept of the callout queue. When we look at the algorithms for paging and scheduling, the callout queue will be discussed again.

Summary

In this chapter, we have examined the mechanism used to make system calls, what a system call number is, and how it can be used. We have also examined some of the

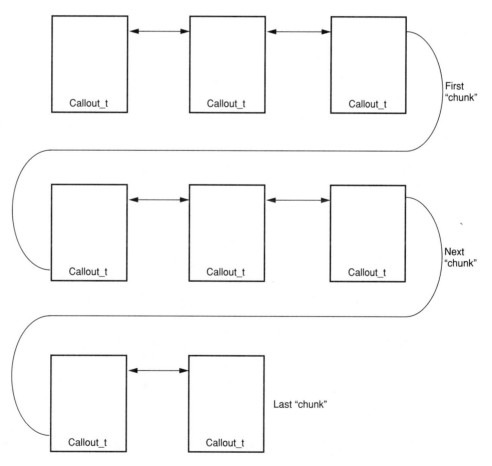

Figure 3.2 Callout queue structures

hardware considerations, such a priority interrupt level, clock interrupt, and the callout queue. The idea of using the priority interrupt level to synchronize processes will be revisited when we examine threads. The code for an actual system call is shown in Appendix A, along with a discussion of how to pass parameters and get return values from a system call.

Thread Architecture

4

Concepts and Theory of Operation

A thread is a sequence of instructions to be executed within a program. A traditional UNIX process has one thread that starts with **main( )** and ends with the **exit(2)** system call. In this sense, all programmers are familiar with the idea of a thread. If several programs are to be used to accomplish a single task or a series of tasks, a programmer will use multiple threads of control. Such multiple threads of control have traditionally been achieved using the **fork( )** system call, while order of execution of each thread (program) was controlled via signals or some other method.

The objective of the following three chapters is to introduce the concepts of threads as implemented by SunOS, the definitions and properties of threads, how to synchronize threads, and most importantly, how the ideas of threads have been used in the SunOS kernel to achieve best performance. This section will not examine any particular kernel thread, but rather give the idea of what a thread is and how it works. Subsequent chapters will examine specific threads and their functions.

This chapter will examine the theory and concept behind threads while, the following two chapters will examine the internal implementation of threads and then some sample user level programs, programming strategies, and debugging hints. Initially, the concept presented will apply to user programs written using the threads interface. On the surface, this may not appear beneficial to understanding the kernel. However, the kernel is a program very much like a user level program in its structure and function. So in this sense understanding user level threaded applications will provide insight to how the kernel does its job. This is particularly helpful since we are not showing any SunOS source code.

What Is a Multithreaded Program?

To understand a multithreaded program, it is necessary to understand what constitutes a thread. As stated before, a thread, or a thread of control, is simply a series of executable steps. Normally, a program has a unique path through the code that defines the thread of control. A thread of control, in other words, is a program in execution. Each thread contains all of the information required to continue its existence, i.e., the stack, the text, and the data segments we examined before. Generally, a process is not accessible from another process, the content of one process stack is not known to other processes and processes execute independently of one another. Of course, there is a whole series of system calls that make such knowledge and communication possible, but without such exceptional help, communication is not possible.

A multithreaded program is a process that contains more than one thread. Each thread within the program acts like a mini-program with exactly the same properties previously attributed to processes.

- Each thread is independent of every other thread.
- There is no way to predict the order of execution or the order of completion of the various threads.
- The number of threads in a program is unknown to other threads.
- Threads are invisible from outside the program.
- Threads have their own identity, i.e., stack, PC (program counter), registers, priority.

As mentioned before with processes, there is a set of calls, in this case library (not system) calls that will enable the various threads to communicate and share information, but the default is that each thread is a stand-alone entity.

Threads communicate via library calls and processes communicate via system calls. If nothing else, based on what you know about system calls and the resources required to run a system call, you should guess that thread communication and execution is faster than process interaction, and your guess would be right. We will look more in detail at the implementation of threads, but for now the important concept is that a thread is a local resource not a system resource. This concept leads to some interesting properties of threads.

- Threads are independent of each other, but actions a thread may take, such as make a system call, will affect other threads in the process. For example, opening a file in one thread makes the file open for all threads.
- Since threads are all part of the same process, sharing data is very easy; all threads have access to global data.
- Exiting a thread (via **exit( )**) will exit *all* threads.

So we can see that threads are a local resource and each thread within the process has its own identity and path of execution, but each thread also has access to the process-wide resources we looked at earlier.

Why Use Threads? Or Why Not?

The question arises, "If threads are the same as processes, why use threads?" This seems a fair question, since at first glance it appears that use of threads does not add new functionality, only a new way to use a model that has been in use for some time. As mentioned before, since threads are a local resource and not a kernel resource, use of threads is faster. To some, this may not be enough incentive to redesign their program. In addition to the speed of threads, here are some additional reasons to use threads:

- Improved efficiency on uniprocessor systems. Normally, when a process encounters a *slow* system call (one that would normally block until completion such as **read( )** or **write( )**), the entire process will stop until the service request is complete. If a program is threaded, only the thread making the request will block. All other threads will continue. This is a large bonus on uniprocessor machines because there is no context switch when the request is made and because it will allow multiple requests to be made from one process without waiting for previous requests to complete.

- Use multiprocessor hardware. With a multiple CPU architecture (SPARC 10, SPARCcenter 1000, SPARCcenter 2000), if a process is not threaded, it will run on only one processor at a time. In other words, there will be no advantage to having multiple processors if your program cannot use more than one CPU at a time.

- Improved throughput. With threads it is a very simple matter to implement asynchronous I/O, that is an I/O request that does not block. This was achievable on earlier releases, but not in such a straightforward manner.

- Program structure. The ability to create a threaded model makes the design of a program a bit more difficult, but results in a more logical design. For example, a window application may allocate one thread to each button on the window. This sort of design becomes easier to maintain if developed properly.

As with most new features, there is a wrong way to use threads. There are two common cases when creating a thread would not be appropriate. First, although threads and thread creation is very cheap, it is not free. Creating a thread that has only 5 lines of code, for example, would not be useful. The second case is creating a compute bound thread on a uniprocessor architecture. If there are many threads in a process that are doing I/O (or any *slow* service request), the threads library will automatically switch between threads to start all of the requests. Conversely, if a thread is compute bound, meaning it uses up all of the time slice without doing any *slow* service requests, then other threads in the same process will starve.

Basic Thread Concepts

At this point, we want to begin to examine the fundamental concepts regarding the internal implementation of threads and how they are used in the SunOS kernel. This will include the ideas of thread creation, synchronization, and lightweight processes.

The Threaded Model Using fork( )

Since a thread of control is a sequence of steps to be executed, a process is a thread. Any task that is completed using more than one such thread can be considered *mul-*

tithreaded. Prior to SunOS 5.2, the only way to accomplish such threaded tasking was to use the system call **fork( )** to create the new thread. The implementation details of what happens with the **fork( )** system call is the subject of Chapter 11 (Scheduling Class and Process Lifetime), however, at this point a preview would be in order.

All processes in SunOS are the result of a **fork( )** system call.[9] Basically, a **fork( )** copies the virtual address space and the new address space (the *child* process) will begin execution on its own. The child process stands on its own and will perform all of its activities independent of its parent. The order of execution and completion of the parent and child processes are not dependent on each other in any way (unless the programmer wants them to be). Each process has its own entry and exit point and a well defined set of steps in between. In this sense, they fit the definition of a thread.

Several processes created in this manner could then communicate via open files, pipes, shared memory segments, or mmap'd files. Figure 4.1 summarizes the traditional model.

The most important thing to notice about Figure 4.1 is that each of the communication methods shown requires use of a system call [**open( ), read( ), write( )** for files; **pipe( )** or **popen( )** for pipes; **shm_get( )** and **shm_at( )** for shared memory segments]. As we have seen, each use of a system call requires intervention by the kernel and can therefore be fairly slow compared to accessing user resources. To achieve the true independence that a new process allows, we are sacrificing some performance.

Threaded Process Model

In the threaded process model, a process no longer has a single entry point and a single exit point. There will be multiple entry points and for each entry point, exactly one exit. Between each entry and exit point there is a discrete set of executable steps to be performed. Each set of steps is called a *thread* and the communication between various threads within a process is accomplished via user resources, not kernel resources. Each thread within a process is independent and separately executable, but since each thread is part of the same process, communication between threads is much simpler and faster. Figure 4.2 summarizes the threaded process model. As Figure 4.2 shows, the shared memory portion is simply a piece of global data.

What does any of this have to do with kernel operation or design? The kernel is a program with the same features and problems of an ordinary program with many, many responsibilities. The kernel must process I/O requests, schedule processes, allocate shared memory segments . . . and so on. Starting with SunOS 5.0 the kernel was a threaded program. This means that instead of a large monolithic program (such as **/vmunix** under SunOS 4.x), the kernel is now a collection of various threads that operate independently (such as **/kernel/UNIX** and the loadable modules of the **/kernel** directory). This means each thread can operate independently and not have to wait for the completion of a piece of the kernel that does not affect

---

[9]To be precise, there are three processes: the pager, the swapper, and the init process that are *handcrafted* at boot time. For purposes of this discussion, though, it is safe to say all processes are born from a **fork( )**.

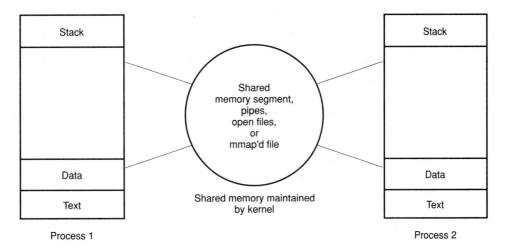

Figure 4.1 Basic process model

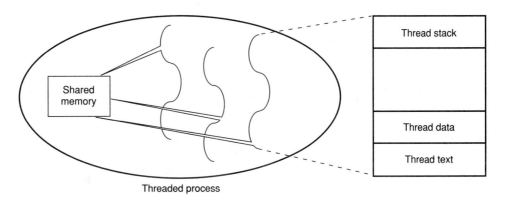

Figure 4.2 Threaded process model

the current request. For example, processing an I/O request is separate from a scheduling request so they may be assigned to different threads. The true benefit of this design becomes apparent with multiprocessor architectures. The I/O request and the scheduling request cannot be processed at the same time!

Operation of Threads

There are three areas that must be examined in terms of the implementation of threads: the user interface, the kernel interface, and the transition between the user mode and kernel mode. When a user creates a thread via the **thr_create(3T)** library call, some allocation is made in the user address space seen earlier. This allocation of space is strictly a library function and does not impact kernel operations directly. In other words, the user (the programmer) may create as many threads as desired and the kernel will have no knowledge of such creations.

On the kernel side, the kernel itself creates a thread with the **thread_create(9S)** kernel support routine, some kernel data structures are allocated to make the kernel thread runable. At any given moment, there is a pool of runable threads that must be scheduled to run on the pool of available CPUs.

At some point though, the set of steps associated with the user thread must be executed. This will require allocation of a CPU and thus a kernel request is made to schedule the thread. When a user thread becomes runable, that thread must be allocated the same structures as the kernel threads and be put into the pool of runable threads. This is accomplished by mapping a user thread onto a kernel thread via a structure called a *lightweight process*.

This is a summary of the operations to make a user thread runable:

- The *kernel* provides a pool of lightweight processes (LWPs) that are scheduled to run by the kernel on the pool of available processors. Each lightweight process will map to exactly one kernel thread.

- The *thread library (**/usr/lib/libthread.so**)* will select an available user level thread to run on the pool of available LWPs. The *library* will also ensure that unblocked threads will run. If a running thread becomes blocked, the library will choose a runable thread to continue processing.

- The *programmer* is responsible for ensuring there is at least one unblocked thread available for execution. A *process* is not blocked until all the threads within the process are blocked.

Figure 4.3 shows the overall scheme.

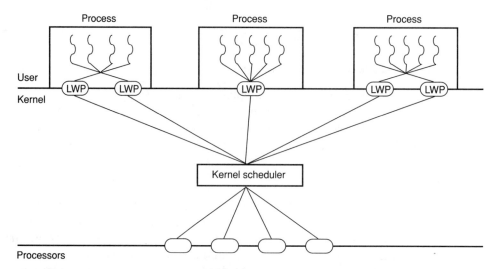

Figure 4.3 Threads, LWPs and scheduling. These ideas are discussed in [4] [5] [6] and [7]. When reading those papers, though, note that they are based on SunOS 5.0 and not the current release 5.3. The concepts are the same, but the function calls and data structures discussed will not be current.

The important thing to note here is that one user thread will use exactly one LWP and one kernel thread. When a user is finished, the LWP will be preserved and potentially used by a different user thread, perhaps even a thread from another process.

Lightweight Processes

With the user level interface to threads programming, namely the library calls found in **/usr/lib/libthread.so**, the user is provided a set of functions that transparently multiplex the various runable threads. In the end, the threads must become known to the kernel so the tasks can be scheduled onto the system processors. Since the focus of this book is not the user interface, the discussion of the implementation of threads will begin with the interface between the kernel and the user, namely the lightweight process (LWP). For now, it is okay to think of the threads library as a user-level scheduler for user threads. The threads library will select a thread (or threads) to run and will build an LWP with the identity (priority, PID, UID ...) of the thread to be run. LWPs are in turn mapped onto kernel threads that are scheduled for execution by the kernel. LWPs are kernel entities (data structures) that have properties of their own:

- LWPs share process space and resources.
- One LWP may execute on different CPUs during its lifetime.
- LWPs are independent of other LWPs.
- Each LWP may run independently on a processor. Therefore, a process with many LWPs may use many processors. In this sense, the LWP appears to the process as a *virtual CPU*.

The threads library and the LWP interface provides for two different types of (user) threads, *bound* and *unbound*. By default, the library will automatically multiplex between the various unblocked threads. This means that the LWP structure can be reused by as many different threads as needed. Such threads do not care which LWP is used and are called *unbound* threads. A thread is unbound by default when created by **thr_create(3T)** unless otherwise specified.

The *programmer* may choose to bind a thread to an LWP for performance reasons. This means that each time that particular thread runs it will always reuse the same LWP data structure and no other thread will use the LWP. These are called *bound threads*. Bound threads and unbound threads may be mixed in the same program.

The reason behind having bound and unbound threads is that it allows programmer flexibility. Creation of an unbound thread is faster than creation of a bound thread, but the thread bound to an LWP will never have to wait again for the creation of an LWP or for an LWP to become available. Additionally, bound threads have the ability to create their own signal stack, or put themselves into a different scheduling class than the original process.

As far as the kernel is concerned, there is no knowledge of an LWPs affinity to a particular thread. The kernel only sees the data in the LWP data structure and uses that information to schedule the thread. The contents of the LWP structure are filled in by the thread library. From the user perspective, having more LWPs means having more CPUs available to work on your program, since each LWP is a schedulable item. In this sense, an LWP can be viewed as a virtual CPU since it *appears* that you have all of the LWPs working toward completion of your task.

Managing the Lightweight Process Pool

Since LWP data structures are part of the kernel address space, it is important to manage the size of the LWP pool to not clutter the kernel area. On the other hand, it is important to have enough LWPs available so a thread will not be blocked due to lack of LWPs. Using the threads library, the size of the LWP pool is managed with two objectives in mind:

- Create enough LWPs so a program will not starve from lack of LWPs.
- Do not leave idle LWPs around to clog the kernel resources.

The first objective is accomplished by using one of the new signals introduced in SunOS 5.x, **SIGWAITING**. If all of the LWPs of a particular process are blocked then the kernel will send the signal **SIGWAITING** to the process. The **SIGWAITING** signal will be handled by a function in the threads library that will determine if the process contains any runable threads. If there are any runable threads, the library code will create a new LWP and assign the waiting thread to the new LWP for execution.

The second objective is achieved by *aging* the LWP. If an LWP becomes idle due to the exiting of a thread or because the thread started an I/O call, for example, the library will search for another thread to assign to that LWP. If no such thread is available, the thread is marked idle and a timer will start. If the LWP remains idle for a period of time (currently set at 5 minutes), the LWP will be removed by the kernel.

With all of this in mind, here is a summary of the steps for manipulating LWPs and unbound threads.

1. A process will start and the threads library will create as many LWPs as needed to execute unbound threads.

2. The LWP will assume the identity of the thread including registers, PC, stack, and priority, and execute the thread instructions.

3. If the thread becomes blocked, the thread library will select another (unbound) thread not currently assigned to an LWP, to run on the newly available LWP.

4. If all current threads (and therefore the associated LWPs) are blocked, the kernel will send the process a **SIGWAITING** signal. The library provides a handler for **SIGWAITING**. The handler detects if there are any runable unbound threads. If so, the handler will create a new LWP for that thread and map it to the runable thread.

5. When a thread is completed, the library will look for other runable threads not currently bound to an LWP. If any exist, the newly freed LWP will assume the identity of the new thread and continue execution. If there are no runable threads, the LWP becomes idle. If an LWP is idle for 5 minutes, it will be destroyed by the library.

The only difference with a bound thread is that the LWP will not age nor be removed, nor will another thread ever be assigned to run on that LWP until **thr_exit( )** or **exit( )** is called.

A Note about Threads and LWPs

In general, the user does not have to be concerned with the number of LWPs since the described mechanisms will, under normal circumstances, ensure that there are enough LWPs but not so many that they would take up kernel resources unnecessarily. However, the programmer interface does provide a means to manually increase the number of LWPs with **thr_create(3T)** (using the **THR_NEW_LWP** flag) or **thr_setconcurrency(3T)**. There are several reasons why the user may want to create additional LWPs.

The default is to create a new LWP each time a thread is created, but if the threads become blocked for a period of time, the LWP will age and be removed. When the threads become runable again, there may not be an LWP available for use. If there are any threads running, the previously described **SIGWAITING** mechanism will not happen and the newly unblocked thread will starve due to lack of an LWP. The solution is to create an LWP with **thr_setconcurrency(3T)**.

Another situation where a new LWP should be created is when a thread has some resources that will not be shared with other threads. Such sharing would occur if the LWP was used for several different threads. In these cases, the user would explicitly create a bound thread (**thr_create(3T)** using the **THR_BOUND** flag) so the resources would not be shared. Examples of this are:

- To start a real-time thread. In order to achieve best results for a real-time thread, it must be set up so the thread will not have to wait for allocation of an LWP. This is accomplished by creating a bound thread.

- When use of an alternate signal stack is needed. Normally, there is only one signal stack for the entire process and therefore one set of signal handlers. If you want a new thread to handle a signal differently than all of the other threads, it must be assigned its own signal stack on its own bound thread.

- When a thread needs a unique timer or alarm. The signal indicating that the timer has expired may not be sent to the correct thread.

It should be noted that the decision to use a bound or unbound thread, or to create or not create an LWP, are user design decisions and not really kernel issues.

Synchronization

When using the multithread model using **fork( )** and **exec( )**, one major task was communicating between the several processes. This was normally done using an open file, a named pipe, a System V IPC mechanism (shared memory, message queue, or semaphore), or an mmap'd file. When using the threaded model and the threads library, the communication between threads is accomplished in a much simpler fashion. Since all the threads belong to one process, they each have equal access to global data.

By default, threads do not have knowledge of or know the identity of other threads in the process. Even though the threads are independent, different threads may want to modify the same data or communicate via some piece of shared information. In the SunOS kernel, this occurs quite often with various kernel data structures. For example, if there are two processes being created via the **fork( )** system call, both calls will result in access to the list of proc data structures. It is essential that the same proc structure is not allocated to two different processes! For this reason, there must be a means to control access to such critical data or code. Such control is termed *synchronization*. This section will describe the types of synchronization primitives used by the SunOS kernel and the kernel interface for using the primitives.

Solaris Synchronization Primitives

The SunOS 2.x Threads library currently supports four different synchronization primitives.

- Mutex locks
- Counting semaphores
- Reader/writer locks
- Condition ariables

Synchronization primitives are implemented as data structures within the process address space. These data structures may be in global memory or inside a file that can be mapped in and thus live beyond the life of the process. There are basically only two operations that can be used on synchronization primitives or locks: **acquire** and **release**. A typical sequence for using the primitives would go as follows:

- Cooperating threads wishing to access a piece of data or code will attempt to *acquire* the lock protecting the data. If the thread cannot acquire the lock, the thread will block. If the thread can acquire the lock, then all other threads attempting to acquire the lock will block.
- When a thread has finished use of the data or completed executing the critical code, it will *release* the lock, thus unblocking other threads.

There are two very important aspects regarding the use of locks. First, all threads or processes using locks must *cooperate*. If a lock is not checked, or is checked and ignored using **mutex_tryenter(9S)**, there are no mechanisms in the library or the kernel to prevent unauthorized access. Second, use of locks is possible only if the lock can be tested and set in one *atomic* operation. An atomic operation is an instruction or a sequence of instructions that cannot be interrupted. If the test/set function could be interrupted, it would lead to the following (dangerous) sequence of steps:

1. Process A would test to see if a lock were available and found out the lock was currently unlocked.
2. Process A is interrupted and Process B would test the lock, see that it was still unlocked and set the lock and assume ownership of the lock.

3. Process A would continue, under the assumption that the lock was not set, set the lock and continue as if it owned the lock.

4. Since Process B has assumed the lock was set and owns it, there are now 2 processes executing thinking they have unique access to the protected resource.

The SPARC assembly language has an instruction to perform the atomic test and set operations that will prevent the above unfortunate sequence; the **ldstub** instruction (**ldstub**—load/store unsigned byte).

The remainder of this section examines in more detail the functionality of the synchronization primitives. The next chapter will examine the actual data structures and library interfaces for each primitive.

Mutex—Mutual Exclusion Lock

A mutex is essentially a binary indication that a lock is in use. The intent is that exactly one thread/process may own the lock and all others attempting access to the lock will block or fail until the lock is released. Mutexes are the fastest and most memory efficient of all of the synchronization types. The basic kernel functions to acquire and release the lock are **mutex_enter(9F)** and **mutex_exit(9F)**. For those familiar with the user threads interface, these calls are different in syntax, but not semantics, from **mutex_lock(3T)** and **mutex_unlock(3T)**. Mutexes are the most common form of synchronization primitive used by the kernel. This is for two reasons: first, the most common synchronization problem is that of multiple threads trying to access the same data or code segment; second, the use of condition variable requires use of a mutex, as we will see shortly.

Semaphores

Counting semaphores were originally described by E. Djykstra in 1968, who defined the operations for semaphores. If the reader is familiar with the use of traditional System V kernel supported semaphores, they will find that the functionalities of the user and kernel support routines are exactly the same. Rather than a binary value as with a mutex, semaphores may be set to an initial value and the value may be incremented or decremented as resources are used. An example follows:

- If there are a number of resources of a given type, say three tty ports, then a semaphore would be set up with an initial value of the number of resources available, in this case three.

- Each process or thread that wished to use one of the resources would decrement the count, or the number of ports available by calling the kernel support routine **sema_p(9F)**.

- Any attempt to decrement the count to less than zero by **sema_p( )** will cause the process to block waiting for the count to become greater than zero.

- When a process is finished using the resource, the count or number of resources will be incremented using the **sema_v(9F)** routine.

(NOTE: The user interface for use of semaphores is **sema_post(3R)** and **sema_wait(3R)**. The System V type semaphores are still available through the system calls **semget(2), semop(2)**, and **semctl(2)**.

Since the value (or lock) being manipulated is a count, rather than just a flag as in a mutex, the operation takes a little longer and the semaphore data structure is a bit more complex. The data structure will be examined in the next chapter.

Reader/Writer Locks

Reader/writer locks are not used a great deal in the kernel, but serve an important function. The intent is to allow coherent access to data by allowing only one function or thread to write a piece of data at a time. Reader/writer locks allow multiple functions desiring to read data access, but only one write request to acquire a lock. Reader/writer locks require more kernel resources because two lists are required, a list of pending reads and a list of pending writes. A typical scenario for use of reader/writer locks would go as follows:

1. Several threads would try to read a piece of data by first acquiring the read lock using **rw_rdlock(9S)**. As long as there are no pending write requests, this call will allow as many threads as needed to access the data.

2. Another thread tries to update the same data as in the previous step by making the call **rw_wrlock(9S)**. This call will block if there are any pending reads *or* pending writes.

3. At this point, all subsequent **rw_rdlock( )** or **rw_wrlock( )** calls will block until the thread that made the **rw_wrlock( )** call executes the **rw_unlock(9S)** call.

The reader/writer locks are available in the user level threads library and are used typically when accessing database data. The reader/writer locks are not as common in kernel use, but may be used by various system calls attempting access to kernel information, such as a PID or UID.

Condition Variables

Condition Variables are used to wait for any arbitrary condition to become true, such as a state change. Condition variable calls **cv_wait(9F)** and **cv_signal(9F)** are used to replace the older mechanisms of **sleep( )** and **wakeup( )**. One of the more common instances in which a condition variable would be used would be in the read/write routines for device drivers. Normally, a device driver read (or write) routine will set up the I/O transfer and then go to sleep and wait for the transfer to complete. The problem that needs to be solved in this scenario is the attempt to start multiple I/O requests for the same device. The driver must make sure that I/O requests do not interfere with each other by marking the device busy until the request is successfully started. In earlier releases of SunOS, this was done by using the **sleep( )** kernel support routine and is now done using the **cv_wait(9F)** call. When the I/O was complete, the interrupt routine would be called and the routine would be awakened by using **cv_signal(9F)** (or **wakeup( )** in the older releases).

Condition variables have a problem that is not encountered by the other synchronization primitives. Since a thread will block waiting for a particular event or condition (device not busy, for example), it is not possible to make that condition occur inside that thread. At least two threads will be involved in the synchronization. All other forms of synchronization require only one thread. For example, one thread may block other threads by using **mutex_enter( )**, perform the critical operation and then unblock other thread with **mutex_exit( )**. Once a thread has made a **cv_wait( )** call, it is not possible to have the same thread make a **cv_signal( )** call.

For this reason, use of condition variable must be controlled by using a mutex. The mutex allows the condition variable to act as a test and set scenario for an undefined condition. Following are the steps and some sample code to demonstrate use of condition variables. This code will build on the driver instance of waiting for a device to be *not busy*.

```
Thread 1
/* the BUSY flag is globally initialized to FALSE */
....
mutex_enter(&m)
if ( BUSY )
            cv_wait( &cv, &m);
BUSY = TRUE;
/* process request... */
mutex_exit( &m);

Thread 2
....
cv_signal(&cv)
BUSY = FALSE;
......
```

1. A process will enter thread 1 and begin by acquiring the mutex and checking the state of the device.

2. If the mutex is available and the device is not busy, then processing will continue by setting BUSY to "true" to prevent other threads from entering this critical code. During this period, all other threads will block because they cannot acquire the mutex.

3. If the lock is available, but the device is busy, then the process will execute the **cv_wait( )** call. The **cv_wait( )** will put the process to sleep and release the mutex.

4. Another process will eventually test if the event or condition of interest has happened and issue the **cv_signal( )** call. The **cv_signal( )** will cause the thread waiting on the event to wakeup and reacquire the mutex, and then test the condition.

Condition variables are the hardest primitive to understand and use, but are actually pretty fast and do not use up much in the way of kernel resources. The following table summarizes the various performance issues with using the synchronization primitives. (1 is best, 4 is worst; ease of use is author's opinion.)

	Speed	Memory	Ease of use
Mutex	1	2	1
Conditional variable	2	1	4
Semaphore	3	2	2
Rd/Wr lock	4	4	3

Summary

This chapter has introduced in some detail the important concepts of threads and a multithreaded program:

- Properties of threads
- Synchronization of thread activities
- Types of synchronization primitives used by the Solaris kernel
- Threads and signals

Subsequent chapters will examine the data structures and algorithms that implement the threads concepts and discuss thread strategies employed by the kernel.

Implementation of Thread Architecture

This chapter will examine the data structures and algorithms used to implement the threaded architecture as described previously. Each data structure discussed earlier will be presented and in the end the pieces will be tied together. One thing to note as you examine the structures is that the field names are always indicative of the structure type. All LWP structure fields begin with **lwp_**, thread structure fields begin with **t_**, and so on. This naming convention will prove useful as the book progresses and will give some insight when scanning the header files. This convention also extends to data types though not as consistently. Some examples are **pri_t** for priorities, **k_sigset_t** for signal masks, **clock_t** for time structures, and **pirec_t** for a priority inheritance record.

The LWP Data Structure

Since every application thread is mapped onto a lightweight process (LWP) and then onto a kernel thread, the first two data items to be examined will be the **klwp_t** and the **kthread_t**. Figure 5.1 shows the general layout of the **klwp_t**. The file **/usr/include/sys/klwp.h** should be referenced for further details.

The LWP is used as an interface between the kernel and the user process and as such has no information the kernel itself needs to continue running. This means this data structure is eligible to be swapped or paged out when memory constraints demand. The first portion of the LWP will contain the information about the context of the LWP so it can be restored when paged or swapped in. Such context includes the process control block (PCB), which has a copy of the registers, the program counter, and a pointer to a context block (1,196 bytes).

Since each thread is capable of making its own system call, each thread must keep track of the arguments to the system call, the error codes for the current system call,

Context information–pcb, context block
System call information–arguments,   error code. . .
Signal information–current signal   signal mask, queued signals. . .
Profiling, accounting, resource usage   and timing
lwp_cv (kcondvar_t)
Pointer to kthread_t–lwp_thread
Pointer to proc–lwp_procp
Pointer to time structure

klwp_t /usr/include/sys/klwp.h

Figure 5.1 Selected fields of `klwp_t data` structure. The entire
structure is 392 4-byte words. The header file should be referenced as needed.

and the status of any **longjmp(2)** system call. This is the contents of the second
block of information in the LWP (52 bytes).

The next block contains signal handling information. Since each individual thread
can be delivered a signal, each thread/LWP combination needs to keep track of the current signal being delivered (**lwp_cursig**), signal queue information (**lwp_curinfo**),
and signals currently blocked (**lwp_sigholdmask**). Total signal information includes
56 bytes.

Following the signal information are 100 bytes of resource usage, profiling, and ac-
counting information. These fields are used to store time stamps, the number of
faults this LWP has taken, the number of swaps for this LWP, the number of context
switches, and other data. As we go through some of the other algorithms for paging
and swapping, these fields will be updated.

Finally, there are three important fields, a condition variable (**lwp_cv**), a pointer
to the proc structure (**lwp_procp**), and a pointer to the **kthread_t** structure (**lwp_
thread**). The pointers are used to reconstruct the threads and process when it is
swapped and paged in or out. The condition variable will be seen again when swapping is covered.

The Thread Data Structure

For user application threads, there will be exactly one **kthread_t** structure and one
klwp_t structure for each currently running user thread. The information could have
been kept in one structure, but there is a large amount of information (total greater
than 1,800 bytes) and too many threads would significantly reduce the amount of

memory available if all 1,800 bytes were locked down with kernel memory. The solution was to put into the **klwp_t** structure less essential information that could be swapped out as needed and put only crucial (non-swappable) information into the **kthread_t** structure to be locked down. The result is a fairly compact **kthread_t** structure—264 bytes—and a larger **klwp_t**—1,568 bytes. The **kthread_t** structure is shown in Figure 5.2.

Threads will appear on one of several lists during their lifetime, the dispatch queue, a turnstile, or a freelist. **T_link** is used as a pointer to the next thread on that particular list.

Since each thread can belong to a different scheduling class, such as RT (Real-time) or TS (Time-share), there is a pointer to scheduling class specific data, such as priority, in the field **t_cldata**. Notice that this is a pointer of type void. This is a common technique for defining pointers that will point to an unknown type. Internally, the pointer will be cast to the appropriate type once the type is known.

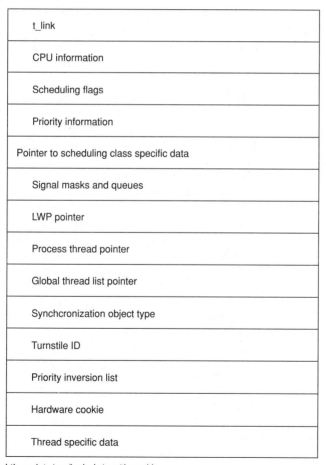

kthread_t /usr/include/sys/thread.h

Figure 5.2 Kernel thread structure (kthread_t) (see thread.h)

CPU information concerns which CPU (if any) this thread is *bound* to. Current architecture does not distinguish between the CPUs in a multiprocessor (MP) system. This means that it does not make a difference if a thread starts execution on CPU 0 and then continues on CPU 1. Being bound to a CPU means that this thread will run on this CPU and only this CPU.[10] If a thread is bound to a CPU, then the **t_bound_cpu** field will be set to a pointer for the cpu structure (see next section) of that CPU otherwise it will be NULL. The system call **processor_bind(2)** will allow a user to specify that a process/thread will run on a particular CPU. This call will set the **t_bind_cpu** field to the CPU specified in the call otherwise it will be −1.

Priority information is held in **t_pri** and **t_epri**. T_pri holds the current assigned priority and **t_epri** will contain the inherited priority. Priorities will be discussed further in the scheduling chapters.

There are two signal masks **t_sig** and **t_hold** to indicate the currently pending signals and signals currently held. **T_lwp** points to the associated **klwp_t** structure for this thread.

There are two sets of forward and back pointers **t_next** and **t_prev** along with **t_forw** and **t_back**. **T_forw** and **t_back** are used to keep a circular doubly linked list of threads in this process. **T-next** and **t_prev** are used to keep track of all threads currently in the system. The global list will be used when scanning for candidate threads to swap out.

When a thread is put to sleep because it could not acquire one of the synchronization primitives (mutex, semaphore, condition variable, read/write lock), the **t_sobj_type** field will be set to the type of synchronization object awaited. Associated with the sleeping thread is the turnstile where the thread can be found when it is to be awakened and stored in **t_ts**.[11] Note this is not a turnstile ID, but a pointer to a turnstile structure.

When priority inversion is discussed later, we will see that a low priority thread can block one or more high priority threads. A list of these threads is kept in a list of priority inheritance records stored in the thread structure, **t_prioinv**.

In the thread field **t_mmuctx** is an opaque data type (or *cookie*) that contains MMU (Memory Management Unit) specific information used for paging and swapping.

The total size of the **kthread_t** structure is 264 bytes. More of the fields will be discussed as they come up during the course of the book.

The CPU Structure

A pointer to the struct cpu was mentioned in the previous sections. The cpu structure is used to indicate which CPU is currently being used to run this particular thread. The cpu structure is defined in **/usr/include/sys/cpuvar.h** and is 580 bytes in length. There will be one struct cpu for each processor installed in the system and

---

[10]Typically, only interrupt threads are bound to a CPU. There is not much reason to bind a thread in the current implementation as this is a *one-way* bind. In other words, the thread will be bound to a CPU, but the CPU will still be running other threads.

[11]A turnstile is simply a pointer to a list of threads waiting for a particular condition or event to occur. All threads waiting for the same event will be on the same list. When a thread is blocked waiting for an event, the address of the turnstile structure is used to locate the list later.

each structure is connected via a doubly-liked list (using **cpu_next** and **cpu_prev**). The beginning of the list of structures is the kernel variable **cpu0** (on Sun4c architecture) or **cpus** (on Sun4m architecture). The important parts of the rest of the structure are used to identify the current thread running on this cpu:

- **cpu_next, cpu_prev**—Pointers to the next and previous cpu structure of the system-wide list of cpu structures

- **cpu_runrun, cpu_kprunrun**—Flags used by the scheduler to indicate a user level preemption or a kernel level preemption

- **cpu_dispthread**—A pointer to the **kthread_t** structure of the currently running thread if this thread was put into execution by the dispatcher

- **cpu_intr_thread**—A pointer to the **kthread_t** structure of the currently running thread if this thread was put into execution as the result of an interrupt

- **cpu_thread**—A pointer to the currently running thread. If this field is not the same as **cpu_dispthread**, it is probably a pointer to an interrupt thread

- **cpu_idle_thread**—A pointer to the **kthread_t** structure for the thread to be put into execution when this cpu is idle. This thread will always have a priority of –1

The cpu structures will be used to track down what is currently running on the system or, in the case of a system crash, what was running when the system died.

The "Big Picture"

There is one more structure that is needed to tie all of the major thread pieces together (no pun intended) and that is the proc structure. The proc structure is the focus of all process activities, such as process start-up, process status gathering, hooks into the virtual address space, and the thread activities. The proc structure is fairly large (776 bytes) and will be revisited many times, particularly during the scheduling chapters. For now, the primary field of interest is **p_tlist**. **P_tlist** is a pointer of type **kthread_t** that will point to the beginning of the list of threads for this process. Even if the programmer does not create any threads via the **thr_create(3T)** call, there will always be at least one thread representing the **main( )** entry point to the program, so the **p_tlist** field should never be null.

When a thread is put into execution, its identity will be loaded into a cpu structure. The "Big Picture" of the threads implementation is illustrated in Figure 5.3

All of the data structures must be present in memory for a process to run. The proc structure and the **kthread_t** structure must be present in memory all of the time. The **klwp_t** structure may be swapped out as needed when free memory is low.

When analyzing the current conditions of a machine or to analyze a system crash file the roadmap pictured in Figure 5.3 should be used.

1. To find the currently running process, start with the cpu structures (cpu0 or cpus).

2. Follow the pointer to the **kthread_t** structure.

3. Follow the thread pointer to the proc structure.

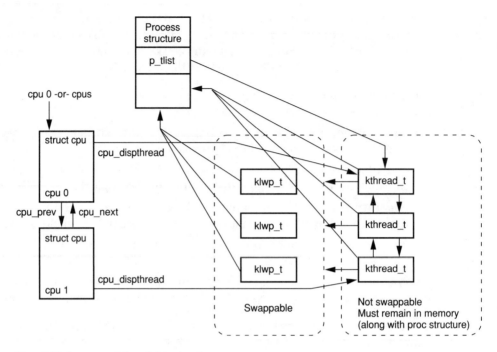

Figure 5.3 Summary of thread data structures

4. Find the user structure inside the proc structure that will contain the command used to start this process.

5. If there is more than one CPU in this system, go back to step 1 and follow the pointer to the next cpu structure (**cpu_next**).

Synchronization Structures

The following section presents the data structures associated with the synchronization primitives. There will be no "Big Picture" for these structures since they are created as needed by the various (kernel and non-kernel) threads. Most of the fields are straightforward and again note the naming conventions: **sema_** for semaphores, **m_** for mutexes, **rw_** for reader/writer locks, and **cv_** for condition variables.

Since each of the data structures have similar fields, they are presented in the same manner. The **waiters** field is of type **turnstile_id_t**, which is 2 bytes and is an index into the turnstile that contains the thread waiting for this particular synchronization object. The count field in the semaphore is the actual count that will be incremented or decremented with the **sema_p( )** or **sema_v( )** calls.

In the mutex, the owner field is the address of the **kthread_t** structure that represents the thread currently holding this mutex. Notice the field is only three bytes and normally addresses are 4 bytes. The three bytes are used to build a four-byte address as follows:

```
1 1 1 < three byte owner field > 0 0 0 0 0
```

This will work because the thread address is always in kernel space and we know from the ABI that kernel address must start at 0xE0000000 or larger, hence the leading ones. The ABI also says the thread address must align on 32-bit boundaries so we can assume the trailing 0s. Since we use only three bytes for the address, the actual lock can be placed in the low order byte of the word and when a lock is released the owner field and the lock can be cleared with one instruction. This byte is accessed by the **LDSTVD** instruction.

For further notations on the structures, it is suggested that you read the comments in the appropriate header files as illustrated in Figure 5.4.

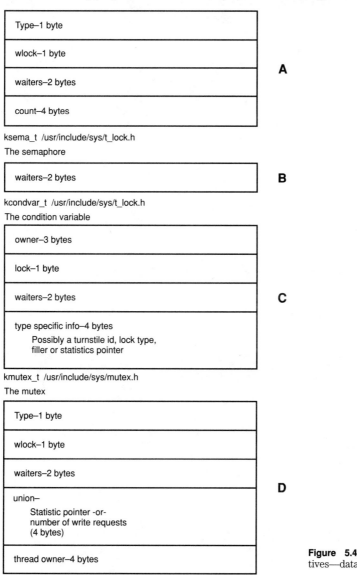

Figure 5.4 Synchronization primitives—data structures

Summary

This chapter has presented the (admittedly somewhat tedious) primary data structures involved in implementing the threaded architecture of SunOS 5.x. The most important information to draw from this chapter is not the actual contents of the structures, but their relationships to each other and their uses. The "Big Picture" presented will be enhanced as we discuss implementation of virtual memory. The references cited in the previous chapter [4], [5], [6], and [7] are somewhat dated and do not really cover the level of detail presented here. The best reference may be the header files themselves.

6

Using Multithreaded Architecture

With the introduction of threaded software architecture, some new issues arise that are not normally found with single threaded processes. Deadlock, which is the stopping of a process due to a resource being unavailable for an indeterminate period of time, becomes a much more easily achievable state. Signals that used to be delivered to a process must now be concerned with which thread within the process is to receive the signal. The advent of hardware with more than one processor also creates problems that are only solvable with threads and synchronization primitives.

This chapter will examine the problems of deadlock, signals, and multiprocessors, as well as examine some generic strategies and potential pitfalls when writing threaded code.

Deadlock

Deadlock is defined as a process or group of processes (or threads) stopped because a resource is being held that will never become available. In SunOS 4.x, all processes were singly threaded and resource requests were made through the kernel. The writers of the 4.x kernel took great pains to make sure deadlock situations would not occur because of ordinary user requests. With SunOS 5.x, and the advent of user-level threads, a thread may now hold a user-level resource needed by other threads and the programmer cannot depend on the protection of the kernel to relieve the problem. There are two typical types of deadlock that must be avoided, *recursive* deadlock and *hierarchical* deadlock. Recursive deadlock occurs when a thread attempts to acquire a lock it already holds. This probably happens when a function calls itself as follows:

```
Function(arglist){
      mutex_enter(&m);
      Function(arglist);
      ...
      }
```

Hierarchical deadlock occurs when multiple threads require two or more of the same locks. If the locks are not acquired in the same order, deadlock can occur. For example, thread 1 and 2 both require locks A and B. If thread 1 gets lock A and thread 2 gets lock B, both threads will stop waiting for the other lock. Always acquire multiple locks in the same order and release them in the same order.

Some notes about deadlock:

- Deadlock shows itself as a hung process or thread and is not easy to detect (no core dumps or terminated processes). More care is required when designing threaded applications and all threads *must* cooperate.

- Accessing global memory without proper locks or synchronization will lead to corrupt data. A strategy may be to build a data structure that contains the data and a lock that must be used to access the data.

- Be sure to use libraries that do acquire and release locks in an unknown fashion. The calling function will not be able to detect any problems.

Strategies for Writing Threaded Code

If there are many threads accessing the same shared data, one method is to have one application-wide lock that is acquired before updating and released after updating. This is most easily done with a mutex. If there are separate threads for reading and writing, perhaps a cleaner solution is to use reader/writer locks to improve performance. If the reader thread is using a mutex, rather than a reader/writer lock, all readers will be blocked until the read is complete. Also, be sure to release any locks before making any *slow* system calls. A *slow* system call is any call that blocks for an undetermined period before returning. Such calls include read, write, select, poll, and others.

An alternate solution is to allow the functions themselves to deal with the synchronization. In other words, create library functions that can be called from any or all of the threads of an application, which handle the locking of data. Such library functions are known as *MT-safe*. The advantage here is that the programmer does not have to worry about acquiring locks or having multiple threads trying to access the same resource. Such a strategy also has the advantage of hiding the synchronization scheme from the developer.

If you choose to design such MT-safe libraries, make sure the libraries do not modify global data that can be modified by any thread. When a piece of global data must be changed, restrict the code that can make the update to one section and protect that code with a mutex to guarantee exclusive access. This idea is known as *code locking*. The kernel provides many examples in the use of code locking. The SunOS kernel is a fully preemptible program with a few non-preemption points. These non-preemption points are guarded by global locks that must be acquired before a preempt may occur.

If data is to be shared with threads outside of the current process, or shared with some unknown number of threads or processes, code locking will not work. Designing data structures with locks built-in and then sharing them via traditional mechanisms, such as files, pipes, or shared memory is known as *data locking*. Data locking is accomplished by building a data structure with the lock and the data to be accessed as shown:

```
struct fubar{
        int data;
        rw_lock lock;
};
```

This way many threads may be in a critical section of code, but only one may update it. These locks may even exist in files that can exist after the life of the process. (Be sure to unlock the data before closing the file!). Once again, this strategy is used by the kernel in SunOS 5.x. Look in the kernel header files (**/usr/include/sys**) to see examples of locks within data structures for use in data locking. In **/usr/include/sys/proc.h**, the proc structure defines a field **p_lock** of type **kmutex_t**. This field is used to guarantee exclusive access to the proc structure. Such a guarantee is needed when updating process resource statistics or when entering or exiting the process.

Properties of Signals in Threaded Processes

The next issue to deal with regarding threads and threaded programming has to do with signals. When using the synchronization primitives, there is little distinction between the kernel and the user interface for the primitives. The calls are slightly different, but the functionality is exactly the same.

With signals and threads the issue is more complex. The purpose of signals is to send notices between processes. With threads there may be more than one thread of control that is sending or receiving signals. The problem is that there is only one set of signal handlers for the entire process. This means that a signal handler installed for a thread is installed for all threads in the process.

For non-threaded processes, the issue is relatively easy, a signal is handled exactly like an interrupt. When a hardware interrupt occurs, the current process (or thread) is suspended while the interrupt is serviced. After the interrupt is serviced, the original thread resumes execution. A signal is just a software interrupt. When a signal is received, the thread will suspend execution while the signal handler code is executed. After the handler code is run, the thread will resume execution. The problem arises with a multithreaded process. When a process has many threads running, which thread will be interrupted to handle the signal? The answer is, it depends on what type of signal was sent.

There are two types to contend with, *synchronous* and *asynchronous*. Synchronous signals are those generated by the user. Examples of synchronous signals are: **SIGSEGV** (Segmentation Violation), **SIGBUS** (Buss error), and **SIGFPE** (Floating point Exception). For synchronous signals, the thread that caused the signal is the one that will be interrupted. This means several threads can handle the same signal simultaneously.

Asynchronous threads are caused outside of the process and may be handled by any thread (chosen by the library) not masking that signal. Examples of asynchronous signals are: **SIGINT** [Interrupt (^C)] or **SIGIO** (I/O Completion notice). Not knowing which thread will be interrupted to handle a signal can be a problem. Take the case where a thread initiates an I/O request and goes to sleep. When the **SIGIO** comes in to indicate the I/O has completed, the handler must be smart enough to continue the correct thread.

There are some important things to note in this model:

- Each thread has its own signal mask. This mask is modified via the **thr_setsigmask(3T)** library call.

- Signals can be delivered to a thread or a process via the **thr_kill(3T)** or **kill(2)** calls.

- Any signal that sets the action for a signal to **SIG_DFL** or **SIG_IGN** will affect the entire process that caused the signal.

Remember though, if the default action for a particular signal is to **exit( )**, as is the case for a **SIGSEGV**, it does not really matter which thread is interrupted since **exit( )** from any thread will terminate all threads in the process.

Signal Handling Strategies

All threads will handle the same signal in the same way, i.e., there is only one signal handler per process, not per thread. There are at least two methods that would allow a thread to handle a signal differently.

The first is to create a bound thread (**thr_create(3T)** with the **THR_BOUND** flag) and install a separate signal handling scheme for that thread using the **sigaction**(2) and **sigaltstack**(2) system calls. The second method would be to code a process wide signal handler that will use the ID of the thread as an index to a table of thread specific handlers.

It may be undesirable to allow the thread library to choose which thread handles an asynchronous signal. This behavior can be changed by having all threads block asynchronous signals [use **thr_setsigmask(3T)**] and creating one thread to handle them using **sigwait( )**.

The Threaded Kernel and Multiprocessors

By now it should be clear that many threads can cooperate and not compromise data or code integrity by using the synchronization primitives and some of the mechanisms described above. This works fine with software, but what about hardware interrupts. If a device has completed its task and interrupts to signal its completion, which CPU is the interrupt delivered to, and does it make a difference? Typically, when a device interrupts an interrupt handler routine is called to service the interrupt request. The problem is that an interrupt handler may want to update a critical data structure access another protected resource.

With only one processor, this action is not really a problem because there will be exactly one piece of code running at any given instant. To make sure that the interrupt handler has exclusive access, the only trick is to make sure no other code interrupts the handler. Under SunOS 4.x, such access was ensured by using a call **spl( )** (for set priority level). The argument to **spl( )** was an interrupt level (see Chapter 3). After making the **spl( )** call, only code running at hardware priority levels higher than the argument would be allowed to run. For example, when a disk drive was complete with an I/O request, the interrupt handler would run and make a call **spl(5)**, 5 being the interrupt level for the disk drive. All other code running at priority levels less than or equal to 5 would be blocked until the service request was complete and a call **splr( )** (set priority level restore) to return the system to the previous priority level.

With multiprocessors, the solution is not quite so simple. If a processor is set to a high interrupt level to block other processes, the interrupt will be delivered to another CPU where the level is set lower. This could result in multiple tasks updating data at the same time. One solution is to set the interrupt level high on all processors to prevent the interrupt from rolling over to another CPU. Alternatively, the hardware could be designed so *all* interrupts go to only one processor. Either way the result would be a bottleneck that would defeat the purpose of having multiple processors.

The solution to this problem is attacked using the synchronization primitives we have already seen, most commonly mutexes. Since a mutex (or any synchronization primitive) is a piece of global data for a process, there will be exactly one copy of the primitive and all processors will have a consistent view of the contents of the primitive. The key, of course, is to make sure all the threads cooperate.

Summary

This chapter has examined some of the issues and strategies for using threaded code, including data locking and code locking, signal handling, and multiprocessor issues. In the *real* world where application code is developed, the most difficult part of writing threaded code will be top-level design issues. Whether to use a single process with many threads or to use many processes [with **fork( )**] to attack a single problem. The deciding factors will be the usual ones, which are the actual hardware platforms used (single or multiprocessor) and a trade-off between performance versus data integrity. Creating a user level thread can be up to 30 times faster than starting a new process via **fork( )**! However, the extra code needed to ensure data integrity may be too much. Imagine a data-base engine with separate threads (running in parallel) to update, read, delete, and insert a record!

Appendix B has several examples of threaded code that are also included on the floppy that accompanies this book. [8] and the AnswerBook that come with the Software Development Kit from Sun have more examples.

Memory Management

7

Hardware Architecture

Part 3 of this book is devoted to the concepts surrounding Virtual Memory (VM) architecture and implementation. The notion of VM is woven into the fabric of all other parts of the operating system: process management, file system management, and interprocess communication. Part 3 will examine the basics of VM and in that examination, we will discover that some of the implementation of the VM architecture is built on threads, which is why the threads discussion was placed first.

The first two chapters will examine terms, definitions, and data structures used to build the VM system. The first chapter looks at hardware concerns and the second is software oriented. The last chapter will look at the actual algorithms used for paging and swapping. Also, in Appendix B, there are some code examples and benchmarks to demonstrate use of the VM architecture to improve program performance.

Definitions and Terms

Many different operating systems use similar ideas and concepts to implement virtual memory. Before going too far into any discussion, it is useful to define exactly what terms are used by Sun and what they mean. This section will define terms used throughout the entire book. Even if you have seen this before it is a good idea to review it here.

Virtual memory

Virtual memory is a set of algorithms that allow the execution of a program that is not entirely loaded into memory. The virtual memory subsystem on Sun will provide the user with a view of virtual memory that does not depend on the underlying physical memory.

The need for virtual memory comes from the fact that a program must be loaded in memory before it can run. This means that if a program is larger than physical memory, allowance will have to be made to load the portions of the process into memory as needed. In the past, programmers had to design such a means on a per process basis. Such programs were called *overlay managers*. An overlay manager would detect that the program needed something not currently loaded in memory and initiate the steps to load the desired portion.

This is exactly the role of the virtual memory subsystem. Instead of building overlay and overlay managers, each process is given the exact same picture of virtual memory to use. The picture of virtual memory is consistent and does not depend on the underlying physical memory limitations. The fact that the virtual memory is consistent for all programs is important to users because system calls can be written that take advantage of the VM subsystem. These system calls (**mmap, memctl, msync...**) will be examined later.

Address space

The address space is defined as the user's view of virtual memory. Each portion of the virtual address space will ultimately be *mapped* into physical memory. Without the use of virtual memory, the address space is simply a list of physical pages where the program is stored. Now the address space is a list of virtual addresses that must be translated to a physical address where the information is stored.

The task of translating virtual to physical addresses is the task of the memory management unit (MMU). When a request for an address is made, which happens when a variable is referenced, the CPU will issue a request for that virtual address. The MMU will translate that virtual address to a physical address transparent to the program and more importantly perhaps, transparent to the programmer.

Page

The short definition of a page is a contiguous collection of bytes. There are two uses for the term *page*, one for hardware and one for software. In either case, the meaning and use are similar. A hardware page is a collection of bytes stored in RAM (random access memory). The size of such a page is determined by the architecture of the system and on Sun hardware the size is either 8K (for Sun4 architectures) or 4K (for Sun4c, Sun4m, Sun4d architectures). All of physical memory is divided into pages known as *frames* and a specific hardware memory address consists of a page frame number and offset within the page.[12] This <page frame, offset> pair is very important as we will soon see. The physical layout showing the page frames is shown in Figure 7.1.

The software definition of a page is similar in the sense it is a collection of contiguous virtual address bytes. The function of the hardware is to enable the mapping of the *virtual* address pages to the *physical* address pages. For now the important concept is the idea of a page.

---

[12]The term *page* is used in a hardware sense and a software sense. Typically, when referring to a hardware page, we use the term *page frame* or *frame*. In the virtual address space, though, a contiguous collection of bytes is also known as *page*.

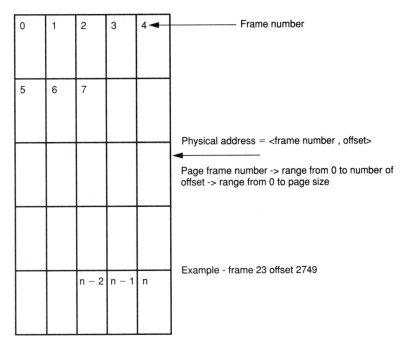

Figure 7.1 Physical memory layout

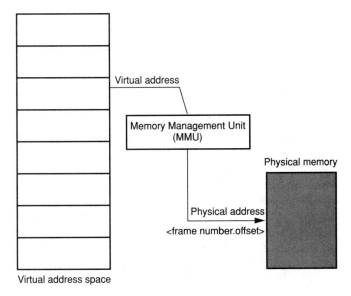

Figure 7.2 Virtual to physical address translation

At this point, the relationship between the address space, the MMU, and physical memory can be seen in Figure 7.2 on the previous page.

Segment

Once again, there are two definitions for this term, one for software and one for hardware. The hardware definition of a segment, which is used by the MMU (Memory Management Unit), is a contiguous collection of physical pages, described above, that can be referenced via a single segment entry in the virtual address. The software definition, as used by the VM subsystem, is a group of (virtual) pages that can be treated in a similar fashion. If you are familiar with the traditional use of the term *segment*, as in *text segment* or *data segment*, you will find that these terms still fit within these definitions.

Context

The context of a process is the list of CPU resources that a process is using at any given moment. Each process has the following that define its context:

- Virtual address space
- Set of registers
- Text, data, and stack

Several processes can be sharing the CPU at any given time, and each process will have its own unique context. Much of the information regarding the context of a process is stored in the stack segment of a process virtual address space.

The MMU uses a different meaning for context. The CPU can run only one context at a time, but the MMU can keep track of more than one context at a time. From the MMU perspective, a context is a set of translations to use for a process. When a process runs, it will be given an MMU context number. SPARC MMU all have a limit to the number of MMU context that can be supported. This means that if that number of processes is exceeded, an MMU context switch is required. An MMU context switch means one of the sets of translations currently stored in the MMU must be unloaded and the set of translations for the new process will be loaded into the MMU. Such a context switch is more complicated than a CPU context switch, which will require only selecting the context number that has been assigned.

Cache

Sun systems contain a hardware cache. Cache is very high speed memory that is used to store frequently used pieces of data. Cache memory is a different type of chip compared to main memory. Cache is SRAM (static RAM), while main memory is DRAM (Dynamic RAM). SRAM has faster access times, but they cost more, use more power, and are larger. These disadvantages make SRAM unsuitable for all of main memory.

System Architecture

Given the above definitions and concepts, we are now ready to describe a generic Sun system. A uniprocessor SPARCstation consists of the following:

- A CPU
- A virtual address cache
- An MMU
- Some main system memory
- Some backing store (swap or disk)

These pieces are connected as shown in Figure 7.3.
The typical sequence of events for a data request goes as follows:

1. The CPU will request data from main memory. This happens on any variable access such as $x = 19;$ in the code.

2. The first step is to check to see if the variable **x** has been referenced recently. If so, the current value of **x** will be stored in the cache and the new value is written in the cache and the data request is satisfied.

3. If **x** is not stored in cache, the virtual address of **x** is passed to the MMU. The MMU will use the virtual address of **x** to look up in its translation tables to see if there is a current valid translation. A valid translation means the physical page that contains **x** is currently in memory. If there is a valid translation, the value of **x** is copied to cache (so it will be there the next time), the new value is written, and the data request is complete.

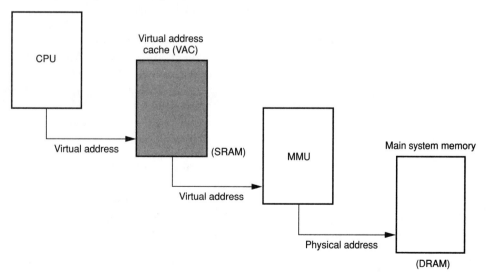

Figure 7.3 System architecture (uniprocessor) 1

4. If there is not a valid translation, this is called a *page fault*. This means that the page containing **x** is *not* in memory and it must be retrieved from the backing store, which is the file somewhere on disk or from swap space. The page containing **x** will be brought into memory and the value for **x** will be updated *and* the value will again be brought into cache.

A quick glance at this scenario will reveal that a data integrity problem may occur because there is a copy of a variable in the cache and another copy in main memory that may be different. Sun currently delivers two types of cache, *write-through* and *write-back* cache. The difference is what takes place when there is a cache **write**.[13] If a value is being changed in cache, write-through cache will also write the new value to the associated memory page. If the cache is write-back, that new value will not be written out until the process is swapped, exited, or there is another request for that cache address.

The write-back cache is faster, but data coherency may be an issue. Write-through cache will be slower, but data will be preserved. In general, Sun uses write-back cache on the smaller machines (SS1, SS1+, SS2, IPC, IPX) and write-through cache on the larger machines (SS10, SPARCcenter 1000, SPARCcenter 2000).

Multiprocessor Architecture and Cache Snooping

A multiprocessor (MP) architecture consists of several (2 or more) CPU modules connected via a bus that allows the modules to communicate with each other and with other components of the system. A CPU module consists of a CPU, a virtual address cache, and an MMU. Each CPU model has access to main memory and the backing store, so each CPU module has all the components of the uniprocessor model shown previously. Figure 7.4 summarizes the MP architecture.

The sequence of steps for resolving data request in the MP architecture is very similar to the uniprocessor, with the exception of the cache lookup. MP architectures employ a technique known as *cache snooping* to satisfy data requests.

When a data request is issued from the CPU, the first step is to look in the cache for that CPU module to see if the data is stored there just like a uniprocessor data request. If the data is not found in the cache, the data request will be forwarded to the other caches on the remaining CPU modules, rather than forwarded to the MMU for resolution. There are several possible scenarios:

- If the data request is a **read** and the data is found in another cache, the data will be copied to the local cache and used. This means that there could potentially be one copy of the data for each CPU.

- If the data request is a **write** and the data is found in another cache, the data is copied to the local cache and then written. All other copies of the data in other caches must then be flushed so there will only be one current copy of the data in all caches.

---

[13]The sequence described here is the same for a **read** or a **write**. If the data is not in cache, look in memory. If it is not in memory, perform the page fault and then load memory and cache.

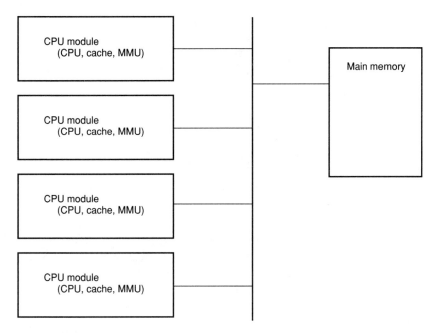

Figure 7.4 Multiprocessor (MP) architecture

- If the data is not found in any of the caches, the data request will be forwarded to the MMU on the CPU where the request originated and the same sequence as a uniprocessor is used.

Performance

From the user perspective, there is little to be done to examine the inner workings of the hardware or to take advantage of the architecture. It would be nice, for example, to have a convenient means of measuring how many data requests are resolved in cache, rather than having to search main memory; unfortunately, there is not. For the most part, the cache hit rate (the percentage of requests resolved in cache) is fairly high, around 90 percent. If a programmer is not careful though, that rate can be reduced significantly.

For example, a program needs to copy a block of data from one location to another. The following code may be used for this purpose:

```
#include <stdio.h>
#include <string.h>

#define CACHE_SIZE (128 *1024)
#define CACHE_LINE 0

char            to[CACHE_SIZE + CACHE_LINE];
char            from[CACHE_SIZE];

main()
```

```
{
        char            *p1, *p2;
        int             index, count;

        memset(from , 1, CACHE_SIZE);
        memset(to , 0, CACHE_SIZE);

        for (count = 0; count < 150; count++) {
            p1 = to;
            p2 = from;
            memset(to , 0, CACHE_SIZE);
            for (index = 0; index < CACHE_SIZE; index++)
                *p1++ = *p2++;
        }

}
```

This code will result in many cache misses. The reason is twofold: the way the compiler assigns addresses and the way entries are placed in cache. First, the compiler will assign the addresses of *to* and *from* consecutively. This means that the address of to[0] will be offset **CACHE_SIZE** from[0]. These addresses are used in assigning the specific location in the cache. Specifically, the location in cache is calculated by dividing (modular divide) the virtual address by the size of the virtual cache as shown.

$$(\text{virtual address of the data}) \% (\text{size of cache})$$

In this case, the calculation for the buffers will be the same, which means they will always be contending for the same location. **to[0]** will be loaded into cache and the request for **from[0]** will be requested and not found, i.e., a cache miss. This will occur for each entry in the buffer.

The solution to this is to offset the address of the buffers by the 32 bytes, the size of a cache block. The CPU will read the size of the cache block not just the amount of the data requested. In the sample program, change **CACHE_LINE** to 32 instead of 0. NOTE: this program assumes a cache size of 128K and a cache line of 32 bytes. Be sure to check the details for your architecture. All Sun architectures have a cache of 128K or 64K and a cache line of 16 or 32 bytes.

Summary

This chapter has provided a brief introduction to the basic terminology and hardware activities that will provide a foundation for the discussion of the implementation of virtual memory in the software. Bear in mind this is a very high level overview of hardware events. Other topics that may be of interest to the hardware oriented reader should be looked at to get a more detailed picture:

- I/O cache
- CPU module memory for read/write buffers
- Mbus, xbus, and xdbus architecture for MP

- Write-through vs. write-back cache
- Virtual address vs. physical address cache

The AnswerBook provides some of these details in the Writing Device Drivers section of the Software Developers Kit (SDK). [18] provides some additional details on Sun hardware.

8

Implementation of Virtual Memory

The SunOS 5.x Virtual Memory (VM) architecture and implementation remain essentially unchanged from SunOS 4.x. The intent of Sun's virtual memory model is to provide an implementation that reflects the actual uses of the resources involved. This section will describe the concepts and properties of the Virtual Memory subsystem in SunOS 5.x, as well as the implementation of the objects and how they are managed. Further reference material can be found in [11].

Concepts, Terms, and Definitions

The basic requirement that a process, or at least the part that is currently executing, must be resident in physical memory (RAM) has not changed. This idea is not new and in the past such an implementation was achieved using overlays. If a process was larger than physical memory, the process would have to unload a portion of itself and load another portion to continue. Each portion of the program to be loaded and unloaded was called an *overlay* and the part of the program set up to direct the loading and unloading activities was called an *overlay manager*. The purpose of the virtual memory subsystem is to provide the functionality of the overlay manager on a system-wide basis and in a fashion that is transparent to the programmer.

The idea of virtual memory is that it *appears* to a process that there is more memory than the actual physical memory that exists on the system. Virtual does not mean infinite, however. In SunOS 5.x, the system virtual memory consists of all of its physical resources including, but necessarily limited to:

- Random access memory (RAM)
- Local and mounted file systems
- Swap space (known as anonymous memory[14])

---

[14]The term anonymous memory will be used to refer to any object that does not have an identity in the file system, such as a file name or a device node. Objects with identity can be seen with ls. Anonymous objects cannot be listed.

A process address space is defined as a set of mappings from objects in the system virtual memory to pages in the process virtual address space. Objects in the system virtual memory are generally one of two types: *named* and *unnamed*. A named object is anything that can be referred to via the SunOS file system, which includes:

- Ordinary files
- Named pipes
- Sockets (or TLI endpoints)
- Directories
- Block or character devices

In general, anything that can be seen with the **ls** command, or can be accessed via an **open(2)** system call, is a named object.

Unnamed objects do not have names and cannot be seen by the file system. Such items may include:

- Copies of private pages
- System V IPC objects (Shared memory, et. al.)
- Uninitialized data segments
- Stack segments

The system provides a pool of structures for managing such unnamed objects (struct anon) and will allocate swap space for storage of these objects.

Every object in the VM pool, named or unnamed, must correspond to some physical object such as a file, a swap space location, or a page of physical memory. In other words, every virtual address in a process virtual address space must correspond to some physical address. This translation is done in an object-oriented specific fashion. For example, an ordinary file is accessed in the same fashion as a device node, although the actual routines may be different. This action is implemented by using call through the data structure that represents the object mapped.

By allowing a program to map objects of different types into the process address space, the programmer is provided a single consistent view of memory and may treat the process space simply as a list of pages; one page of the process address space will map directly to exactly one object in the virtual memory. However, the reverse is not true. One object in virtual memory may be mapped by any number of processes. For example, an ordinary file (a named object) may be accessed by many processes or a shared memory segment (an unnamed object) may be attached by many processes. This means that an object does not become the *property* of the process that maps it, nor does the object even know it has been mapped.

By providing such a view of virtual memory, the programmer can now directly access objects that formerly could only be accessed via **read(2)** and **write(2)**. The disadvantage is that since any number of processes may do the same thing, data integrity becomes a large issue. By allowing the shared mappings, the groundwork for providing shared libraries has also been laid.

Virtual address space

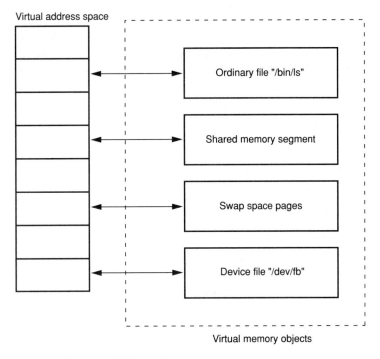

Virtual memory objects

Figure 8.1 Summary of VM mapping

In summary of the conceptual framework then, the virtual memory system is used to build a process address space by creating a set of mappings to allow access to differing object types in a consistent fashion. Virtual memory mapping is shown in Figure 8.1.

Implementation

As we have seen, virtual memory is the act of mapping physical objects onto the virtual address space. The data structures and algorithms involved in implementing this concept correspond very closely to the conceptual layout shown in Figure 8.1. For example, a process virtual address space consists of an address space; an address space is a set of segments; each segment is broken up into a set of pages; and each page corresponds to a physical object. The actual implementation of the virtual memory is very much the same. A process address space (starting with a struct proc) consists of an address space (struct as); an address space consists of segments (struct seg and an object specific segment structure); each segment will map onto pages (via a struct vnode or struct anon that point to struct page); and each page will contain object specific addressing (via the hat [hardware address translation] layer). The following section will describe each layer of the virtual memory scheme.

The Address Space

Each layer of the VM system (address space, segment, pages, and physical objects) supports a set of functions for manipulating that layer. For the address space layer, there are two sets of routines, one for manipulating the entire address space and another for manipulating a subset of the address space or a range of virtual addresses. Some of these are listed here. (For a complete set of address space functions, look in the file **/usr/include/vm/as.h**.)

- **as_map( )**—for the **mmap(3)** call
- **as_free( )**—for the **exit(2)** call
- **as_dup( )**—for the **fork(2)** call
- **as_swapout**—for swapping an entire process
- **as_alloc**—for the **exec(2)** call

These functions are not part of the address space structure, but do take a struct as for an argument. The actual structure is fairly small (48 bytes) and consists of some locks (**a_contents, a_cv, a_lock**), the number of pages in use by this address space (**a_rss**) and three very important fields:

- **a_segs**—a pointer to the beginning of the list of segments that make up this address space.
- **a_seglast**—a pointer to the last segment that was used in this address space.
- **a_hat**—a pointer to a hat structure that points to a list of all of the physical MMU mappings for this address space.

The **a_hat** field points to structures that are machine dependent and known as the *hat*, or hardware address translation layer. The structures in the hat layer are separate from the other layers of the VM system and contain information specific to this machine's MMU. The hat layer consists of data structures and functions that load and store valid address translations to and from the MMU when a context switch is encountered.

The **a_seglast** field is used as a hint concerning where to find the segment associated with a particular virtual address. Typically, addresses are used sequentially, so rather than begin a search for a virtual address at the beginning of the segment list (**a_seg**), a *hint* as to where to start the search is kept in **a_seglast**. **a_seglast** will normally point to the last segment where a virtual address was found.

Kernel Address Space

Normally, the as structure is pointed to by the proc structure. However, there is one process that does not have a proc structure associated with it, the kernel itself. Since the kernel is a program with the same structure as any other program, there is a special as structure that is the entry point for the kernel segment list, **kas**. The as layer, kas, and hat layer are shown in Figure 8.2.

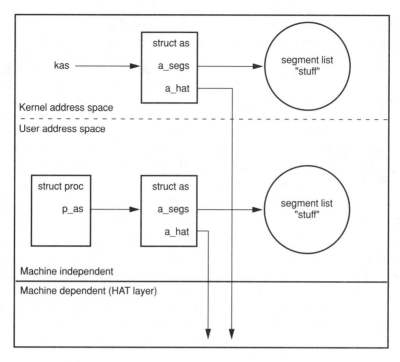

Figure 8.2 Summary of address space management

Segment Descriptions

As mentioned earlier, the address space structure points to a list of segments. A segment in the virtual memory context is not the same as the text, data, and stack segments mentioned in Part 1. A segment in the VM system is a range of contiguous virtual address of the same type or object. For example, there may be two sections of virtual memory allocated by the call **malloc( )** that could be contiguous, but will be in different segments in the VM system because of the objects that are mapped into the spaces. A typical address space for even a simple program may have ten or more such segments.

The segments on the segment list will be arranged in ascending order by virtual address and each segment will require two data structures to fully define the segment: a public portion and a private portion. The public portion (**struct seg**) will contain information common to all segments (see **/usr/include/vm/seg.h**). Following is a list of some important fields of a **struct seg**:

- Starting virtual address for this segment (**s_base**)
- Size of the segment in bytes (**s_size**)
- A back pointer to the as structure (**s_as**)
- Pointers to the next and previous segments in the list (**s_prev** & **s_next**)

- A pointer to a set of routines for manipulating this segment type (**s_ops**)
- A pointer to the private portion of the segment definition (**s_data**)

These fields are pretty straightforward, but a special note should be made about the **s_ops** field. In a mode similar to the address space, there is a set of routines for manipulating segments. The implementation is a little different because there are five different segment types, as we will see, and each requires its own set of routines. Instead of a common set of routines, there is a pointer in the segment structure that will point to routines for using this segment type. This is object-oriented programming at its best. Hiding the routines in the data means the kernel itself does not need to know about the object type, only how to access it.

Segment Types

Even though a segment may span many pages, all of the pages within the same segment will map to the same object type. That is the definition of a segment in the VM system. The private portion of the segment description will contain information specific to that segment type and along with the segment specific functions from the public portion of the segment definition, constitute what is known as a *segment driver*.

There are currently five different types of segment driver defined by the SunOS kernel:

- **segvn**—for vnode segments
- **segdev**—for device mappings
- **segmap**—for kernel use in transient mappings
- **segkmem**—for mapping kernel text, data, and stack segments
- **segkp**—for kernel mapping of user spaces

A user process will use only **segvn** and **segdev** segments, while the kernel will use only **segmap, segkmem,** and **segkp** segments. The most widely used segment type in the system is the **segvn**, which is used to map ordinary files and unnamed objects such as the stack and copies of pages. Each segment type has its own data structure that will be pointed to by the **s_data** field of the segment structure. The structures are named **segvn_data, segdev_data, segmap_data, segkp_data,** and **segkmem_data** for **segvn, segdev, segmap, segkp,** and **segkmem** segments respectively. Since the **segvn** segment is the most commonly used segment type in the system (about 90%), we will summarize the segment definition using the **segvn_data** constructs as shown in Figure 8.3.

The most commonly used segment driver on the system is the **segvn** or vnode driver. The vnode will be used to map all ordinary files as well as any unnamed objects. We will examine the contents of a vnode structure later in the file system management section, but its concepts and uses are similar to what we have already seen. The segment structure contains routines to manage and manipulate segments and the vnode contains routines to manage and manipulate the objects being mapped.

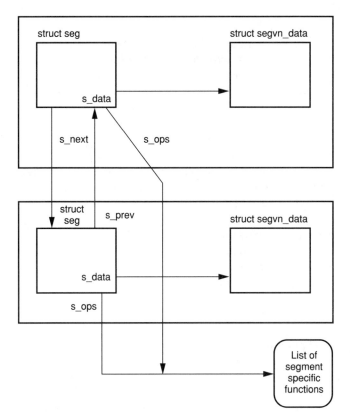

Figure 8.3 Summary of segment definition

For example, if the object is an ordinary file, the vnode will search for and manage the inode for that file. If the contents of the file are mapped directly to user space, the vnode will manage the list of pages for the file.

Anonymous Memory

If the object is unnamed (such as stack space), the vnode will manage a pool of *anonymous* pages.

Anonymous pages or anonymous memory will be used to back up any object that does not have permanent file space, i.e., does not have identity in the file system (hence the term *anonymous*). In normal operations, there are three major pieces of a process that will use anonymous memory:

- Stack segments
- Uninitialized data segments
- Copies of private pages (Copy-on-write or COW)

Copy-On-Write (COW)

The first two object types mentioned have already been discussed, but the third, *copy-on-write*, warrants further explanation. All address spaces, segments, and vnodes ultimately map to a page or a series of pages. Each page is designated as either *public* or *private*. Public pages are pages that can be shared with other processes and thus can have more than one mapping. Examples of public pages are text sections and shared libraries. Private pages cannot be shared and will have exactly one mapping. Examples of private pages are stack segments and parts of the data segment.

This scenario makes sense if you think of it in terms of a process such as **vi**. Each invocation of the editor will use the same code (the text segment), but each instance will be editing a different file (the data and stack segments). This means that when a process is copied (when a **fork(2)** occurs) the public pages will simply be shared while the private pages must be copied. The COW (Copy-on-write) facility has been introduced to make such copying more efficient. COW is a policy that says that a private page will not be copied until it is written to by any of the processes needing the page. This way if a page is never written on, it will never be copied and it can continue to be shared even though it is a private page.

Pages

The page is the focal point for all memory activity in the VM system. As far as virtual memory is concerned, all of physical memory is a pool of page structures to be managed for the purpose of mapping objects to process virtual address spaces. The VM system uses the page data structure to manage the pool and there will be one page data structure for each page of physical memory. The pool of page structures is allocated at boot time and is sized according to the size of physical memory minus the portion of memory used by the kernel. The block of page structures is pointed to by the kernel variable **pages**.

Within the static block of pages, there will be several logical lists of pages and each page may be on more than one list at a time. There are three lists we are most interested in:

- The freelist
- A vnode page list
- The page hash list

The kernel symbol **page_freelist** points to the head of the list of available page structures. As each segment is mapped to a process, a list of pages representing that segment will be built and attached to the vnode by taking structures off of the freelist. When a segment is destroyed, the list of pages attached to that segment is returned to the freelist. By allocating structures from the front of the freelist and returning them to the end of the freelist, a least recently used (LRU) algorithm is implemented.

A page hash table is used to implement a quick lookup for a particular page. A page identity is determined by the vnode a page it is currently attached to, and the offset within the vnode (Note the similarity with the page frame & offset identity in the hardware memory mapping). This identity is used to put a page structure in a hash bucket in the page_hash[ ] array. Figure 8.4 shows the page table and list management of the page structures.

Note that it is possible and even reasonable that a page be on two vnode lists at the same time. This would happen when two processes are sharing a text page or perhaps a shared library. With this summary, we can look at the fields of the page structure itself from **/usr/include/vm/page.h**:

- **p_vnode**—pointer to the vnode for this page.

- **p_offset**—offset in bytes from the beginning of the range represented by this vnode. The **p_offset** and **p_vnode** fields are used to create a hash identity for the **page_hash[ ]** array.

- **p_hash**—pointer to the **page_hash** table.

- **p_next, p_prev**—pointers to the next/previous page if on the freelist.

- **p_vpnext, p_vpprev**—pointers to the next/previous page on this vnode list.

- **p_mapping**—pointer to the HAT information for this page.

The Virtual Memory Roadmap

All of the data structures defining the virtual memory system have now been described. By placing them all together, we have what is shown in Figure 8.5.

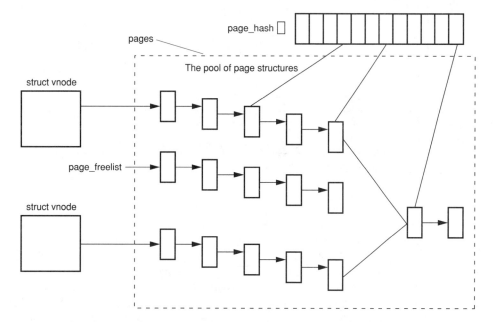

Figure 8.4 Summary of page management

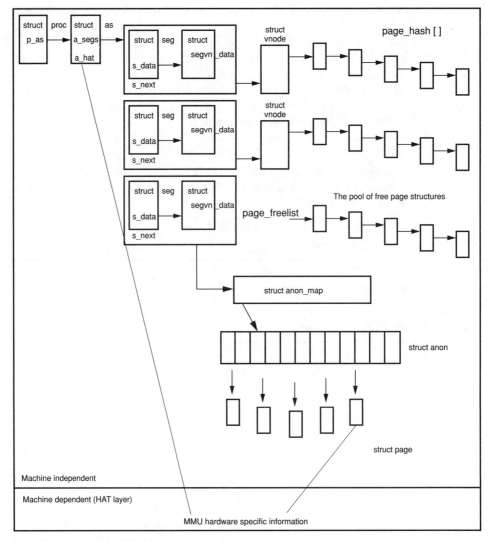

Figure 8.5 Summary of all VM data structures

The only portion of Figure 8.5 that may need further explanation is the segment that uses the anon structure instead of a vnode. Anonymous memory is managed in a manner very similar to virtual memory. There is a pool of anon data structures for each page of anonymous memory. The anonymous memory pool will consist of all swap space disk partitions and any files that have been designated as swap. (A list of swap spaces can be seen with the **swap −l** command.) When a need for anonymous memory arises, one of the structures will be used and linked into an **anon_map** structure that is then attached to the segment. The anon structures must still ultimately point to a page structure because the data must be in physical memory when it is used.

All of these data structures and roadmaps are interesting, but why have we shown all of this? The major function of the virtual memory system is to allow many different types of objects to be faulted into memory without the operating system having to understand the inherent nature of the object. With the system laid out as described, it is now possible to show how this functionality works. The following steps are used to fault in an object. (The function shown within parentheses is the kernel routine that handles this step.)

- A virtual address is requested by the process. This will result in the address space layer fault routine being called (**as_fault**). Also at the address space layer, protection and permission checking for the requested operation will be handled (**as_checkprot( )**).

- The segment list will be searched using the virtual address and the segment driver fault routine will be called (**seg->s_ops->fault( )**). If the address is not in the current list for the address space, a new segment will be created.

- For a vnode segment (**segvn**-the others vary slightly), page permissions and protections are checked (**seg->s_ops->getprot( )**).

- If this segment will use anonymous memory, then an anon-map structure will be allocated (**anonmap_alloc( )**).

- Use the vnode driver to retrieve the object. This may mean accessing a device driver or reading a file, however this will all be transparent to the VM system, since the calls will be made in an object oriented fashion through the vnode.

- Once the object is loaded and allocated a page structure and a page in memory, place the information in the HAT layer (**hat_memload( )**).

Notice the use of the object-oriented type call **seg->s_ops->fault( )**. By using this technique, it is possible to expand the list of object types used since the kernel uses object through the data structure interface (**s_ops**) and does not hard-code the object type in the kernel code.

Summary

This chapter has reviewed the basic *roadmap* of the virtual memory system. Since the objective of this book is to show how the system works *and* to provide useful means to take advantage of such knowledge, you may be asking, "Where is the usefulness of this (large) tidbit of knowledge?"

Three objectives have been accomplished here:

- The groundwork for *all* other pieces of the kernel has been established by defining terms and concepts of virtual memory.

- By precisely laying out the roadmap, previously for threads and now for virtual memory, we have a very powerful means of analyzing crash and core files using **adb** and **crash**. These utilities and crash analysis methods will be explained in Appendix A of this book.

- By building the virtual memory system the way it is, there is a set of powerful routines that can be used to directly map objects to user space. These routines will be used to write faster and more flexible programs than the traditional read/write routines can provide (see [15]). Such functions include **mmap( ), memctl( ), madvise( ),** and others. Explanations of these functions and code samples with benchmarks are provided in Appendix B of this book.

The primary references to further research these topics are [11], [19], and [20]. [2] (BSD internals) provides some groundwork that was eventually used in Sun's implementation. More about virtual to physical address translations can be found in the AnswerBook section on writing device drivers. As usual, the header files (in **/usr/include/vm**) are most helpful.

Global Memory Management

Up to this point, we have examined how a single process would access and, if needed, fault a page in from backing storage or swap space. The remaining question to examine is: How did a page get into the swap area in the first place? Or to phrase it a different way: If a page has been faulted in, how or why would it get removed from memory (not necessarily moved to swap)?

How the system manages the entire pool of physical memory pages is the subject of this chapter. How the pool of anonymous pages is managed is examined in a section titled "Virtual swap implementation" found in Chapter 15 concerning file systems. How the system selects which processes to swap out is examined here.

Global Paging Concepts

When a page is requested by a process and the request results in a page fault, there are two possible situations. First, if there is a free page of physical memory, the requested page uses the free page and is mapped into the process virtual address space. Second, if there is not a free page of memory, the system will have to decide which page (or pages) to move to make room for the new request. This sequence of moving pages into and out of physical memory is known as *page in* and *page out* and these activities are managed by the pager process (process ID 2).

All page in requests occur the same way, the process tries to access a virtual address that has a mapping in the virtual memory system, but does not currently have a mapping to a physical object. (Remember, if a page does not have a mapping in the *virtual* memory system, attempted access will result in a segmentation violation.) As each request for a page comes in, the following occurs:

- Check the virtual address cache (VAC) to see if there is an entry.
- Check the MMU to see if there is a valid page translation.

- If the page is not resident, allocate a page from the freelist, perform the I/O and set up the mapping.

The problem is that each process that starts up or is running cannot keep requesting maps to physical pages. Eventually, the pool of physical pages (the freelist) is empty. Therefore, the kernel imposes a policy of *page replacement* in order to control the activities of the pager and swapper to ensure that pages are available when needed.

An analogy to memory management is that of an instructor presenting a topic on the board. The board is initially empty. As the lesson continues and the instructor writes on the board, space for continued writing becomes scarce and decisions on what part of the previous writings should be erased must be made. It is the same with physical memory. As processes start and continue to request pages, physical memory fills up and decisions on which pages to free up must be made.

The burden of keeping pages available for use is not the responsibility of one process, but rather a set of actions that make pages available. For example, the **exit(2)** call will free all of the pages it was using. The **unmmap(3)** indicates that a set of pages is no longer needed by a process and eligible to be freed. If memory is in very high demand, the swapper (process ID 0) will move all of the anonymous pages to backing store (probably the swap partition) and free up some physical memory. The page daemon (process ID 2) will start the actual I/O sequence when it is determined when a page must be moved or removed from main memory.

System Paging Strategy

The system strategy for managing memory revolves around two kernel variables, *minfree* and *lotsfree*, and one algorithm called the *two-handed clock algorithm*. Minfree and lotsfree are kernel variables that are set based on the amount of physical memory available for use. This is the amount of physical memory minus the pages that are locked for the kernel and possibly the process **kadb(1)**. Minfree and lotsfree set as follows:

- **minfree** = available memory / 64
- **lotsfree** = available memory /16

When the system is booted, all pages of memory are free. After the kernel is loaded and locked into memory, processes will begin running and demand use of memory. Since there is plenty of memory for all demands, no memory management is needed. Much as when the instructor begins writing on an empty board, there is no need to erase anything.

Four times per second, the amount of memory left is tested by the kernel and if the amount left plus any pending requests is less than lotsfree, in other words, memory is starting to run out, the pageout daemon is started using a **cv_signal( )** call. The pageout process or page daemon (process ID 2) was created at boot time and has been sleeping, waiting for the **cv_signal** call. The pageout process consists of two threads, the first will scan memory and create a list of pages to page out and the

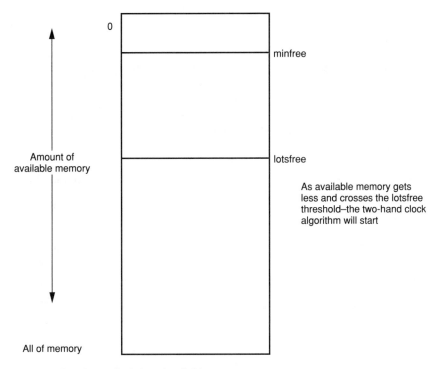

Figure 9.1 Lotsfree and minfree thresholds

second will perform the actual I/O based on the list created by the first. The thread that scans memory is what is commonly known as the two-hand clock algorithm.

Figure 9.1 summarizes this process.

The two-hand clock algorithm is so named because of its activities. A pointer (the fronthand) will sweep through all of the pages in memory (using the page structures) and reset (set to 0) the bit in the structure that indicates if a page has been referenced. Some period of time later a second pointer (the backhand) will sweep through memory and check the same bit. If the bit is still 0, this means the page has not been referenced lately and it will go on the list to be paged out. If the bit has been set to 1, the backhand will simply continue scanning. Bear in mind, these pointers will scan only *available pages*, which means kernel locked pages will not be scanned.

There are two basic parameters that define the scanning of pages.

- **scanrate**—how many pages are scanned per second, in other words, how fast are the *hands* of the clock moving

- **handspreadpages**—how far behind the fronthand is the backhand

As the amount of free memory decreases, the system will become more desperate to locate pages that can be moved out. The scanrate is set to vary linearly as the amount of free memory changes. The more memory that is available (closer to lotsfree) the slower the scanrate; the less memory available (closer to minfree) the faster the scanrate. The scanrate varies linearly between two values, *fastscan* and *slowscan*, which are constants fixed at boot time based on memory size. A faster scanrate means the system is looking for available pages more urgently.

Handspreadpages is expressed as number of bytes, but it can be thought of as the time period in which a page has to be used. Handspreadpages is a constant fixed at boot time based on the amount of physical memory. If handspreadpages is too small, the window of opportunity to use a page will be too small and pages will be marked for pageout before they have had a chance to be used, in short, too much paging will occur. Two-handed clock parameters are shown in Figure 9.2.

In summary, the pageout process consists of two threads, the first thread searches the page list to find pages available for paging out (the two-hand clock algorithm). This first thread has the following properties:

- The speed at which the pages are scanned varies between slowscan and fastscan.
- The time period during which pages have a chance to be referenced is controlled by handspreadpages.
- The thread will begin when the amount of free memory falls below lotsfree.
- The thread will stop scanning when the entire list of pages is scanned two times and no pages are found to page out.

The second thread of the pageout process is used to perform the pageout of the pages on the list built by the first thread. The second thread will start when there is a non-NULL list of pages and will end when the list is empty.

Remember, the overall global paging objective is to keep the amount of free memory between minfree and lotsfree.

Swapping Control

The next question that arises is "What if the methods above do not keep paging levels where they should be?" The pageout daemon is running and the scanrate is increased to find more pages to move, but processes are starting so fast that memory

List of pages

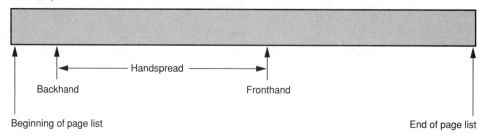

NOTE: The page list is circular

Figure 9.2 Two-hand clock parameters

demands cannot be satisfied by the pageout daemon. The solution is to swap entire processes (threads). Swapping a process is the act of moving *all* of the pages (and swappable data structures such as the LWP) for that thread or process out of main memory and into anonymous memory.

The swapper is part of the **sched** (process ID 0) routine and runs once every second. There are three kernel flags that control the activities of the swapper:

- **nswapped**—the current number of threads swapped out.
- **runout**—a flag used to indicate there is no work for the swapper.
- **runin**—a flag used to indicate there is a need to swap a process in, but there is no room in main memory. In other words, there is work for the swapper, but it cannot be done at this time.

There is also one tunable variable that can be user defined:

- **tune_t_gpgslo**—a tunable variable that is set to indicate the memory level where *desperation swap* will occur.

The basic swapping algorithm (swap out) is as follows:

1. When the system has determined there is a memory condition that requires a thread to be swapped out, a scheduling class specific (TS or RT) swapout routine is called.
2. Each class specific routine will select one thread to be swapped out based on a number of criteria such as: is the thread sleeping or running, is the thread being debugged, is the thread exiting anyway, is this thread locked down.
3. Each nominated thread is presented to the swapper and the swapper will select the lowest priority thread.
4. The kernel stack and the LWP structure for that thread will be moved to the swap area. If this were the last LWP for a process, the swapout routine for the entire address space will be called to move the pages to the swap area. **Nswapped** will be incremented.

To swap *in* a thread, basically the opposite will occur:

1. When the system has determined there is sufficient memory, a scheduling class specific swap in routine will be called for each class that has a thread swapped out.
2. Each class specific routine will nominate one thread to be swapped in.
3. The nominated threads are presented to the swapper and the highest priority thread will be swapped in. **Nswapped** *will be decremented.*

The key to both of these sets of steps is the phrase, "When the system has determined . . .." How does the system detect severe memory conditions that require swapping?

Once per second the flags **runin** and **runout** will be checked and, if needed, the swapper thread will be moved to the front of its dispatch queue to be executed. **Runout** is a flag that will be set if anything has been swapped out. Each time a thread is swapped in, **runout** will be decremented and when it is 0, this is an indication that there are no more threads to swap in and the swapper thread can be moved to the sleep queues.

Runin is a flag that is set when there is a need to swap a thread in, but it had to be delayed because there was not enough available memory. Additionally, each time a thread is swapped out, **nswapped** is incremented and each time a thread is swapped in, **nswapped** is decremented. There are now two conditions that will start the swapper:

- If **runin** is set (not equal to 0) meaning that a thread attempted to swap in earlier, but could not due to memory limitations, the swapper will be put on the dispatch queue and will run in turn. If there is still insufficient memory, the swapper will try again in one second.

- If memory is low (free memory < **tune_t_gpgslo**), or anything needs to be swapped in (**nswapped** > 0), and anything needs to be swapped out (**runout** > 0), then the swapper is started.

The swapper will go to sleep:

- If there is nothing to swap in
- If there was an attempt to swap in, but there was no room

Summary

We have looked at the algorithms for global memory management. In general, there is no way to take advantage of this information from within a program. However, since this is a system-wide issue, each of the variables discussed can affect system performance. Here is a summary of the variables that could be examined:

- **lotsfree**
- **minfree**
- **handspreadpages**
- **fastscan**
- **slowscan**
- **tune_t_gpgslo**

Remember, the objective is to control the amount of paging and swapping the system will perform. For the most part, anything that increases paging will reduce the amount of swapping and conversely; anything that reduces paging will in turn increase swapping.

For example, if lotsfree were made larger, the pager would be turned on sooner and more paging would occur and relieve the need to swap as often. **Vmstat(1M),** **iostat(1M)** and **sar(1)** are tools to measure the current amount of free memory, number of processes waiting to run, and the amount of swapping going on. In Appendix A, there is a shell script to help find the current values for the tuning parameters discussed and how to change them.

Process Management

10

Scheduling Concepts

The introduction of Solaris 2.x brings major changes to the process scheduling and control algorithms of the operating system. One of the major new features of scheduling in SunOS 5.x is the bounded dispatch behavior for designated processes or even a class of processes. In order to achieve bounded dispatch behavior, more commonly referred to as *real-time*, the kernel was designed to be fully preemptive. With the advent of preemptive kernel processing, the possibility of deadlock or severe performance degradation exists because of priority inversion.

This module will discuss the features of bounded dispatch scheduling, the preemptive kernel, scheduling classes, symmetric versus asymmetric multiprocessing, and the table driven scheduling in SunOS 5.x, along with guidelines and commands for using real-time processes.

Definitions

Before a discussion of scheduling is meaningful, it is important to fully understand some of the features and terms of the SunOS processing environment.

Tightly coupled vs. loosely coupled OS

In a multiprocessor environment, there are some choices to be made as to how to implement the operating system for processing system requests. This topic was discussed in the chapter on multithreaded architecture, but is worth reviewing again from the scheduling perspective.

There are basically only two possible configurations for building an operating system that manages more than one processor: *loosely coupled* and *tightly coupled*. In a tightly coupled operating system, there is one copy of the operating system and the various processors share a clock and memory. Since management of resources is centralized and all processors work with the same copy of shared memory, many management issues such as the order of requests, are simplified. The drawback is that with a job mix of predominately system requests, the operating system could become a bottleneck.

In a loosely coupled operating system, processors will each have their own local memory and local clock. The primary advantage with this design is that each processor can handle its own system requests. The drawback is that without a great deal of overhead in communicating with other processors system management issues, such as order of requests, can lead to major problems, including deadlock.

All of Sun's implementation of multiprocessor operating systems, starting with release 4.1.2, have been tightly coupled implementations. There is exactly one copy of the operating system that communicates via shared memory. This will prove to be true even when the kernel is threaded into many pieces.

Symmetric vs. asymmetric multiprocessing

Once the decision on how to implement the software has been made (tightly or loosely coupled), a choice on how to organize the software in the hardware environment must follow. Since we know we are using only one copy of the kernel, the immediate solution is to simply dedicate one of the processors to the operation of the kernel. This processor will have the task of handling all system requests, such as I/O, scheduling, virtual memory operations, and management of system resources, i.e., all system calls. In this case, one of the processors is designated the master. The master processor is responsible for all system requests while all other processors manipulate user functions. This sort of processing arrangement is known as *asymmetric multiprocessing* (ASMP) because the kernel always runs as standalone and there is no concurrency or symmetry in the kernel. Figure 10.1 shows a typical ASMP arrangement.

There is a variation of the master-slave processor scenario. In this variation, there is still one copy of the kernel that will run to the exclusion of all else on a processor. The difference is that it does not matter which processor is used for that purpose, i.e., the kernel will not be dedicated to a particular processor and, in fact, may not be running at all. If, at any moment in time, there are no system requests pending, all processors will be running in user mode. When any process makes a system request, the kernel will begin operation on that processor, continue until all system requests are done, and then release the processor for use in user mode.

Since the kernel is still run as a stand-alone process, this variation is still considered asymmetric. It is more efficient, however, because there is not a processor set aside for dedicated use. This variation is exactly the way SunOS 4.1.2 and SunOS 4.1.3 handle multiple processors.

The disadvantage of the asymmetric model is that performance suffers when there are a large number of system requests. It will be particularly true when there are a large number of I/O bound processes. It is fairly easy to see that if many processes make *slow* system calls, all of the processors will be blocked waiting for the one processor to handle all of the requests. In short the kernel becomes the bottleneck.

The advantage of the asymmetric model is that it is easy to implement because the kernel designers do not have to deal with issues such as protection of critical data

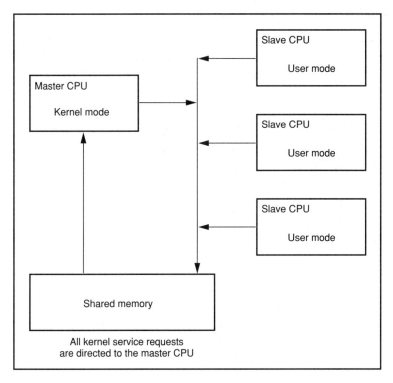

Figure 10.1 Master-slave MP architecture

structures, code, or the ordering of system requests because of the centralized nature of the design.

At the other end of the spectrum from ASMP, is *symmetric multiprocessing* (SMP). In the SMP model, the kernel is split into pieces, or in the case of SunOS 5.x, threads. Each thread is an independent flow of control that can perform a specific function. Each one of these threads can operate on any of the available processors. Thus the kernel, or at least different pieces of the kernel, can operate concurrently or symmetrically on more than one processor at a time. The more threads that are available to run independently, the more *symmetric* the kernel. SunOS 5.x is a highly symmetric operating system with more than 150 threads available to run concurrently in the system.

Figure 10.2 illustrates symmetric multiprocessing.

Preempts and interrupts

Although the terms *preempt* and *interrupt* are well-known, they are often misused. It is important to understand the distinction and when each activity can happen. Preempting occurs when a process takes over control of the CPU and continues to run on its own behalf. The preempt can occur for several reasons, but preempts generally occur when a process of priority higher than the currently running process be-

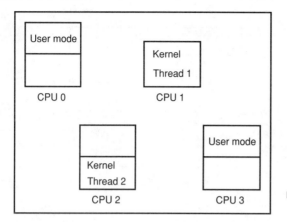

Figure 10.2 Symmetric MP

comes runable. When this happens a context switch will take place and the preempt is complete.

An interrupt is the sequence where a process (or thread) is stopped momentarily to service some form of request. The request may be from hardware, such as the completion of disk I/O or network protocol, or the interrupt may be of the software variety as in the case of a signal. In either case, when the interrupt comes in, the currently running process is stopped, the interrupt is serviced, and the original process will continue. The important thing to note is that the original task does not lose control of the processor.

Generally, interrupting a process is not as critical as preempting a process. Since the original task is not switched out, all of the relevant information is still handy and starting it up after the interrupt service is not so difficult. With preempt, there are other issues. Suppose the preempted task were in the middle of a critical update that other processes depended on having completed. It is not just a matter of doing the context switch.

With traditional UNIX systems and SunOS 4.x, only processes running in user mode were preemptible.[15] This meant if a process were executing in user mode, any other process of higher priority could become runable, initiate the context switch, and take over the CPU. If the CPU was running the kernel, such a preemption could not occur. By defining the limits of preemption this way, scheduling became a little easier. Since the kernel could not be preempted, there was never a need to worry about critical data being lost, or in a multiprocessor environment, concurrent updates of critical data. A major disadvantage to this plan is that real-time scheduling is not possible because a process may have to wait for the kernel to complete what could be a very long task on behalf of another process.

---

[15]Generically, it is said that SunOS and older versions of UNIX were not *real-time* capable. There are other issues to being real-time, but the inability to take the CPU away from the kernel was a major hurdle to real-time. Products that identify themselves as real-time UNIX kernel are nothing more than scheduling executive programs, not an entire operating system.

Under 5.x, both user mode *and* kernel mode processes (threads) are preemptible. The implications of this are far reaching because now even kernel activities may be switched out to run higher priority tasks. This is a necessary, but not sufficient condition to running real-time activities. The ability to preempt the kernel is one requirement for real-time performance. The other requirement is the ability to lock pages in memory. It turns out that real-time scheduling will not give the desired performance if the process has to wait for a page fault. To aid in this cause, the **memctl( )** system call is now available. This call is discussed in detail later.

Real-time vs. bounded dispatch latency

As operating systems and applications perform more and more operations in a shorter period of time, the question arises, "What about real-time processing?" Real-time scheduling can have a rather broad definition, but is typically defined as the ability to gain control of (or one of) the processor(s) within a very short bounded period of time. Depending on your application, this "very short" period of time could be anywhere from several instruction cycles to a matter of seconds. SunOS advertises the ability to perform real-time processing by allowing access to a processor within a bounded period of time. The actual time is dependent on the specific task and architecture, but the current published benchmarks are between 2 and 5 milliseconds on a SPARCstation 2 (one processor).

Such performance is possible because Sun provides a fully preemptible kernel. This means that any process needing use of a processor, with appropriate permissions and priority, can gain almost immediate control of the processor. The problem with preempting the kernel is the same as preempting an ordinary process, i.e., the kernel may be in the process of doing a critical operation that cannot be disturbed.

In order to be completely accurate then, the SunOS kernel is defined as fully preemptible with several non-preemption points. A non-preemption point is a point where the kernel cannot be preempted and thus cause a delay to a process attempting access. However, these, non-preemptible sections of code execute very quickly (for example, a high priority interrupt).

Because of the existence of these non-preemption points, SunOS scheduling cannot guarantee *real-time* access to a processor. Rather, it guarantees access within a bounded period of time. The period of time a process may have to wait to gain access to a processor is called *latency*. The starting up of a process is called *dispatching* in SunOS 5.x, hence the term *bounded dispatch latency* is sometimes used rather than *real-time*. This means that a process designated as *real-time* is guaranteed to gain access to a processor in a bounded period of time. There are other issues regarding real-time that will be examined later in Chapter 13 concerning real-time programming.

Fundamental Scheduling Concepts

As the next generation of software applications develop, there is increased demand for time-critical applications to have control over their scheduling behavior. Applications such as virtual reality and multimedia will be divided into schedulable pieces, some of which require real-time access, while other pieces will not. One of the goals of the SunOS 5.x environment is to provide a standard interface to the programmer that allows such *mixed-mode* scheduling behavior.

With this goal in mind, two features have been included in SunOS 5.x that are available to the programmer for manipulating the scheduling behavior of processes:

- Deterministic scheduling
- Standard system call interfaces

Deterministic scheduling means that the kernel will schedule tasks based on priority and scheduling class. In SunOS, the basic entity to be scheduled is a thread. The programmer will be able to decide the initial priority of a thread as well as the scheduling class to which the thread belongs. Once a thread has entered a class, its behavior is well-defined, i.e., deterministic, because of a dispatch table associated with that particular class. The make-up of the dispatch table is also configurable by the (super)user or system administrator. The table will determine if a thread will be time-sliced, how long the time-slice will be, and what the new priority will be if the time-slice expires.

The standard system call interface provided for these manipulations is **priocntl( )**. **Priocntl( )** can be used to change scheduling class as well as set priority within the class. The table that is used to determine priority changes through the lifetime of the process is manipulated by **dispadmin(1M)**. Use of **dispadmin( )** is discussed in Chapter 14.

Scheduling Implementation

Scheduling in SunOS is built on the internal architecture of a process, namely the threads and lightweight process structures that compose a process. At any given moment during the running of the system, there is a set of runable threads that are stored in a system-wide dispatch queue or for multiprocessor architecture, a set of dispatch queues, one for each processor. A dispatch queue is an array of pointers each pointing to a linked list of threads (**kthread_t** structures).

Each list will have all of the threads runable at a particular priority. The dispatch queue structure is shown in Figure 10.3.

Each thread has associated with it information for accessing files, user credentials, signal context, and other information. The kernel itself consists of a set of threads that are responsible for a multitude of tasks including paging, swapping, and servicing STREAMS requests. There is also an idle thread that will be selected for execution anytime there is no other runable thread available. The idle thread will be switched out whenever any other thread becomes runable. This is achieved by designating the priority of the idle thread as –1.

In addition to user threads, kernel threads, and idle threads, there are interrupt threads. The difference between a kernel thread and an interrupt thread is that all interrupt threads run at a higher priority than all system or kernel threads, even higher than real-time threads.[16] Interrupt threads become runable when a device interrupt occurs.

---

[16]The system is delivered with the basic three scheduling classes: TS, RT and SYS. The system is designed to allow other scheduling classes to be built and loaded. Interrupt threads are guaranteed to the highest priority threads, regardless of the number and type of scheduling classes loaded.

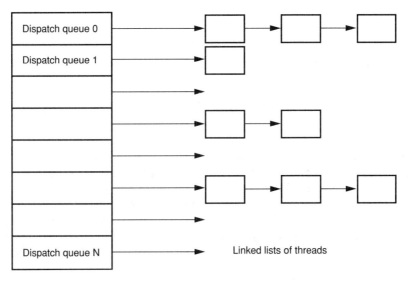

Figure 10.3 Dispatch queues

Since threads have enough information in the thread local stack to be self-contained, it is possible for interrupt threads to be blocked using the same synchronization objects (mutexes, et.al.) as other threads. Also, interrupt threads will be bound to the processor to which the interrupt was delivered and will not migrate to another processor. This characteristic is called *processor affinity*. All other threads have no processor affinity and will move from processor to processor as needed to complete processing.

Priority

Associated with each thread is a priority. The priority is initially assigned based on application parameters and potential command line options. In most cases, the initial priority will be the same as the thread that created the new thread. The priority is used to index into the array of dispatch queues.

A dispatch queue is a linked list of runable threads that have the same dispatch priority. The scheduler will look at an array of such dispatch queues and select the first thread on the first non-empty dispatch queue, which by design will be the highest priority thread available for running.

Typically, a new thread or a thread just completing its time slice will be added to the end of the list of the appropriate dispatch queue. Threads will be taken from the front of the list and put into execution. Thus, a round robin algorithm is implemented among threads on the same queue, i.e., the same priority.

If a thread is waiting on a synchronization object(a mutex lock, for example), it will not be found on one of the dispatch queues. Instead, it will be found on a sleep queue, also known as a *turnstile*. A sleep queue is a linked list of threads waiting on the same priority. Thus, when a synchronization object becomes available, the highest priority thread waiting for it will run first.

Scheduling Classes

SunOS 5.x is delivered with three different scheduling classes:

- Time-share (TS)
- System (SYS)
- Real-time (RT)

Each of these scheduling classes is a separate kernel module that is loaded as needed. Unless specific programs have been started with real-time priority, only the TS and the SYS scheduling classes are loaded at boot time. These kernel modules can be found in **/kernel/sched/ts** and **/kernel/sched/sys**.

Attributes for each class are determined by the class specific functions provided in each scheduling module. Certain attributes are determined by the general rules for scheduling. For example, one rule says that the higher the priority value, the higher the priority of that thread.[17] On the other hand, a scheduling class is free to decide on the range of priorities used by that class or even if threads in that class will time-slice. A thread will initially inherit the class of process that created the thread and any class specific data within the parent. A thread may change the class using the **priocntl( )** system call.

The timeshare class is the most widely used class for scheduling. All user mode (non-real-time) threads will run in the TS class. The timeshare class uses a time slice method for sharing the processor(s). In other words, a thread will run only for a designated period of time before it is switched out to allow another thread to run. The time slice in the timeshare class, by default, will vary from 20 to 200 milliseconds. The length of the time-slice changes based on the priority, which changes every time a context switch occurs. The default can be changed by updating the dispatch table with the **dispadmin(1M)** command. The TS class uses this round-robin scheduling method to ensure all user level threads get a chance to run.

The SYS class is set up to run kernel threads. Threads running in the SYS class have a fixed priority and are not time sliced. This means that once a thread is put into the SYS class at a specific priority, the thread will run until it is blocked, preempted, or completed.

A user may not move a user thread to the SYS class, however, user level threads will be automatically moved to the SYS class on execution of a system call. Since there is no time-slicing in the SYS class, there is no dispatch table to manipulate.

The real-time (RT) scheduling class is also a fixed priority scheduling class that *does* do time-slicing. Real-time threads are scheduled based only on their priorities. Once a thread has been put into the RT class at a specific priority, the priority will remain the same. The thread will run for the time period indicated by the RT dispatch table and then check to see if it is the highest priority thread. If so, the thread will continue to run for another time-slice.

---

[17]If you are familiar with SunOS 4.x, you will note this is reversed from those releases where the *lower* the priority value the higher the priority of the process. Also, priorities were fixed between 0 and 127 (0 being the best).

Interrupt threads are not really a separate scheduling class in the sense that they do not have a table or class functions. Interrupt threads are guaranteed to be the highest priority thread running in the system. This means if a scheduling class is loaded dynamically, interrupt thread priorities will automatically be recomputed. The recalculation is really pretty simple. The interrupt priorities will simply be raised by the number of priorities used by the new class. For instance, by default the RT class is not loaded and the interrupt thread priorities are 100 to 109. As soon as the RT class is loaded, which uses 60 priority levels, the interrupt threads will have a priority range from 160 to 169.

The ranges and the global priorities are shown in Figure 10.4 for each of the classes described.

Process States

At this point we have described the elements and the attributes of the elements involved in scheduling. Before we can describe the scheduling model, we need to describe the concept of process state. Threads can be in one of three states; blocked, runable, or running, while they are in execution. There are two additional states, idle and exited that are used during start-up of a process and when a process has exited (made the **exit( )** system call). A process will be in the idle state exactly once and once it leaves the idle state it will not return. A process will be in the exited state exactly once and once it enters the exited state it will not leave. This means the states of primary interest are runable, running, or blocked.

We have already seen that all runable threads will be stored on one of the dispatch queues, ordered by priority. All blocked or sleeping threads will be stored in one of the turnstiles, ordered by the event for which the thread is waiting. Figure 10.5 shows the overall picture of queues and process states.

There is no list or queue that keeps track of idle threads. A thread is moved from the idle state to the runable state by the **fork** system call. As we will see in the next chapter, when the **exit( )** call is made, a thread will move to the exited state, but it is not quite *dead* yet. There is some cleanup to be done by the **wait( )** system call. After the cleanup, all exited threads will be kept on a list called **thread_deathrow**. **Thread_deathrow** is actually a list of proc structures that have been previously

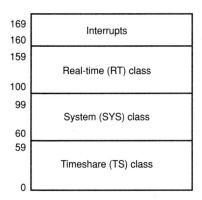

Figure 10.4 Scheduling classes with default priorities

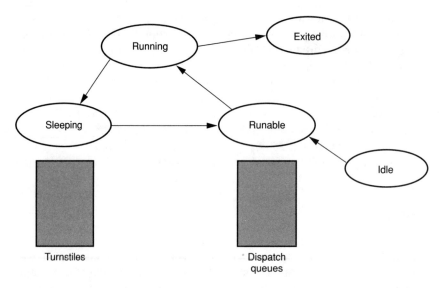

Figure 10.5 Process state model

used for now defunct processes. When a new process is started, a proc structure can be reclaimed from the **thread_deathrow** list, which will be faster than allocating a new structure. This reclaiming procedure will also keep deathrow from growing too large.

Scheduling

Keeping in mind the previous priority and the process state diagram, the scheduling model now becomes reasonably straightforward. The kernel scheduler will select the highest priority thread from the dispatch queues and place it into execution. Remember the following guidelines will apply:

- Interrupt threads will always have the highest priority and will preempt all other threads except higher priority interrupt threads.
- If there are no runable threads in the dispatch queues, the processor(s) will run the idle thread.
- The kernel will always select the highest priority runable thread. In other words, the dispatch queues will be manipulated so the highest priority thread will be on top of the list.

When a process is running, one of several things may happen:

- The thread must sleep waiting for a resource (I/O, locks, timers . . .).
- The thread can use up all of its allocated time-slice.
- The thread can be preempted by a higher priority thread.
- The thread can exit.

Each of these events will result in a state change. Blocking or waiting for a lock will move the thread to a turnstile. Normally, this will happen when the **sleep(2)** system call is encountered, or if any of the synchronization primitives (mutex, semaphore, reader/writer lock, or condition variables) are blocked waiting for a lock or condition to become true.[18] Being preempted or having the time slice expire will move the thread back to the dispatch queues. Exiting will move the thread to **thread_deathrow**. Earlier, we stated that once in the exited state, the thread will never leave and once back in the dispatch queue, the sequence of events will start over. The only state change left to examine is moving from the sleeping state to runable. This will happen when the event waited for occurs, i.e., the lock is available or the I/O is complete.[19] At this point the thread can go back to the dispatch queues, or if the priority is enough to preempt a currently running thread, back to the running state.

Summary

We have examined the basic life cycle of a thread, terminology, and scheduling concepts. The next chapter will examine the internal details of the events shown in this chapter. The basic life cycle has not changed in the UNIX environment for some time and references [1], [2], and [3] give very good examinations of this. SunOS 5.x specifics can be looked at in [5] and [9].

Addendum for Solaris 2.4

The final editing of this book came very close to the release of Solaris 2.4, so I am adding some information on the scheduling for this release. Solaris 2.4 has one additional new class, the IA (interactive) class. From the basic structure of scheduling, you can see that while a new class is relatively easy to add, one needs to write the class-specific routines to implement the class. As it turns out, the IA class shares most of its class-specific routines with the TS class (0–59), but it uses a different dispatch table. The intent of the IA class is to provide a priority boost to the window currently being used. This is accomplished by placing the window server in the IA class; therefore, all the children of the window server will be in the IA class. As the mouse moves and the window focus changes, the IA class-specific routines will raise the priority of that window by 10 (default). This will give a little better performance to window applications.

---

[18]In SunOS 4.x, the internal call to move a process from the running state was **sleep( )**. Under SunOS 5.x, these calls have mostly been replaced by **cv_wait(9)**.

[19]Again, the typical SunOS 4.x method was to use a function named **wakeup( )**. Under SunOS 5.x, the usual method is to use a **cv_signal(9)**.

Scheduling Class and Process Lifetime Implementation

So far we have examined the global scheduling concepts and implementation in the form of scheduling classes and process states and their associated lists. In this chapter, we will examine exactly what happens to an individual process during its lifetime. We will explore the internal details of data structure and algorithms used by the system calls that directly affect process lifetime **fork( )**, **exec( )**, **exit( )**, and **wait( )**.

The focus of attention for all processes and these specific calls, is the proc data structure. The proc structure has been referenced in previous sections when discussing threads and virtual memory, but now will be examined more closely. Use of scheduling classes is transparent to the process lifetime, since the class specific functions for scheduling are used in an object oriented fashion. The first part of this chapter will examine how this is accomplished and then we will look at the process lifetime system calls.

Scheduling Class Implementation

Since the ability to add new scheduling classes is a feature of SunOS 5.x, there must be a scheme for implementing a scheduling class in a nonoperating system dependent fashion. Such a plan is ideal for an object oriented solution. In the kernel, there is an array of structures of type **sclass_t** (see **/usr/include sys/class.h**). The array will contain one entry for each of the available scheduling classes. Each class entry contains the following:

- Class name
- Class initialization function
- Pointer to class functions
- Reader/writer lock

When the system is loaded, the initialization functions for each of the classes to be loaded is called. For example, the timeshare class is loaded by calling the timeshare class initialization function **ts_init( )**, but actual implementation hides the class details by making an object oriented call as follows:

```
(*class->cl_init)(arguments...)
```

where *class* is a pointer to an *sclass* structure. The initialization function returns information regarding the priority range the class will cover and a pointer to the class specific functions that will be called later.

Once the classes have been set up, each thread (**kthread_t**) will have associated with it a class-specific data structure. For timeshare threads, this will be a pointer to a **tsproc_t** (**/usr/include/sys/ts.h**) and for real-time threads, a pointer to an **rtproc_t** (see **/usr/include/sys/rt.h**). This addition leads to the changes to the overall picture of the threads model shown in Figure 11.1.

The most important items in the **tsproc_t** and **rtproc_t** structure are the time left in the time slice allocated and the priority information. There are some flags and pointers to maintain lists as well, but our most immediate concerns will be with the time slices and priorities.

Now that the class is loaded and we can identify the class from a field in the proc structure, we can move on to the specifics of starting and terminating a process.

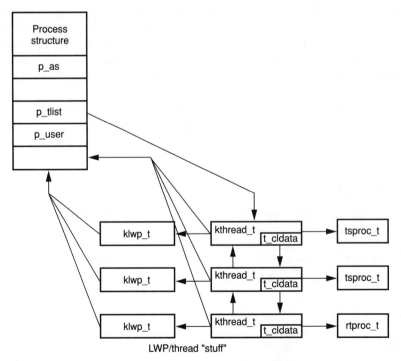

Figure 11.1 Updated threads model showing scheduling class data

The Proc Structure

The proc structure is the center of all activities regarding process management and it must remain in memory at all times. The entire definition of the proc structure (**typedef'd** to **proc_t**) can be found in **/usr/include/sys/proc.h** and is 776 bytes in length. The largest piece of the structure is the user area (340 bytes) that we will examine later. The remainder of the structure has fields that fall into several categories:

- Thread and LWP information—**p_lwptotal, p_lwpcnt, p_lwprcnt, p_lwpblocked, p_zombcnt**.
- Signal information—**p_sigmask, p_sig, p_ignore, p_siginfo**.
- Condition Variables and mutexes—locks to make sure the integrity of the structure is held across competing threads.
- Family tree information—**p_parent, p_child, p_sibling, p_nextofkin, p_link**.
- Memory management—**p_as, p_stksize, p_brksize, p_brkbase**.
- Timing management—**p_utime, p_stime, p_cutime, p_cstime**.
- Debugging (/proc entries) and profiling—**p_sigmask, p_fltmask, p_rpof_timerid**.

For a complete list of the fields, you should look in the header file. Some of the more important fields of interest are discussed here. **P_stat** is the state or status field and relates directly to the process state diagram. Possible values for the **p_stat** field are:

- SSLEEP
- SRUN
- SZOMB
- SSTOP
- SIDL
- SONPROC

Each of these corresponds to one of the states of the process state diagram except for SSTOP, which is used by the debugger when a breakpoint is encountered.

P_cred is a pointer to a credentials structure (struct cred) that contains a process real and effective user id, real and effective group id, and a list of groups to which this process belongs.

The **p_flag** field is a 32-bit number with various bits set to indicate the current operational state of a process. Most of these flags are used by the kernel to indicate temporary conditions during context switches, such as **SLOAD** for loaded in memory. Several flags are used for tracing processes (**SPREXEC, SPROCTR, SPRFORK, SKILLCL**). We will describe the use of each flag as it is encountered in further discussions. All of the flags are listed below. Included are the comments from the header file.

```
SSYS       /* system (resident) process */
STRC       /* ptrace() compatibility mode set by /proc */
```

```
SNWAKE      /* process cannot be awakened by a signal */
SLOAD       /* in core */
SLOCK       /* process cannot be swapped */
SPREXEC     /* process is in exec() (a flag for /proc) */
SPROCTR     /* signal,fault or syscall tracing via /proc */
SPRFORK     /* child inherits /proc tracing flags */
SKILLED     /* SIGKILL has been posted to the process */
SULOAD      /* u-block in core */
SRUNLCL     /* set process running on last /proc close */
SKILLCL     /* kill process on last /proc close */
SOWEUPC     /* owe process an addupc() call at next ast */
SEXECED     /* this process has execed */
SPASYNC     /* asynchronous stopping via /proc */
SJCTL       /* SIGCLD sent when children stop/continue */
SNOWAIT     /* children never become zombies */
SVFORK      /* process resulted from vfork */
SVFDONE     /* vfork child releasing parent as */
EXITLWPS    /* have lwps exit within the process */
HOLDLWPS    /* stop lwps where they're cloneable */
SWAITSIG    /* SIGWAITING sent when all lwps block */
COREDUMP    /* process is dumping core */
```

The User Area

Those familiar with BSD UNIX or SunOS 4.x will be accustomed to seeing a separate user area that was pointed to by a field in the proc structure. The strategy has changed with SunOS 5.x and the user area is now included as part of the proc structure. This has happened for two reasons. First, the user area is smaller than it used to be (320 bytes) and management is easier if it is included in the proc structure. Second, much of the information that used to be stored in the user area is now kept in the **kthread_t** or **klwp_t** structures, or allocated on the fly in kernel memory as needed. There is a performance boost here since now the user area will never be swapped out. Although there is not any information in the user area that is needed while the process is swapped out, there will be no time spent retrieving the user area.

The most useful information in the user area are the arguments passed to the process and the list of file descriptors open for this process.

The "Big Picture" Revisited

Figure 11.2 reviews the major data structures we have examined so far (adding the user area) and their relationships.

Notice that the major sections of Figure 11.2 have been blocked off. The Virtual memory information, address space (as), segment (seg), and vnode structures comprise the first part and the thread and LWP information the second major piece. The portions are marked off because they will be manipulated as a group when the process lifetime system calls (**fork( )**, **exec( )**, **exit( )**, and **wait( )**) are run.

Process Creation with the fork( ) System Call

All processes are the result of a **fork( )** system call. The only exceptions to this are three processes [**init, sched** (the swapper), and **pager**], which are *hand-crafted* at boot time. All other processes can trace their heritage back to the **init** process. For example, a typical *family tree* may resemble Figure 11.3.

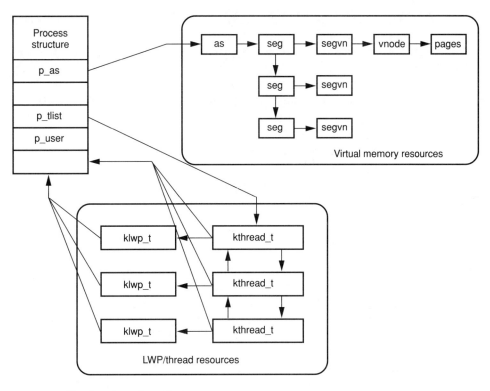

Figure 11.2 The "big picture" revisited

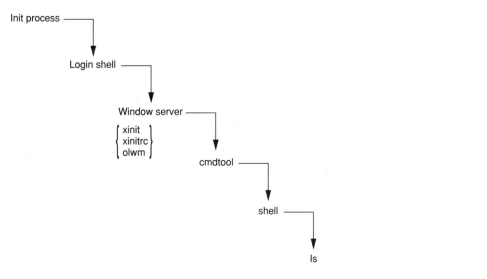

Figure 11.3 Family tree of typical process (ls)

After a fork call is completed, there will be a new process that is called the *child* process while the original, creating process is called the *parent*. The child process will be an exact duplicate of the parent process and the child and the parent will pick up execution at the instruction after the **fork( )**. The return value to the parent process will be the process id of the child and the return value to the child process will be 0. A typical sequence for parent-child code may look like this:

```
...
switch( fork() ) {
     case -1:
     /* process error condition */
     break;
     case 0:
     /* process child activities *
     break;
     default:
     /* process parent activities */
     break;
}
...
```

This code will allow two exact copies to perform different tasks based on the return value from **fork( )**. Making a duplicate of the original implies that all of the structures shown in Figure 11.2 must be copied to build a new process. This is almost true, a new process structure must be allocated and initialized, but there are optimizations so all of the copying will not have to be performed. The first of these optimizations is the Copy-on-Write (COW) policy we examined in the virtual memory sections. This means new pages will not actually be allocated to the child process, rather a pointer to the same pages will be used until the page is actually changed.

A second optimization is the use of the **fork1( )** system call. **Fork1( )** is a new call in SunOS 5.x and its purpose is to speed up the normal fork call. Since a **fork( )** is copying all of the parent process, this means copying all of the thread and LWP structure that were running at the time of the fork. This could be a large waste of time in the case where the next task will be to exec a new process. The system would end up copying structures that are going to be immediately destroyed by the **exec( )**. **Fork1( )** will copy only the thread that makes the actual call. The current system call interface supports **fork( )** and **fork1( )**; future POSIX implementations will support **fork( )** and **forkall( )**. The POSIX **fork( )** will be the current **fork1( )** and the POSIX **forkall( )** will be the current **fork( )**. The underlying implementation will be the same, only the entry points will be different.

The third call commonly used in creating a new process is **vfork( )** or *virtual* fork. **Vfork( )** was intended to be a fast fork for older UNIX systems where the creation time was very long. It was faster because the copies of structure were not actually made, rather pointers to structure were used. With Sun's virtual memory implementation this is exactly what happens anyway, so the benefits of **vfork( )** are gone and there is seldom a need to use it.

Steps in Process Creation

The major steps performed in process creation are:

1. Allocate and initialize a new proc structure.

2. Duplicate the context and virtual memory resources of the parent.

3. Duplicate the LWP and thread resources of the parent.

4. Schedule the child to run in an appropriate scheduling class specific manner.

Fork( ), **fork1( )**, and **vfork( )** all call a common fork routine **cfork( )** with a flag to indicate which flavor of fork is being used. **Cfork( )** performs the following steps:

- Ensure that the LWPs that are to be copied are not swapped out during the operation by marking them as not swappable.

- Perform error checking—Do not allow one user to have too many children, do not use up the last proc structure unless the User ID (UID) is 0 (root).

- Allocate kernel memory for proc structure and PID structures.

- Determine a new Process id (PID) by incrementing the last PID used. If the new PID is greater than **MAXPID** (30,000), start with the first unused PID beginning with 0.

- Initialize the new proc structure by copying most of the parents information. Fields about resource usage, LWP count, and timers will be cleared to zero. Parent process ID (PPID) will be set to PID of parent. Pointers to sibling and parent processes will be set appropriately. **P_stat** will be set to SIDL (idle).

At this point, the process has the form shown in Figure 11.4.

Now that **cfork( )** has completed the first step in creating a process, the next task is to copy the parent's virtual memory resources, followed by copying the parent's LWP/thread resources. At this point, the flag **isvfork**, which was passed as a parameter, is checked to see if this call was the result of a **vfork**. If so, the child **p_as** field, the address space pointer, will be set to point at the parent's address space. If **isvfork** is not set then the routine **as_dup( )** is called to duplicate the parent's address space and segment structures.

Before copying the parent's LWP/thread resources, another flag, **isfork1**, is checked to determine if only one LWP or all of the LWPs must be copied. When the

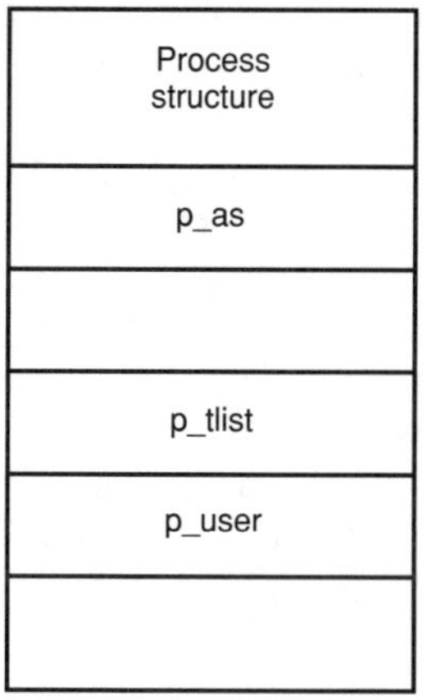

Figure 11.4 New process after first part of cfork( )

POSIX change is made, this flag will always be set to indicate that only the LWP that made the call should be copied.

The last step in process creation is make the child runable. This is done by calling the (scheduling) class specific fork routine. Remember, a new thread (or process) will be in the same scheduling class as the original process. This means the appropriate class routine can be found by using the **t_cldata** field in the thread structure and tracking down the class functions to determine the correct routine to call. This may sound complex, but the call is made in an object oriented way and the kernel does not really know which class is involved. A glance at the **/usr/include/sys/class.h** header file will reveal macros used to make the calls transparent:

```
#define CL_FORK(tp, ctp)   \
         (*(tp)->t_clfuncs->cl_fork)(tp,ctp)
```

In this case, **tp** and **ctp** are pointers to threads. Making a process runable involves placing the processes associated thread on the dispatch queue and letting the scheduler take over. The next chapter will examine exactly how the scheduler does its job.

Process Termination

Process termination occurs when any thread of a process encounters the **exit( )** system call. This can happen voluntarily, by explicitly making the call, or involuntarily when a signal is received. Once a process has terminated, the remains of the child must be picked up by the parent by executing a **wait( )** system call. Note that **exit( )** does not have to be called explicitly. It will be automatically called when a process is finished with its last line of executable code.

The major tasks for the **exit( )** system call are as follows:

1. Release the thread resources currently in use.
2. Close all currently open files.
3. Release all of the virtual memory resources in use.
4. Give up children for adoption to the **init( )** process.

One thing that does *not* occur is that the proc structure is not freed up for use by another process. This will ultimately be done by the **wait( )** call. The proc structure contains resource usage information (timing, page faults, system calls, context switches, etc.) that may be reclaimed by any process doing a **wait( )** call for this process. The **wait( )** call will collect the data in the **p_ru** (resource usage field) and then free up the proc structure for use elsewhere.

The first step, releasing the thread and LWP resources, is fairly simple. If any of the threads were running, they will be stopped, and if there are any threads on the timeout queue, they will be removed. These steps will be taken on all threads except the thread making the call to **exit( )**, or the main thread in the case of the implicit **exit( )** call. Also, at this point all signals in all threads will be ignored. This should make sense since the process is exiting, any signal actions will not be seen anyway.

At this point, all of the open files will be closed. Since the file closing is an integral part of the **exit( )** call, it is not necessary to call **close( )**. If extra file descriptor *chunks* had been allocated, they will be freed up and returned to kernel memory. After the files have been closed there will be no need for any user resources and all of the virtual memory resources can now be freed up. Remember, the code for **exit( )** is kernel code so it is not affected by freeing up the text segment, which is user code. Even if an exit handler was installed with the **atexit(3C)** call, the function registered with **atexit( )** will be executed first and completed before the call to **exit( )**.

If the current process has any children (**p_child** != NULL), then for each child process (found by following the **p_sibling** field of the process), change its parent process ID (**p_ppid**) to 1, the init process. When a process dies, it will send a signal (**SIGCLD**) to its parent. Since the current process is exiting, changing the child parent PID to the init process, ensures that the child will get cleaned up properly, even though its original parent has died. If this exiting process is tracing any running processes, as with a debugger, the traced process will also exit.

Finally, the process will send the signal to its parent and the current thread can be released. The only remains of the process are the proc structure itself. The state (**p_stat**) of this process has been set to SZOMB to indicate it is a zombie process. The term *zombie* means *undead*, which is appropriate for processes in the zombie state. They are alive in the sense that they can be seen with **ps** (because the proc structure exists), but they are "not quite dead yet" (apologies to Monty Python) in the sense that all of the resources needed to continue running (virtual memory and threads) have been released. Such processes are *dead*, but *not dead*, hence the term *zombie processes*.

Process Cleanup with wait( )

The wait system call works by searching its *family tree* (**p_child** and **p_child-> p_sibling**) for any processes that have their state filed set to SZOMB. There are several user interface variations on the **wait( )** system call.

- waitid
- waitpid
- wait3
- wait4
- wait

Wait3( ), **wait4( )**, and **wait( )** are the traditional ways to wait for a child and **waitid( )** and **waitpid( )** are the newer POSIX compliant ways to wait for a child process. In any event, all of the calls end up in the same place in the kernel, a routine named **waitid( )**.

The flags passed as parameters to **waitid( )** will determine exactly which processes are candidates for status collection. Normally, you will wait for the death of a specific process or any child you have created. However, by changing the parameters to **wait(2)**, you may indicate a process or any member of a process group some other subset of *interesting* processes that should be "wait( )'d" for. Once the set of interesting processes has been identified, they are scanned for their state (SZOMB) and cleaned up. Cleaning up involves two steps:

- Capturing the resource usage from the proc structure.
- Freeing up the memory used by the structure.

Capturing the resource usage information, or *reaping* the status of the child, as it is sometimes called, involves transferring the information from the child proc structure to the return value in the **wait( )** call. It is then up to the user to examine the return value. Since the proc structure was allocated using **kmem_alloc(9)**, a kernel version of **malloc(3)**, it is freed up using **kmem_free(9F)**, a kernel version of **free(3)**.

Creating a New Process

The last piece of process lifetime to look at is how to start a new process. The **fork( )** call only copies the original process and continues execution in the child. The **exec( )** system call, and its variations **execve( ), execle( )** and so on, will actually build an entirely new process on top of the space where the original process once lived. This involves mapping the indicated executable file onto process's virtual address space. The following are the major steps in processing an **exec( )** system call:

- Exit[20] all LWPs except the one making the call.
- Search the file system for the executable file to run.
- Verify permission to run the file.
- Allocate a vnode for the file to be included in the virtual address space.
- Determine executable type by looking at the magic number.
- Verify other resources such as setuid, quotas, tracing, or debugging that may be needed.
- Exit the current thread.
- Clear any pending signals (they were meant for the original process), restore signal masks, and restore alternate signal stacks to default.
- Close any files that were marked close-on-exec.
- Set initial values for registers and hardware context.

In short, all of the virtual memory resources and thread resources are erased and rebuilt with the new process file. Entries in the proc structure that were related to

---

[20]In this and later steps, exit means simply to release any resources held by this thread/LWP.

the original process, such as signals and file descriptors, are reset so the new process can proceed on its own.

Summary

At this point, we have examined the scheduling class structures and the algorithms for creating and terminating a process. All of these steps occur anytime a command is entered on the command line. The command line processor, probably a shell of some variety does a **fork( )** and then does a **wait( )** for the child process. Meanwhile, the child process does an **exec( )**, and on completion does an **exit** to inform the parent of the status of the command. These steps are shown in Figure 11.5.

Since all processes are the result of a **fork** from another process, this life cycle holds for all processes. In the next chapter, we will examine how the kernel scheduler ensures that all processes (threads) get a chance to run.

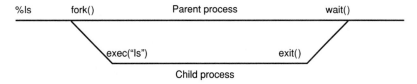

Figure 11.5 Summary of process lifetime

Chapter

12

Process Scheduling

The previous three sections covering multithread architecture, virtual memory implementation, and process lifetime have all described building blocks associated with getting a process into existence. Now, the objective is to place the completed pieces into the scheduling mechanisms and get a share of the CPU resource to complete a task. This chapter will cover the structure of the dispatch queues, the turnstiles, and how a process runs in both single and multiprocessor architectures.

In a more practical vein, at the end of the chapter we will examine how to manipulate the dispatch parameter table for both the real-time and the timeshare scheduling classes and the use of **priocntl( )** to control priority of a single process.

Before proceeding to the topics of this chapter, it may be helpful to review the process state model presented in Chapter 10 (Figure 10.5). As far as scheduling goes, the only relevant states are runable, blocked, or executing. These states are stored in the thread structure field **t_state** and will equal **TS_RUN**, **TS_SLEEP**, and **TS_ONPROC**, respectively (see **/usr/include/sys/thread.h**).

The Dispatch Queues

After a process has been completely built as a result of the **fork( )** (and probably **exec( )**) system calls, it will be marked as runable (**p_stat** == SRUN). Any threads that are made runable as a result of the fork will have their state (**t_state** in the thread structure) set to TS_RUN and will be placed on a dispatch queue. Remember, a process consists of a set of one or more runable threads, so the entity to be scheduled and run is a thread, not a process. Initially, there is only one thread, the one that starts with **main( )** and ends with **exit( )**. If the threads library is used and any **thr_create( )** calls are made, there will be more. In any event, on return from the class specific fork routine, the main thread at a minimum, has been placed on the dispatch queues.

The structure of a dispatch queue entry can be found in the header file **/usr/include/sys/disp.h**. The structure is of type **dispq_t** and consists of three fields:

- A pointer to the first thread on the queue.
- A pointer to the last thread on the queue.
- An integer field indicating the number of threads on this queue.

This structure is summarized in Figure 12.1.

All of the threads on one dispatch queue entry will be of the same priority. Threads on the same queue entry will use the field **t_link** (in the thread structure) to point to the next thread.

One dispatch queue consists of a linked list of runable threads of the same priority. There is a set of dispatch queues (one queue for each priority level) for each CPU in the system.

The Turnstiles

Turnstiles are lists of threads that are sleeping for some reason. Threads sleep because they are blocked waiting for a *slow* system call or are waiting for a synchronization primitive to become available. The definition of a turnstile structure can be found in **/usr/include/sys/turnstile.h** and consists of the following:

- An array of sleep queues
- A Turnstile ID
- Some Flags
- A lock

The most important part of a turnstile is the sleep queue pointer. A turnstile actually contains a pointer to an array of sleep queues. The number of sleep queues available is **NTSILE_SQ** (#define **NTSTILE_SQ 2**). A sleep queue is a linked list of threads. A **sleepq_t** definition (**/usr/include/sys/sleepq.h**) is a pointer to a thread. The remainder of the list of threads is built using the **t_link** field of the thread structure.

The term *turnstile* comes from the fact that a turnstile allows only one thread to pass regardless of how many "lines," or queues, there are, just as a turnstile at a stadium allows only one customer to pass at a time, regardless of how many people are waiting. The same is true here. No matter how many sleep queues are attached to a turnstile, only one thread will "pass" (be awakened) at a time.

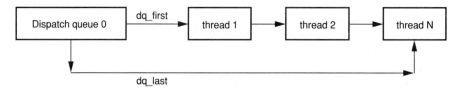

Figure 12.1 Dispatch queue entry structure

An important part of scheduling is moving the thread to and from one of the turn-stiles. The kernel will place all threads waiting on a particular item (the same mutex, for example) on the same sleepq in the same turnstile. This means all threads wait-ing for the same item will be on the same list. The identity of the turnstile (a **turn-stile_id_t**—an unsigned short) is a field in all of the synchronization primitives, mutex, semaphore, reader/writer lock, and condition variable. This id is used to find the thread when it is time to wake the thread up.

Since many threads can be waiting on the same item, there is an ordering to the turnstiles. A thread will be placed on the end of a sleep queue and it will be removed from the front, which in effect implements a first-in first-out scheme for the queues. The exception to this is when a **cv_broadcast(9)** or **cond_broadcast(3T)** call is en-countered. In these cases, *all* threads waiting on the specified item will be awakened.

There is one final point to be made regarding turnstiles. A turnstile is actually a pointer to a set of sleep queues. In all cases except for reader/writer locks, only one of the sleep queues is actually used. With the reader/writer lock (**rw_lock**), there will be two sleep queues, one for the list of threads waiting for read locks, and one for the list of threads waiting for write locks. In either event, the turnstile id field of the **rw_lock** structure will be the same.

Thread Scheduling

One of the last actions taken before a **fork( )** system call returns to the user is to place the newly runable thread onto one of the dispatch queues. The particular dis-patch queue is chosen based on the priority of the thread. Remember the priority of the thread is the same as the parent unless changed by **priocntl( )**.

If a CPU is idle, the kernel will look to see if there are any runable threads by checking to see if there are any non-empty dispatch queues. If there are any runable threads, the highest priority thread will be put into execution. If all of the CPUs are busy, then the kernel will call a class specific function for each thread currently in execution to see if that thread's time-slice has expired. The call will be made every clock tick (100 times per second). Each call will decrement the amount of time left in the thread's time slice (**ts_timeleft**). If the time left is greater than 0, it will con-tinue execution. If the time left in the time slice is 0, the following will occur (This will not occur if this is a timeshare thread currently running in kernel mode because time slicing does not apply in kernel mode):

1. A new priority is assigned based on the timeshare dispatch parameter table (de-scribed in the next section).

2. A new time slice will be assigned based on the new priority.

3. The thread will be moved to the back of a dispatch queue based on its new priority.

4. The thread will give up the CPU.

If the current thread is a real-time thread, the only thing to be done is to decre-ment the amount of time left. If it is 0, the thread will be put at the end of the dis-patch queue. Priority never changes for a real-time thread, so when a real-time thread has used all of its time-slice, it will simply be placed at the end of the queue for that priority.

Preemptive Scheduling

Generically, selecting a thread to run is fairly straightforward. The scheduler will look for the highest priority thread currently loaded in memory and execute the context switch to place the thread on the CPU. Since we have stated several times that all threads (kernel threads, real-time threads, timeshare threads) are preemptible, we need to examine how and when such preemption occurs.

The internal routine to handle preemption is called **preempt( )**. **Preempt( )** will be called any time a thread is made runable that has a higher priority than the currently running thread, or in the case of multiple CPUs, higher than any of the currently running threads. **Preempt( )** will also be invoked when a thread's time-slice has expired by setting the **cpu_runrun** or **cpu_kprunrun** flags. One or both of these flags will be set when a thread becomes runable with a sufficiently high priority. They are set to indicate that a preemption needs to occur and they are cleared after the preemption has taken place. The flags are checked any time a thread is made runable.

The reason two flags are needed is the requirement to indicate whether a kernel level preemption is needed or a user-level preemption. In terms of what happens next, there is no real difference between a user-level preemption and a kernel level preemption. In either case, **preempt( )** will be called which in turn will call a class specific (**ts_preempt( )-, rt_preempt( )**, or **sys_preempt( )**) preemption routine. From **/usr/include/sys/class.h**:

```
#define CL_PREEMPT(tp) \
      (*(tp)->t_clfuncs->clpreempt)(tp)
```

The major function of each of the class specific routines is the same, namely place the outgoing thread on the appropriate dispatch queue (according to class and priority) in the appropriate position within the queue. If a thread is preempted because it ran out of its time slice, it will be placed on the end of the dispatch queue. If a thread was preempted because a higher priority thread became runable (a real preemption), the thread will be placed on the front of the dispatch queue. This mechanism means a thread will get its entire time slice before other threads of the same priority are run.

The system class preemption is very simple since there is never a time-slice expiration or priority change. The thread is simply put back on the front of the dispatch queue it came from. This means a system class thread must voluntarily give up the CPU before another thread of the same priority can run.

The real-time class preempt checks for a time-slice expiration as mentioned above and returns the thread to the same dispatch queue. For the timeshare class, if this is a time-slice expiration, the time slice and the priority will be reset according to the timeshare dispatch table (described in the next section). Changing the priority will cause the thread to be placed on a different dispatch queue.

CPU Selection in an MP Architecture

If there is only one CPU, there will be only one set of dispatch queues. In an MP (multiprocessor) environment, there will be one set of dispatch queues for each CPU. When a preemption occurs (due to a preempt or a time-slice expiration), the routines that place threads on the dispatch queues have to decide on which set of dispatch queues to place the thread. Once again, this is done in a class specific manner. From **/usr/include/sys/class.h**:

```
#define CL_CPU_CHOOSE(t, pri) \
        (*(t)->t_clfuncs->cl_cpu_choose)(t, pri)
```

As far as the hardware is concerned, it makes no difference which CPU is used to run a thread. However, there will be a reduced amount of traffic on the CPU bus (Mbus, xbus or xdbus), if the thread is run on the same CPU it ran on previously. For this reason, the timeshare class choosing routine will place the thread on the same set of dispatch queues it came from originally. If the thread is moving dispatch queues because it has not run in awhile (**ts_maxwait** has expired), **ts_cpu_choose( )** will examine all of the CPUs and place the thread on the dispatch queue of the CPU that has the lowest priority thread currently running.

Attempting to choose the same CPU is enforcing a policy known as *loose affinity*. With the real-time class, such affinity is not enforced and **rt_cpu_choose( )** will always select the dispatch queue associated with the lowest priority CPU.

The Final Scheduling Pieces

At this point, the preempt routine has moved the preempted thread to a dispatch queue in a class specific fashion. **Preempt( )** continues by vacating the CPU and selects a new thread to run on this CPU. Since the dispatch queues were all arranged with the scheduling class in mind, the selection of a new thread need not be class specific. The steps for selecting the thread to run are summarized here:

1. Search all of the dispatch queues for a thread with real-time priority and choose the highest of those.

2. If there are no real-time threads, select the highest priority thread from the dispatch queue of the CPU just vacated.

3. If the current queue is empty, scan the other dispatch queues for the highest priority thread.

4. If there are no other runable threads, select the idle thread for this CPU.

Once a thread has been selected, all that remains is to load the thread on the CPU. It is possible that the same thread that was just preempted is the thread that is selected to run. This will most likely happen when a real-time thread has run out of its time slice and is still the highest priority thread. In this event, there is no loading required because it has not yet been unloaded.

The entire scheduling sequence is shown in Figure 12.2.

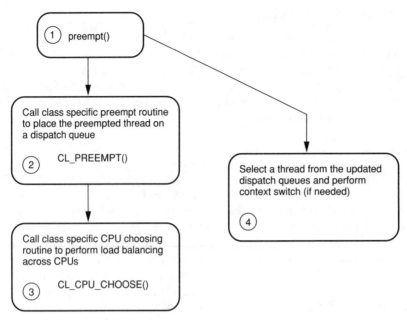

Figure 12.2 Summary of scheduling

Interrupt Handling

We have looked at how a thread becomes runable, how a thread is placed into execution, and how thread preemption occurs. All of this works well with threads that
run within the parameters of a scheduling class. There are, however, a significant
group of threads that do not run within the framework of a class, and those are interrupt threads.

When an interrupt occurs, it will be delivered to a particular CPU and the thread
that was running on that CPU will be *pinned*. A pinned thread cannot move from
one CPU to another and it does not lose its context. It is simply suspended until the
interrupt has been processed. The CPU will know which thread to run to service the
interrupt because it will have a list of interrupt threads associated with the cpu
structure for that CPU (**cpu_t->cpu_intr_thread** in **<sys/cpuvar.h>**).

A device driver will add the interrupt routine for that device to the list by calling
the kernel support routine **ddi_add_intr(9F)**. The **cpu_intr_thread** field in the
cpu_t structure is a pointer to a linked list of interrupt threads. Since the interrupt
routine is a thread, it has all of the properties of thread, meaning it will have its own
stack, set of registers, program counter, and so on. This is very important because this
means an interrupt thread can block, acquire mutexes, sleep, and all of the other things
noninterrupt threads can do.[21] In short, an interrupt thread had its own context.

---

[21]For device driver writers, this is a major change from SunOS 4.x. Under 4.x, an interrupt had no context and therefore could not call **sleep( )** for fear of hanging the system. It is still not a good idea to sleep
in an interrupt handler, but it is now less dangerous.

Since an interrupt handler is a thread, it makes the scheduling of interrupt threads fairly easy. When the interrupt comes in, the thread associated with that interrupt is placed into execution at a very high priority. In fact, interrupt threads are guaranteed to be the highest priority threads in the system, regardless of other classes that have been added or invoked. The only thread that can preempt an interrupt thread is a higher-priority interrupt thread. Priorities for interrupt threads are assigned based on hardware interrupt levels. An interrupt thread servicing a level 5 hardware interrupt has a priority of the highest class plus 5. For example, if the TS and SYS classes are currently loaded, the highest priority is 99. A level 5 interrupt thread will have priority 104 (99 + 5). A level 10 interrupt (the time-of-day clock) will have priority 109 (99 + 10).

This mechanism is in place for interrupts of interrupt priority level 10 or less (See interrupt levels in Chapter 3). When a *high-level* interrupt occurs (level 11 or higher on a SPARC), the interrupt handler will run without a context, i.e., no thread. High-level interrupts will simply acquire the CPU, run to completion, and return to the pinned thread. There can be no sleeps when running such interrupt service routines because there is no context.

Priority Inversion

With the advent of the synchronization primitives, a condition known as *priority inversion* is possible. In general, when two threads are requesting the same mutex, for example, there is a race condition to determine which thread actually acquires the mutex. The other thread (or threads) will block waiting for the mutex to be released. Priority inversion occurs where two or more threads of different priority are contending for the same lock (mutex, semaphore . . .). If the lower priority thread acquires the lock, the higher priority thread will block as usual, but the wait could be much longer than expected because the lower priority thread may not get to run as often, or as fast, and not release the lock in a timely manner. The solution to this is *priority inheritance*. Priority inheritance means the lower priority thread will temporarily use (inherit) the priority of the other thread to speed up release of the lock. An example of priority inheritance follows:

1. Thread A has a priority of 147 and thread B has a priority of 92.
2. Both thread A and thread B are performing a **mutex_lock** for mutex Z.
3. If thread B acquires the mutex, thread A will block.
4. For as long as thread B holds the mutex and thread A waits, thread B will run at a priority of 147.
5. As soon as the lock is released, thread B will resume at priority 92.

There are variations on this same problem, such as a blocking chain. Thread A holds a lock needed by thread B, while thread B holds a lock needed by thread C. This means thread C will have to wait for thread A to complete. All of this inheritance is implemented by using a field in the thread structure—**t_epri**.

In the strictest sense, this is not a problem for the scheduling subsystem. A thread will be placed in the dispatch queue according to priority and will run on that basis. It is up to the locking and unlocking routines to make sure the priority is set correctly.

Use of dispadmin(1M) to Control Scheduling

As a practical matter, one of the most powerful ways to influence scheduling behavior in SunOS 5.x is by adjusting the dispatch parameter table(s). This section will examine the details of the table and use of **dispadmin(1M)** to administer them.

It was noted earlier that scheduling in SunOS 5.x is table driven. This means that a scheduling class and initial priority have been established for a particular process; all other scheduling parameters, such as time slice, priority after a wakeup, and so on, are all determined by looking at a class-specific table that outlines those features. Each scheduling class has such a table that can be modified by using the **dispadmin(1M)** command. The easiest way to change the table value is to redirect the output of the –g option to a file. Edit the new file to reflect the changes you want and then use the –s option to read the new values into the system.

```
# dispadmin -l
TS SYS
# dispadmin -c TS -g > /tmp/tc_table
# vi /tmp/ts_table
        Make changes as needed
# dispadmin -c TS -s /tmp/ts_table
```

The values and meaning for the real-time and timeshare dispatch tables are on manual pages **rt_dptbl(4)** and **ts_dptbl(4)**. In the real-time class, the table is simple with only two values, the priority and the time slice. The following shows a sample RT class dispatch parameter table. Associated with each priority is a time quantum (expressed in $\frac{1}{1000}$ of a second units):

```
# dispadmin -c RT -g
# Real Time Dispatcher Configuration
RES=1000

# TIME QUANTUM                          PRIORITY
# (rt_quantum)                          LEVEL
1000                    #                  0
1000                    #                  1
1000                    #                  2
1000                    #                  3
1000                    #                  4
1000                    #                  5
1000                    #                  6
1000                    #                  7
1000                    #                  8
1000                    #                  9
 800                    #                 10
 800                    #                 11
 800                    #                 12
 800                    #                 13
 800                    #                 14
```

```
800                    #                    15
800                    #                    16
800                    #                    17
800                    #                    18
800                    #                    19
600                    #                    20
600                    #                    21
600                    #                    22
600                    #                    23
600                    #                    24
600                    #                    25
600                    #                    26
600                    #                    27
600                    #                    28
600                    #                    29
400                    #                    30
400                    #                    31
400                    #                    32
400                    #                    33
400                    #                    34
400                    #                    35
400                    #                    36
400                    #                    37
400                    #                    38
400                    #                    39
200                    #                    40
200                    #                    41
200                    #                    42
200                    #                    43
200                    #                    44
200                    #                    45
200                    #                    46
200                    #                    47
200                    #                    48
200                    #                    49
100                    #                    50
100                    #                    51
100                    #                    52
100                    #                    53
100                    #                    54
100                    #                    55
100                    #                    56
100                    #                    57
100                    #                    58
100                    #                    59
```

The timeshare class dispatch table is more complex. Each priority level has 6 entries:

- **priority**—the dispatch priority.

- **quantum**—the number of CPU ticks this process will be allowed before being switched out (remember 100 ticks per second).

- **tqexp**—the new priority of this process the next time it runs if it used all of its time slice this time. This will generally be lower and has the effect of preventing CPU hogs from remaining at a high priority.

- **slpret**—this is the priority a process will be assigned when it becomes runable after sleeping. This is generally higher and has the effect of preventing CPU starvation.

- **maxwait**—this is the maximum number of seconds a process will wait before getting its full time quantum. This field is used in conjunction with the **lwait** field.

- **lwait**—if a process has waited maxwait and not used its allocated quantum, it will receive the **lwait** priority. This also has the effect of trying to prevent CPU starvation.

```
# dispadmin -c TS -g -r 100
# Time Sharing Dispatcher Configuration
RES=100
# ts_quantum  ts_tqexp  ts_slpret  ts_maxwait  ts_lwait  PRIORITY LEVEL
        20        0        59          0          50        #     0
        20        0        59          0          50        #     1
        20        0        59          0          50        #     2
        20        0        59          0          50        #     3
        20        0        59          0          50        #     4
        20        0        59          0          50        #     5
        20        0        59          0          50        #     6
        20        0        59          0          50        #     7
        20        0        59          0          50        #     8
        20        0        59          0          50        #     9
        16        0        59          0          51        #    10
        16        1        59          0          51        #    11
        16        2        59          0          51        #    12
        16        3        59          0          51        #    13
        16        4        59          0          51        #    14
        16        5        59          0          51        #    15
        16        6        59          0          51        #    16
        16        7        59          0          51        #    17
        16        8        59          0          51        #    18
        16        9        59          0          51        #    19
        12       10        59          0          52        #    20
        12       11        59          0          52        #    21
        12       12        59          0          52        #    22
        12       13        59          0          52        #    23
        12       14        59          0          52        #    24
        12       15        59          0          52        #    25
        12       16        59          0          52        #    26
        12       17        59          0          52        #    27
        12       18        59          0          52        #    28
        12       19        59          0          52        #    29
         8       20        59          0          53        #    30
         8       21        59          0          53        #    31
         8       22        59          0          53        #    32
         8       23        59          0          53        #    33
         8       24        59          0          53        #    34
         8       25        59          0          54        #    35
         8       26        59          0          54        #    36
         8       27        59          0          54        #    37
         8       28        59          0          54        #    38
         8       29        59          0          54        #    39
         4       30        59          0          55        #    40
         4       31        59          0          55        #    41
         4       32        59          0          55        #    42
         4       33        59          0          55        #    43
         4       34        59          0          55        #    44
         4       35        59          0          56        #    45
         4       36        59          0          57        #    46
         4       37        59          0          58        #    47
         4       38        59          0          58        #    48
         4       39        59          0          58        #    49
         4       40        59          0          59        #    50
         4       41        59          0          59        #    51
         4       42        59          0          59        #    52
         4       43        59          0          59        #    53
         4       44        59          0          59        #    54
         4       45        59          0          59        #    55
```

4	46	59	0	59	#	56
4	47	59	0	59	#	57
4	48	59	0	59	#	58
4	49	59	0	59	#	59

A close look at the default TS table will reveal that higher priorities have a shorter time quantum, while lower priorities have a large quantum. This generally means that CPU-intensive, noninteractive processes will end up with lower priorities, while user-intensive processes will have a higher priority. Since user-intensive processes are sleeping most of the time anyway, this seems to be an equitable system.

Summary

This chapter has examined in some detail how a thread becomes runable and how its priority is adjusted over its lifetime. Interested users should examine the system calls **priocntl(2)**, **processor_bind(2)**, and **p_online(2)**. For global changes to the system, knowledgeable system administrators should look at the use of **dispadmin(1M)**. For further reading, [5] and [9] can provide some insight. Also, a more detailed example for table manipulation appears in Appendix B.

13

Real-Time Programming

Since the use of *real-time* programming may be new to many UNIX/SunOS programmers, this chapter is intended as a practical introduction to the use and hazards of real-time programs. It will examine exactly what real-time means to SunOS and the overall system performance impact that may result from poor programming techniques.

Components of Dispatch Latency

Most common definitions of real-time include the idea of guaranteeing access to a CPU within a bounded period of time. What exactly is that bounded period of time and what will it be on a SunOS based architecture? The period of time it will take to respond is known as the *dispatch latency period* and consists of three basic components:

- Interrupt scheduling and processing
- Dispatch processing
- Application response time

If an interrupt is currently running when the real-time task is started, the new task must wait until the interrupt is scheduled and processed. After the interrupt is handled, the real-time task can begin its dispatch sequence. This involves being placed on the dispatch queue and preempting a current process. Finally, the real-time task may have to wake up lower priority tasks and have them run to give up resources that are being held (*priority inheritance*). Given all of these parameters, a bounded period of time can be attached to the start-up of a real-time task. The period of time, dependent on the system architecture, is shown in the following table. (This data is taken directly from the System Services Section of the SunOS AnswerBook.)

Workstation	Bounded Time	Unbounded Time
SPARCstation 1	< 2.0 ms	4.5 ms
SPARCstation 1+	< 2.0 ms	4.0 ms
SPARCstation IPX	< 1.0 ms	2.2 ms
SPARCstation 2	< 1.0 ms	2.0 ms

The bounded time column is a time when there is a bounded number of processes running on the system. For SS1, SS1+, and the IPX, the times shown are for fewer than eight processes; for the SS2, fewer than sixteen processes. The unbounded time is for any number of processes.

There are some situations that will *invalidate* the guarantee of performance. Any interrupts that occur after the start of the dispatch period must be serviced and will delay the start of the real-time task. Also, if there are other real-time tasks at higher priority, they could adversely affect dispatch latency of new real-time tasks.

There is one other problem with real-time performance in SunOS. The virtual memory model used by SunOS does not guarantee that the page which is needed by the process is going to be loaded in memory. If the page needed is not loaded, the process may gain access to a CPU only to wait for the page fault to be processed, thus defeating the purpose of having a real-time priority.

Prior to SunOS 4.1 there was no way to guarantee that a particular page was loaded. The **memctl( )** system call started with 4.1 and is included in 5.x. The **memctl( )** system call can take an address range and lock the relevant pages in memory. The pages are also marked so they are not subject to the usual page out criteria.

Basic Guidelines for Running Real-Time Applications

From an administrator's perspective, a process must have three conditions present to gain real-time response from the scheduling system:

- The process must be running in the RT scheduling class as described above. This can be done from the command line when the process is started with the **priocntl(1)** command or within a program with the **priocntl(2)** system call.

- All of the pages of the process's virtual memory address space must be locked down. This is done programmatically with the **memctl(2)** system call or the **mlock(3)** library call. This will assure the process is not delayed due to page faults.

- The process must be statically linked when compiled. This is done using the N option to the C compiler command. Optionally, an environment variable, **LD_BIND_NOW**, may be set non-NULL and this will force all of the shared library pages to be faulted in at process start-up time. Static linking must be used because dynamic linking could result in delay due to page faults.

Once these conditions are true, the process will gain access to a CPU within a bounded period of time, typically several milliseconds. This time is compared to several hundred milliseconds for time-share processes. Once a process in the RT class is running, it will continue to run as long as it is the highest priority runable process. This statement has two major implications for overall system performance.

First, a real-time process (or thread) is not guaranteed to be the highest priority process in the system. There may be other real-time processes with higher priority within the RT class or there may be another class with higher priority than all RT processes. Also, interrupt threads will always have higher priority than RT class threads.

Second, there are several things that could make the real-time process not runable. As with all threaded applications, a thread, and thus potentially the entire process, may be blocked waiting for synchronization objects to become available.

These concepts lead to the following general guidelines for running real-time processes:

- Overall system performance degrades if a real-time process performs synchronous I/O, i.e., the process blocks waiting for the completion of an I/O request.

- When starting multiple real-time processes, only one can be the highest priority. Therefore, other real-time processes may suffer from CPU starvation.

- Interrupt processing does not favor real-time processes. In other words, an interrupt for a device controlled by a real-time process is not done ahead of an interrupt for a device controlled by a timeshare process.

- Use of shared libraries can save large amounts of memory. The trade-off is that the library usage could cause a page fault when used. Real-time processes can use shared libraries *and* avoid the page faults by setting the **LD_BIND_NOW** environmental variable to non-NULL. The trade-off here is an increase in process start-up time.

Runaway Real-Time Processes

If a real-time process is stuck in a loop or some other runaway condition, the system can stop or degrade to the point where the system appears to be stopped. There is no easy way to regain control of the system because the process will not respond to control-C or any other signals such as **SIGKILL**. To regain access to the system, use the **L1** (stop) and 'A' keys on the keyboard to return to the prom monitor mode. If this is a persistent problem, you may wish to boot the system with **kadb** installed to help debug the problem. **Kadb** is discussed in more detail in Appendix A.

File System Management

14

File System Architecture

One of the important features of a UNIX operating system is the operating system itself has no knowledge about hardware devices or pseudo-devices. This means that when a program issues the **open(2)** system call, the operating system does not know if the open is for a pipe, a disk file, a character device, or some other peripheral device. This transparency is accomplished by using object oriented techniques inside the kernel. The next three chapters will examine the internal architecture of how file systems are implemented, the architecture of some commonly used file system types, and how operations are carried out on a file system.

This chapter in particular will look at how a local file descriptor is hooked into the kernel file system architecture, how directories are structured, and how a file lookup occurs. This will include examination of inodes, vnodes, vfs structures, and superblocks. There was extensive discussion of the vnode in the virtual memory (VM) model discussed in Part 2 that should be reviewed if needed.

The Vnode (Virtual Node) Structure

The vnode structure in SunOS (all versions since 4.0.x) is the focus of all activities with regard to I/O as well as virtual memory (VM). A vnode is used to map pages of memory into the address space of a process and to permit access to all different types of file systems. The term vnode is an abstraction from an inode (index node). While an inode is used to map processes to UNIX files, a vnode can map a process to an object in any file system type. In this way, system call need not understand the actual object being manipulated, only how to make the proper object oriented type call using the vnode interface. Figure 14.1 illustrates these relationships.

Use of a layer such as a vnode provides distinct advantages:

- A well defined interface between file systems and the kernel.
- Support for non-UNIX based file system without modification to the kernel.

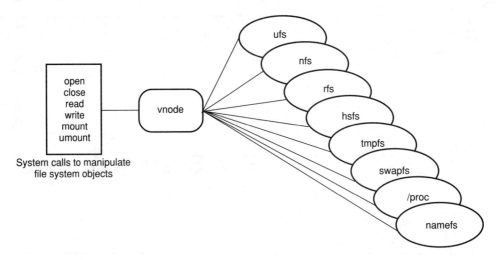

Figure 14.1 Vnode layer

A vnode structure is 56 bytes in length and its definition can be found in **/usr/in-clude/sys/vnode.h**. A partial listing of that file is shown here:

```
/*
 * The vnode is the focus of all file activity in UNIX.
 * A vnode is allocated for each active file, each current
 * directory, each mounted-on file, and the root.
 */

typedef struct vnode {
        kmutex_t        v_lock;                  /* protects vnode fields */
        u_short         v_flag;                  /* vnode flags (see below) */
        u_long          v_count;                 /* reference count */
        struct vfs      *v_vfsmountedhere;       /* ptr to vfs mounted here */
        struct vnodeops *v_op;                   /* vnode operations */
        struct vfs      *v_vfsp;                  /* ptr to containing VFS */
        struct stdata   *v_stream;               /* associated stream */
        struct page     *v_pages;                /* vnode pages list */
        enum vtype      v_type;                  /* vnode type */
        dev_t           v_rdev;                  /* device (VCHR, VBLK) */
        caddr_t         v_data;                  /* private data for fs */
        struct filock   *v_filocks;              /* ptr to filock list */
        kcondvar_t      v_cv;                    /* synchronize locking */
} vnode_t;
```

There will be one vnode for each active file, directory, socket, stream, or mounted file system. The fields of most interest that implement the object oriented features are **v_op** for the vnode operations and **v_data**, which is a private data structure that will point to a different structure depending on the object being represented. As each object is attached via the **open(2)** system call, a vnode is allocated and the **v_op** field will point to a list of routines for handling objects of the type just opened. For devices, this will ultimately lead to the open routine inside the device driver for that device. All the operating system sees is an object oriented call as shown here:

```
From /usr/include/sys/vnode.h
#define VOP_OPEN(vpp, mode, cr) \
```

```
        (*(*(vpp))->v_op->vop_open)(vpp, mode, cr)
struct vnode_t *vpp;
int mode;    /* the mode from the open call */
int cr;      /* credentials */
```

For each of the various system calls that manipulate file-like objects, there is an associated object oriented call similar to the one above.

The **v_data** field is used in a context specific manner. For a UFS object, **v_data** will point to an inode, for a distributed file object it will point to an rnode structure, and for device file object **v_data** it will point to an snode.

An rnode is an abstraction of an inode used for remote files on remote systems. The definition of an rnode can be found in **/usr/include/nfs/rnode.h**. An snode, or special node is used to describe special files in any file system. The definition of an snode can be found in **/usr/include/fs/snode.h**.

The remaining fields of a vnode will be discussed as needed later. The important thing to note is there will be one vnode for every file system object, no matter its type, a local file, a remote file via NFS or RFS, or a special block or character device file. Also, each vnode contains a pointer to a list of routines for manipulating objects of that particular type.

Virtual File System (VFS) Structures

Just as vnodes are used to describe individual file system objects, vfs (virtual file system) structures are used to describe entire file systems. There will be exactly one vfs structure for each mounted file system, along with routines to manipulate that file system. As with a vnode, the vfs structure provides an object oriented interface so the operating system itself does not need to understand the underlying file system type, only how to make the calls.

The following shows a partial listing of the vfs definition from **/usr/include/sys/vfs.h**.

```
typedef struct vfs {
       struct vfs       *vfs_next;          /* next VFS in VFS list */
       struct vfsops    *vfs_op;            /* operations on VFS */
       struct vnode     *vfs_vnodecovered;  /* vnode mounted on */
       u_long           vfs_flag;           /* flags */
       u_long           vfs_bsize;          /* native block size */
       int              vfs_fstype;         /* file system type index */
       fsid_t           vfs_fsid;           /* file system id */
       caddr_t          vfs_data;           /* private data */
       dev_t            vfs_dev;            /* device of mounted VFS */
       u_long           vfs_bcount;         /* I/O count (accounting) */
       u_short          vfs_nsubmounts;     /* immediate sub-mount count */
       struct vfs       *vfs_list;          /* sync list pointer */
} vfs_t;
```

In a fashion similar to vnodes, the **vfs_op** field points to a list of routines used to operate on entire file systems. Such operations include mount, umount, swap, sync, and others (see **vfs.h**). The following shows the macro from the header file (**vfs.h**) to translate a mount call into the file system specific mount call using the **vfs_op** field.

From **/usr/include/sys/vfs.h**

```
#define VFS_MOUNT(vfsp, mvp, uap, cr) \
    (*(vfsp)->vfs_op->vfs_mount)(vfsp, mvp, uap, cr)
```

There is also a private data field, **vfs_data**, in a vfs structure that will point to a context specific object depending on the file system type. In the case of a UFS (UNIX file system), **vfs_data** will point to a ufsvfs structure.

The **vfs_next** field is a pointer to the next vfs structure in the linked list of vfs structures. There is always at least the root file system, so the beginning of the list is pointed to by the kernel symbol **rootvfs**, which will point to the vfs structure that represents the root file system. Each subsequent vfs structure will represent another mounted file system, either local or remote of any type. This is summarized in Figure 14.2.

There is another pointer of interest in the vfs structure, **vfs_vnodecovered.** The mount command syntax is as follows:

```
#mount <file system> <mount point>
```

The first argument is the file system to be mounted and can be a local or a remote file system. The second argument is the mount point. The mount point is a local file that must exist in a currently mounted file system. For example, the command

```
#mount hosta:/example /opt
```

means that the directory, /opt, must already exist in a local file system. Since a directory is a file system object like any other, it must be represented by a vnode. So for every mounted file system, the **vfs_vnodecovered** field will point to the vnode that represents the mount point for that file system.

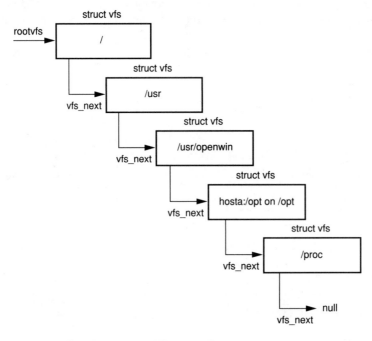

Figure 14.2 Sample vfs mounted file system list

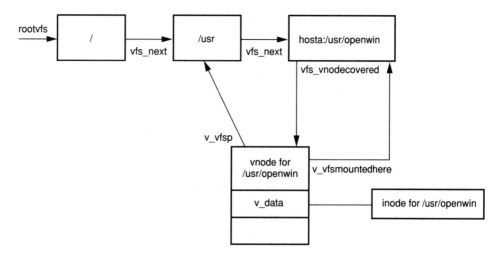

Figure 14.3 Summary of vfs/vnode mounting structures

The vnode structure has two fields that will help locate file systems, **v_vfsp** and **v_vfsmountedhere**. If a vnode is representing a directory that is a mount point for a file system, **v_vfsp** will point to the file system being mounted and **v_vfsmountedhere** will point to the file system where the mount point exists.

As an illustration, use a typical plan of mounting **/usr/openwin** from **hosta** onto **/usr/openwin**. The command to do that is

```
#mount hosta:/usr/openwin /usr/openwin
```

In this case, **/usr/openwin** will be a directory that is part of the local **/usr** file system and there will be a vnode to represent that directory. Vnodes that do not represent mount points can be distinguished because the **v_vfsmountedhere** field will be NULL. The data structures to implement this mount are shown in Figure 14.3.

Looking Up Files

All of these data structures and pointers are used to help the system look up a file. Whenever the **open(2)** call is encountered, there will be a lookup in the file system(s) to find the requested file. There are two routines, one from the vfs structure; **vfs_root( )**, and one from the vnode structure, **vop_lookup( )**; which are used to conduct the search. Remember, these calls are file system specific and called in an object oriented way as shown earlier.

The goal of a file search is to find the file and create a vnode in memory that represents that file. The first possibility for a file search is to look for an absolute path name that starts with a "**/**." The following steps will use **/usr/openwin/fubar** as an example.

1. The lookup routine for the root file system (or each component of the file name) will be used first. The lookup routine will find that **/usr** is a mounted file system because the vnode for **/usr** has a non-null pointer for **v_vfsmountedhere**.

2. The search will continue using the lookup routine in the vnode for **/usr**. Again, the lookup routine will discover the next component of the path **/usr/openwin** is a mount point.

3. Following the **v_vfsmountedhere** pointer, the search will continue on the remote file system.

4. The search on the remote file system is successful and a vnode is created on the local system representing **/usr/openwin/fubar**.

A variation on this search is when the file name starts with "**..**" as is **../home/fileb**. The search mechanism is similar except when the "**..**" is encountered in the path. If we are currently looking at the root of a mounted file system, the "**..**" will mean we have to go to the parent of the file system. We will know this is a root for a file system because the flags field of the vnode will be set to VROOT (see **vnode.h**). In this case, follow the **v_vfsp** pointer to continue the search in the parent file system.

Local Structures and Links

So far we have seen how the kernel manages files and file systems. The real objective with an **open(2)** call, is to create a local access to the file. The return value from the **open(2)** is a file descriptor. In the case of **fopen(3)**, a file pointer is returned that is a pointer to a file descriptor. This section will examine how a file descriptor at the local level is linked into the kernel structures we have just examined.

File Descriptors

The first structure of interest is the file descriptor structure. When a file is opened, a file descriptor is returned to the user. The file descriptor is of type **int** and is used as an index into a table of open file descriptors. The table is stored in the user area portion of the proc structure. In previous releases, the file descriptors were stored in a statically sized table within the user area. The problem with this was that the table could get full and the user could not open more files. In SunOS 5.x, this restriction no longer applies. File descriptors are now allocated in *chunks* of 24 (**#define NFPCHUNK 24 /* <sys/user.h> */**). The file descriptor table is a list of *chunks* linked together. The start of this list is pointed to by the **u_file** field in the user structure. Each entry in a chunk is a field of type struct file that is defined in **/usr/include/sys/file.h**. The first 24 file descriptors are stored in the user area itself. If there are more than 24, the **uf_next** pointer in the ufchunk structure is used to find the next chunk.

Following is a partial listing of **file.h**:

```
struct ufchunk {
       struct file *uf_ofile[NFPCHUNK];
       char uf_pofile[NFPCHUNK];
       struct ufchunk *uf_next;
};

/*
 * One file structure is allocated for each open/creat/pipe call.
 * Main use is to hold the read/write pointer associated with
```

```
 * each open file.
 */
typedef struct file {
      struct file     *f_next;          /* pointer to next entry */
      struct file     *f_prev;          /* pointer to previous entry */
      ushort_t        f_flag;
      cnt_t           f_count;          /* reference count */
      struct vnode    *f_vnode;         /* pointer to vnode structure */
      offset_t        f_offset;         /* read/write character pointer */
      struct cred     *f_cred;          /* credentials of user who opened it */
      caddr_t         f_audit_data;     /* file audit data */
      kmutex_t        f_tlock;          /* short term lock */
      kcondvar_t      f_done;
      int             f_refcnt;
} file_t;
```

The **file_t** structures are allocated as needed in kernel memory. For the purposes of our discussion, the most important fields in the file structure are:

- **f_next** and **f_prev**, pointers to the next and previous file descriptors.

- **f_offset**, an offset in bytes from the beginning of the file where the next read or write will take place. The offset will change each time a read or write takes place or when the **lseek(2)** call is used.

- **f_vnode**, a vnode pointer that completely describes the open file.

- **f_count**, a count that is incremented when using the **dup(2)** or **dup2(3)** call and decremented when using a **close(2)** call.

Figure 14.4 illustrates file descriptor components.

There is another advantage to allocating file descriptors in this manner. Under previous releases (before 5.x), the total number of files open by all processes at a given time was limited to the size of a static table known as the *System Open File Table* (SOFT). The SOFT was a table of file structures. With SunOS 5.x, there is no static table and the number of file structures can grow dynamically as needed. Since the file structures are allocated in kernel virtual memory, the only limit is the size of kernel virtual memory not in use, a very large number.

The open( ) System Call

With all of the pieces in place, we can now examine how the open system call uses the pieces to do its job. The following steps are completed in opening a file:

- Allocate an entry in the local file descriptor table.

- Allocate an entry for the file in the ufchunk structure.

- Using the lookup scheme described earlier, search the vfs and vnode structure until the file to be opened is located.

- Allocate a vnode and point to it through the file structure.

- Using the **v_op** routines verify permission (**VOP_ACCESS**) and then open (**VOP_OPEN**) the file.

- Return a file descriptor index to the user.

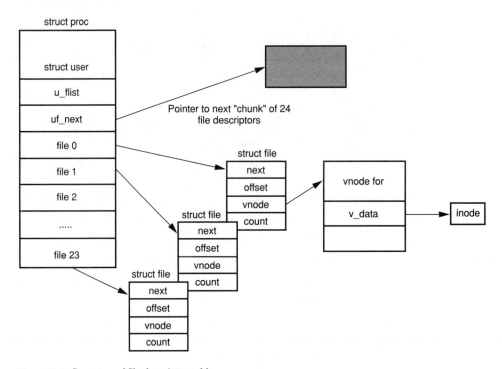

Figure 14.4 Summary of file descriptor table

If any of the steps fails along the way, structures that have been created will be destroyed.

Summary

We have looked at the data structures (vfs, vnode, file, and ufchunk) and one algorithm (for **open(2)**) that are used by the kernel for looking up files, mounting and operating on file systems, and operating on files. The next topic will examine the actual structure of a disk partition and a pseudo file system. Although the actual structures are not discussed, [10] contains an excellent description of the Fast File system and performance benchmarks.

15

File Systems

Solaris 2.x provides support for all of the file systems previously released with SunOS except the Translucent File System. Additionally, some new file system types have been added, the most notable of which is the pseudo file system type, **/proc**. Also, the concept of virtual swap has been made a standard part of SunOS 5.x. This chapter will examine the various types of file systems, and examine in detail two examples of file systems that use the Virtual File System (VFS) interface described earlier, **/proc** and virtual swap. Later chapters will look at the algorithms used to transfer data from applications and memory to the file systems.

File System Types

SunOS 5.x supports three basic types of file systems: disk-based, distributed, and pseudo file systems. Disk-based file systems are stored on physical media such as a hard disk drive, floppy disk, or CD-ROM. Each type of media has its own format. Currently, SunOS 5.x supports three different types of disk-based files systems:

- **ufs**—UNIX file system. Sun bases this file system on the Berkeley Software Distribution (BSD) 4.2 Fast File system. Some extensions have been added since it was first used by Sun at SunOS release 4.0. These changes and extensions are discussed below.

- **hsfs**—High Sierra file system. Hsfs is typically used on CD-ROM and supports Rock Ridge extensions. Hsfs provides all of the UFS semantics except writability and links.

- **pcfs**—Personal computer file system. As the name implies, pcfs file systems support reading and writing of MS-DOS formatted disks.

SunOS also supports the notion of a distributed file system. A distributed file system is one that can be shared via the network to appear as if it were local to your workstation. Commands and files to administer distributed file systems have been consolidated into the directory **/etc/dfs** for the most part. The intent is that a user or administrator will not have to learn a new set of commands and files for each new distributed file system type. Currently SunOS supports two distributed file system types:

- **nfs**—Network file system. This is the default distributed file system type used by SunOS 5.x. It is virtually unchanged from previous releases of nfs.

- **rfs**—Remote file system. It has been the default distributed file system type for AT&T UNIX implementations.

Conceptually, rfs is the same as nfs in that files or file systems can be shared via the network to appear local to a given workstation. There are two significant differences from nfs. First, rfs supports the notion of domains. This feature allows an rfs file system to be shared among a restricted group of users or workstations.

Second, rfs supports the sharing of physical devices by sharing the block or character device file. In this way, a shared tape drive, for example, can appear local to your workstation.

A *pseudo* file system is used to gain access to kernel specific information using the UFS style of file names and system calls without using any additional disk space. Typically, this is accomplished using the Virtual Memory (VM) resources of the kernel or swap space. SunOS 5.x supports the following pseudo file systems:

- **tmpfs**—Temporary file system. Tmpfs is a memory based file system that uses the structure of the VM system rather than a dedicated piece of physical memory. Normally, the **/tmp** directory is mounted at boot time as type tmpfs. This version of tmpfs is the same as previous releases of tmpfs[14].

- **proc**—Process file system. The proc file system is new to SunOS 5.x, but has been part of System V, Release 4 (SVR4) for some time and is implemented on SunOS the same as SVR4 systems. Its purpose is to provide an interface for debugging and gaining easier access to more general process information, such as memory maps. The proc file system is discussed in more detail later.

- **lofs**—Loopback file system. Lofs is used to create a virtual file system that is a copy of another file system or to overlay an existing file system. For example, **/usr** may be a read-only file system, but it is desired to write on **/usr/local** (assuming **/usr/local** is not a separate partition). The administrator may use lofs to mount **/usr/local** to another mount point as read-write to gain access without making all of **/usr** read-write.

There are several other pseudo file systems that are derived from the SVR4 world. These file systems do not have a visible interface to the user and are used by programmers and will not be discussed at length here.

- **fifofs**—First-in-first-out (FIFO) file system entries are made when named pipes or anonymous pipes are used. This is an improvement over previous releases in that one piece of common code is used for both types of pipes. Therefore, the kernel level code to execute this is reduced.

- **fdfs**—File descriptor (fd) file systems allow access to files using a file name space. The three entries used by fdfs are:
~/dev/stdin
~/dev/stdout
~/dev/stderr

  These entries correspond to /dev/fd/0, /dev/fd/1, and /dev/fd/2.

- **namefs**—The name file system is used primarily by the STREAMS interface for files. Namefs will allow the mounting of any file descriptor on top of any file name. For example, mounting a file name on top of **/dev/console** has the effect of redirecting console output to the named file.

The BSD Disk-Based File System

The most commonly used file system in SunOS is the BSD 4.3 Fast File System. The basic SunOS 5.x file system is a modification of the file system released with the Berkeley Software Distribution (BSD) at release 4.2. This has been the standard for all releases of SunOS since the release of SunOS 4.0. The default disk-based file system in SunOS is known as the *Fat Fast File System* (fffs) with System V enhancements. To understand the adjectives *fat* and *fast*, it is necessary to compare the current disk geometry with the original that was based on the AT&T disk model.

The disk drive geometry developed by AT&T places exactly one file system on each partition of the disk. The specific layout and contents of the file system are contained in a data structure called the *superblock*. Among other things, the superblock contains a count of the number of files, a count of the number of data blocks, and a pointer to the list of data blocks not currently in use.

The contents of the file system is a set of files and a set of data structures called *inodes*. Inode stands for *index node*. The directory entry for a file contains a number that is an index into the table of inodes for this file system. An inode contains the basic parameters to describe a file, including some time stamps, the size of the file, file permissions, the type of the file, and most importantly, a list of addresses that represent the location of the data blocks containing the actual data within the file. The definition of an inode can be found in the file **/usr/include/sys/fs/ufs_inode.h**. For now, we will look at the role of the inode. In the next chapter, we will examine the details of the contents of an inode. Figure 15.1 depicts the directory/inode relationship.

One thing to note is that the name of the file is *not* one of the items stored in an inode. The only place the inode number and the file name are connected is in the directory file. This means that if the directory entry is deleted, there is no way to retrieve the file because there is no way to find the correct inode.

The traditional (AT&T) file system is laid out with one superblock, a table of inodes, and a table of data blocks. The data blocks range in size (by powers of 2) from 512 bytes to 2048 bytes. There is also space for a disk label and a boot program in the first 8K of the disk. This produces the layout shown Figure 15.2.

This layout has several disadvantages. The first is the small size of the data block. For large files, this requires many searches to the disk to fetch all the data for one file. Next, the layout of the data blocks is not efficient. Over time, data blocks for one

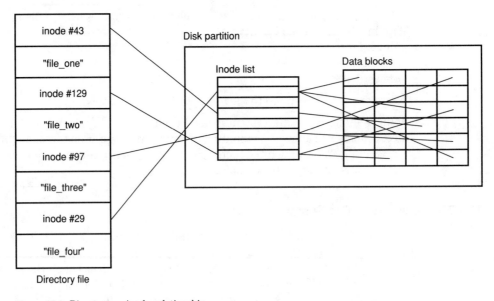

Directory file

Figure 15.1 Directory -> inode relationship

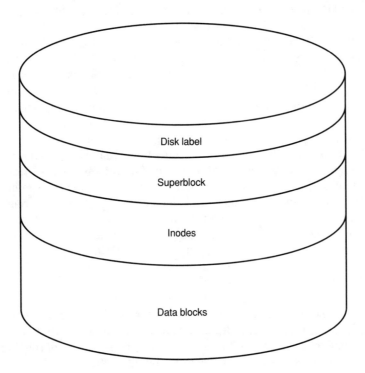

Figure 15.2 AT&T disk layout

file will be spread out all over the partition as the file grows. This means seek times grow also. The same is true for inodes. As a directory grows, the inodes representing the files in that directory are spread out and seek time increases for certain directory operations. Last, since there is only one copy of the superblock, there is the potential for catastrophic loss of the contents of a file system if the superblock is damaged.

Using the AT&T layout, performance degrades rapidly as the size and number of files increases. One way to restore performance is to dump the file system, reformat the disk, and then restore the contents. This will rearrange the inode and data blocks in an efficient manner, but the problem will reappear as files and directories grow.

Work at Berkeley has lead to a better disk geometry[10]. The new layout calls for a disk partition to be divided into cylinder groups. A cylinder group is a group of consecutive cylinders on the disk. By default, on Sun file systems, a cylinder group is 16 cylinders although the number of cylinders per cylinder group is an option to be used with the **mkfs** command. Within each cylinder group there is a redundant copy of the superblock, a set of inodes, and a set of data blocks. To keep each cylinder group manageable, there is also a cylinder group summary structure that has the location of free inodes and free data blocks. This new disk geometry is shown in Figure 15.3.

The methods for where to place new data blocks and new inodes are also changed from the original. All of the data blocks for one file will be kept within the same cylinder group (if possible) and all of the inodes for the same directory will be kept within the same cylinder group (if possible). These improvements will greatly reduce seek

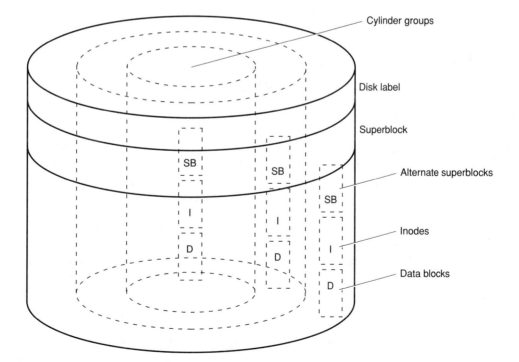

Figure 15.3 BSD ffs file system layout

time for files and prevent file datablocks from becoming spread out on the disk. The default data block size was increased from 1K byte to 8K bytes. This means fewer data blocks to fetch for a large file.

The drawback to a large data block is that small files will waste space by using an entire data block. The new file system will prevent that by allowing a data block to be divided up into fragments, typically 1K byte within an 8K data block.

It should be noted that the default data block size and the default fragment size were established when the file system was created with the **newfs(1M)** or **mkfs (1M)** command. With the large data blocks and the small fragments, the new file system gets the speed improvements attributable to a large block and the space efficiency from the smaller fragments.

These improvements have been designed to use a much larger bandwidth of the available disk transfer rate and, additionally, the performance does not degrade over time. Hence the adjective *fast* file system. What about the *fat* part? With Sun's original implementation of the file system, there was a calculation done with the **newfs (1M)** command to determine the number of inodes that would be allocated for each cylinder group. The default was to allocate one inode per every 2K bytes of data. This calculation was made and the smaller of the calculation or 2K was used as the number of inodes per cylinder group. This number of inodes could lead to a problem if there were a large number of small files. The file system would run out of inodes before the file system was full.

At SunOS 4.1, the calculation for the number of inodes was not truncated at 2K and the number of inodes per cylinder group grew. Now there are many more inodes than should ever be needed, hence the adjective *fat* file system.

System V Enhancements and EFT

With the release SunOS 5.x, the basic Fat Fast File system remains the same. This means all SunOS 5.x file systems are compatible with SunOS 4.x file systems. The only exception to this is in the case of SunOS releases prior to 4.1. Prior to SunOS 4.1 the file systems were not *fat* and attempts to mount 5.x file systems on releases prior to 4.1 will not work correctly.

There also has been a small change to the label on the disk to make SunOS file system completely compliant with the System V standards. This additional information is called the *Volume Table of Contents* (VTOC). The VTOC is a 512 byte sector in the label that contains a volume name, partition tags, and partition flags to identify permissions for particular partition. The values are explained more fully on the manual page for **format** and in [21].

Also, added to SunOS 5.x file systems are *Extended Fundamental Types* (EFT). These values are used for major and minor number on devices and for user IDs. In the past, major and minor device numbers were expressed as one sixteen-bit word, eight bits for the major number and eight bits for the minor number. This meant that the largest major number for a device was 255. As the potential number of devices has grown, the need for a larger possible value for major and minor number has grown. Now the major and minor number for a device is expressed as one 32-bit number, eighteen bits for the major number and fourteen bits for the minor number.

This means the largest value for a major device number is now 256K and the minor device number can range up to 16K. Also expanded is the value for a user ID (UID). In the past, 16 bits were allowed for UID or a maximum of 64K, now the UID uses 32 bits for a maximum 4Gb value.

Generally speaking, these changes to the label in the VTOC and the EFT for devices and UID, do not affect compatibility of 4.x and 5.x file systems. The VTOC is not used by 4.x so if it is set by a 5.x system, the file system is still mountable and the VTOC will be ignored. If EFTs are used, they will be truncated when using earlier releases. The only issue for compatibility is the changes introduced for the *fat* part of the file system. The increase in the number of inodes means the file system will not be backwards compatible to 4.0 systems. The following information summarizes the file system compatibility issues for SunOS disk-based file systems.

Export Mount	5.x	4.1	4.0
5.x	OK	OK	OK
4.1	OK*	OK	OK
4.0	no	no	OK

*EFTs may be truncated

Pseudo File Systems

The previous sections have examined the most commonly used file system with SunOS, the BSD Fast File System, more commonly known as *ufs*. The following sections will examine two examples of other types of file systems. The first is **/proc**, which is used to provide a general interface to all types of processes, **a.out**, ELF, or executable shells. The second file system type to be described is called *virtual swap* or swapfs. Virtual swap was designed to prevent some of the problems associated with running out of swap space, without increasing the size of the physical swap partition.

/proc file system

With the introduction of the threaded process model and the use of a new executable image format (ELF instead of **a.out**), it has become necessary to define a new interface to the process that does not depend on its underlying type. In other words, it is important to be able to model a process no matter if it is an **a.out**, ELF, executable shell process, or whatever type may be defined in the future. The original purpose of the process file system was to define a standard debugging interface for all processes to replace the **ptrace(2)** mechanism. **/proc** has now evolved into a generic interface to the process as a file that can respond to standard system call requests, such as **open(2)**, **close(2)**, **read(2)**, **write(2)**, **lseek(2)**, and **ioctl(2)**.

The process file system shows all currently running processes as files whose name is the process ID (PID) of the process. Normally, these files live in the directory

/proc, but they can live in any file system entry specified as type "proc" in the **/etc/vfstab** file. A sample vfstab file entry follows:

```
From /etc/vfstab
#device     device      mount       fs      fsck      mount      mount
#to mount   to fsck     point       type    pass      at boot    options
/proc       -           /proc       proc    -         no         -
```

A listing (**ls -l**) from a sample **/proc** directory is shown here:

```
total 128216
-rw-------  1 root      root               0 May 30  1994 00000
-rw-------  1 root      root          696320 May 30  1994 00001
-rw-------  1 root      root               0 May 30  1994 00002
-rw-------  1 root      root               0 May 30  1994 00003
-rw-------  1 root      root         1081344 May 30  1994 00102
-rw-------  1 root      root         1601536 May 30  1994 00110
-rw-------  1 root      root         1142784 May 30  1994 00216
-rw-------  1 jrg       other         839680 May 30  1994 00217
-rw-------  1 root      root         1069056 May 30  1994 00220
-rw-------  1 root      root         1208320 May 30  1994 00221
-rw-------  1 jrg       other         663552 May 15 09:45 00244
-rw-------  1 jrg       other        1433600 May 15 09:45 00248
-rw-------  1 jrg       other        7839744 May 15 09:45 00249
-rw-------  1 jrg       other         659456 May 15 09:45 00250
-rw-------  1 jrg       other        1417216 May 15 09:45 00258
-rw-------  1 jrg       other        3084288 May 15 09:45 00265
-rw-------  1 jrg       other        2719744 May 15 09:45 00268
-rw-------  1 root      root         2248704 May 15 09:45 00270
-rw-------  1 jrg       other        1855488 May 15 09:45 00272
-rw-------  1 jrg       other        3022848 May 15 09:45 00273
-rw-------  1 jrg       other        3203072 May 15 09:45 00281
-rw-------  1 jrg       other        3256320 May 15 09:45 00283
-rw-------  1 jrg       other         839680 May 15 09:45 00286
-rw-------  1 jrg       other        3235840 May 15 09:45 00288
-rw-------  1 jrg       other         811008 May 15 09:45 00291
-rw-------  1 jrg       other        3239936 May 15 09:45 00293
-rw-------  1 jrg       other         811008 May 15 09:45 00296
-rw-------  1 jrg       other         626688 May 15 09:50 00322
```

There are some things to be noticed in this listing. The owner and group of the file are the real UID (user ID) and the real GID (group ID) of the process, but notice the permission is read-write only for the owner. Also notice the size of the file. The size listed for each file is the size of the swappable portion of a process. Process PID 0, 2, 3 (the swapper, the pager, and the update daemon) are not swappable, so the size listed for these three processes is zero.

The only user level utilities that access the **/proc** file system are **ps(1M)** and **truss(1)**. **Ps(1M)** (process status) opens a process file, takes a snapshot of the current status, and displays it to the user. **Truss(1)** replaces **trace(1)** from SunOS 4.x and intercepts system calls during the execution of a process to display the exact calls being run. This is done with no effect on the running process except to slow it down.

More generally, access to the virtual memory map of the process is gained programmatically using the **ioctl(2)** system call. For example, to access the memory map of a process, the following code fragment might be used:

```
#include <sys/types.h>
#include <sys/signal.h>
```

```
#include <sys/fault.h>
#include <sys/syscall.h>
#include <sys/procfs.h>
#include <sys/stat.h>
#include <fcntl.h>
#include <stdlib.h>

void            *p;
int              retval;

int             convert_file_name(char *, char *);
main(argc, argv)
      char          *argv[];
      int            argc;
{
      char           filename[6];
      char           fullname[12];
      int            i, length;
      int            n_mappings;
      int            fd;
      prmap_t        *prmaps;

      memset(filename, '0', 5);
      memset(fullname, 0, 12);
      filename[6] = '\0';
      strcpy(fullname, "/proc/");
      if (argc != 2) {
            printf("Usage: procfs <PID>");
            exit(2);
      } else {                    /* convert argument to filename */
            convert_file_name(argv[1], filename);
      }
      strcat(fullname, filename);
      fd = open(fullname, O_RDWR);
      if (fd < 0) {
            perror("bad file open\n");
            exit(4);
      }
      ioctl(fd, PIOCNMAP, &n_mappings);
      printf("Number of mappings for this proc - %d\n", n_mappings);
      prmaps = (prmap_t *) malloc((n_mappings * sizeof(prmap_t)));
      ioctl(fd, PIOCMAP, prmaps);
      for (i = 0; i < n_mappings; prmaps++,i++) {
            printf("%10x\t", prmaps->pr_vaddr);
            printf("%10dK\t", prmaps->pr_size/1024);
            if (prmaps->pr_mflags & MA_READ)   /* check segment flags */
                  printf("read ");
            if (prmaps->pr_mflags & MA_WRITE)
                  printf("write ");
            if (prmaps->pr_mflags & MA_EXEC)
                  printf("exec ");
            if (prmaps->pr_mflags & MA_SHARED)
                  printf("shared");
            printf("\n");
      }
}
```

The buffer will be filled by the **ioctl** call and will contain a list of the memory mappings which can then be printed out and may look like this:

```
Number of mappings for this proc - 30
     10000              8K    read exec
     21000              8K    read write exec
```

```
      23000           240K      read write exec
   ef410000            12K      read exec
   ef422000             4K      read write exec
   ef430000           384K      read exec
   ef49f000            20K      read write exec
   ef4a4000            16K      read write exec
   ef4b0000             8K      read exec
   ef4c1000             8K      read write exec
   ef4d0000           340K      read exec
   ef534000            32K      read write exec
   ef53c000            16K      read write exec
   ef550000            52K      read exec
   ef56c000             8K      read write exec
   ef570000           328K      read exec
   ef5d1000            16K      read write exec
   ef5e0000             4K      read exec
   ef600000            20K      read exec
   ef614000             4K      read write exec
   ef620000            44K      read exec
   ef63a000             8K      read write exec
   ef640000          1384K      read exec
   ef7a9000            52K      read write exec
   ef7b6000            12K      read write exec
   ef7d0000            68K      read exec
   ef7f0000             4K      read write exec
   ef7f1000             4K      read write exec
   ef7fe000             4K      read write exec
   efff3000            52K      read write exec
```

To a system administrator more interested in a global picture of things, this may not be of great interest. To a programmer interested in the inner workings of their program, however, this is invaluable.

The process file system is an example of a file system implemented using the Virtual File System (VFS) interface defined by the SunOS virtual memory architecture described earlier. For a complete list of the flags used by the **ioctl(2)** interface and the uses of the **ioctl** commands, refer to **/usr/include/sys/procfs.h** and the manual page for **proc(4)**. For a more complete discussion of the **/proc** file system, read [16].

Virtual swap implementation

The current implementation of the SunOS virtual memory subsystems uses the concept of mapping physical objects, namely pages of physical memory are mapped into the virtual address space of an individual process. Common examples of such objects that are mapped are files, shared libraries, and device nodes. Typically, the mapping occurs when the **mmap( )** system call is encountered. Figure 15.4 depicts the mapping of physical objects into virtual memory.

In the case of a file or a shared library, the object being mapped in has an identity in the file system, i.e., a file name such as **/usr/lib/libc.so** or **/kernel/unix**. However, not all objects mapped have such an identity. Since these objects have no name in the file system, they are known as *anonymous memory*, or more commonly, *swap*.

When a process begins execution, it is known that some amount of swap space or anonymous memory will be required, although the exact amount is not known. Under the current system of VM, when a process is started it will reserve the maximum number of pages it may need from available swap space. This will assure the process

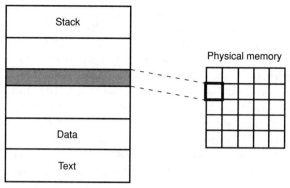

Figure 15.4 Mapping a physical page to virtual memory

that sufficient swap space is available before running the process. These reservations decrease the amount of swap space available to other processes.

Restaurant reservations provide a fine analogy. You call the restaurant and make a reservation for 20 people for dinner. The head waiter would then set aside twenty seats and make them unavailable for other patrons. What happens if you arrive for dinner with only 12 people? The seats cannot be used because reservations were denied based on your using 20 seats.

The problem is the same for a process reserving swap space. What if your process does not use all of the pages of anonymous memory it has reserved? As it turns out, this is exactly what does happen! About one-third of the reservations made are never used. This means a new process may not be able to start because it cannot make a reservation even though there is space that may never be used.

One solution to the problem is of course to make the restaurant (the swap partition) larger. Another solution is to make the restaurant (available swap) *appear* larger. This is the concept of *Virtual Swap* (or a virtual restaurant!)[12]. When a request for a reservation arrives, the system will count as available pages of swap, in addition to swap partitions and files designated as swap, pages of memory not currently in use.

To use the restaurant analogy, it is like saying there are seats in the kitchen if needed, but we are counting on the fact that some people who made reservations will not show up and the kitchen seats will not be needed.

Performance and Swap Partition Size

The objective of introducing virtual swap was primarily to reduce the need for very large swap partitions and to take advantage of I/O subsystems hardware during paging and swapping operations. The performance objective was to *not reduce* overall system performance.

The problem with making a swap partition too small is that physical memory will be full of anonymous pages that cannot be freed for use by processes. In the virtual restaurant, this is analogous to clogging up the kitchen with customers and not having room for the cooks to prepare new meals. Performance benchmarks showed that, depending on the workload, swap partitions as small as 20% of the size of main memory showed very small performance slowdowns on standard benchmarks.

However, if you read the documentation for SunOS 5.x, it is recommended that the size of the swap partition be sized at three times the size of main memory. This is reinforced by the **Suninstall** program that will select default sizes for swap as three times main memory. The reason for this size selection is that the standard benchmarks do not account for the unusual demands placed on swap caused by pseudo file systems such as **/proc**. Remember, *virtual* does not mean *infinite*. Processes can still fail due to lack of swap space even with virtual swap in use.

An important point to note is that the use of virtual swap is transparent to the user or administrator. There is no way to turn off this feature or to force swapping to be done to memory pages rather than disk pages. The only way to examine how many pages of swap are currently in use is with the **swap –l** command. The intent is twofold: first, to make more efficient use of swap by delaying the allocation of pages until needed rather than when they are reserved, and second, to allow the swap partition to be a little smaller than the old swap mechanism demanded.

The real answer to sizing swap is to experiment with your typical workloads to see if there are performance gains or losses when changing the size of swap partitions.

Summary

This chapter examined the basic terminology, types, and mechanisms used by the Solaris file system. There have been some changes to the file system layout since SunOS 4.x, including the Volume Table of Contents (VTOC) and Extended Fundamental Types (EFTs). These items are incorporated into the **format** that correctly reads and writes these data structures. Also discussed was the concept of virtual swap and pseudo file systems, such as **/proc**.

For further examination of these topics, you should consult [12], [13], [14], and [16], along with the following manual pages and AnswerBook search entries:

```
fsck(1M)
mkfs(1M)
newfs(1M)
format(1M)
swap(1M)
prtvtoc(1M)
vfstab(4)
fs_ufs(4)
proc(4)
mount(1M)
```

File System Operations

Previously, we have examined how the kernel builds data structures to keep track of open files and mounted file systems and the actual geometry of a typical UFS disk partition. This chapter will look at the pieces that tie the two topics together, namely file system operations such as **read(2)** and **write(2)**. To start, we will examine the data structures involved in maintaining the file system integrity. Then, we examine what happens when the system calls are invoked and how the kernel chooses where to write a block of data on the disk.

Data Structures for File Systems

Each disk drive consists of one or more file systems. Each file system (with the BSD FFS scheme) is made up of cylinder groups. Each cylinder group is made up of inodes and data blocks. The focal point for all of the information regarding a file system (inodes, data blocks, and cylinder groups) can be found in the superblock. Each of the data structures of interest are discussed in the following sections.

Superblocks

As we have seen earlier, the superblock is a critical structure and there are several copies within the file system. The definition for a superblock is found in **/usr/include/sys/fs/ufs_fs.h**. A superblock is a very large structure (1,380 bytes). The highlights of the contents of a superblock are listed below:

- As each file system is mounted, the superblock for that file system is faulted into memory. Each superblock has links that point to the next and previous superblocks currently mounted.

- Generic parameters about the file system include: number of cylinder groups (**fs_ncg**), size of data blocks (**fs_bsize**), size of fragments in data blocks (**fs_fsize**), amount of free space (**fs_minfree**), rotational speed and delay of disk (**fs_rotde-lay** and **fs_rps**), optimization choice (time or space, **fs_optim**), sizes of cylinder groups (**fs_cgsize**), flags (**fs_flags**), and state (**fs_state**). Many of the fields are calculated using the other fields, but are included so the calculations only need to be done once.

- An array of pointers to cylinder group summary structures (struct csum) that contain data regarding number of free inodes and data blocks for each cylinder group (**fs_csp[]**) and a summary structure for all of the cylinders (**fs_cstotal**).

Cylinder group structures

There are two structures of interest needed to describe information for cylinder groups **struct csum** and **struct cg**. Both are defined in **/usr/include/sys/fs/ufs_fs.h**. A struct csum or cylinder group summary structure contains only four fields (16 bytes total):

- **cs_ndir**—the number of directories in this cg.

- **cs_nbfree**—the number of free blocks in this cg.

- **cs_nifree**—the number of free inodes in this cg.

- **cs_nffree**—the number of free fragments in this cg.

Each of these fields will be used when determining where to allocate new directories and data blocks for files in an attempt to balance the inodes and data across cylinder groups.

The struct cg is basically a small (172 bytes) superblock describing the contents of this particular cylinder group. Information such as number of cylinders in this group, number of inodes, and the number of data blocks for this cylinder group are kept here. The most important fields in the cg structure are two bit maps one for unused/used inodes and one for unused/used data blocks. When it comes time to place an inode or data block in this cylinder group, these bit maps will be consulted to find the location of free blocks.

The cylinder group block structure will be found on the disk immediately after the backup superblock that has been placed in that cylinder group. Each cylinder group block structure has built into it a cylinder group summary structure and each superblock has a summary structure for all groups. The incore superblock is pointed to through the vfs structure for that file system. All of this leads to the two figures below. Figure 16.1 shows the data structures laid out in memory, while Figure 16.2 shows the layout of structures on the disk.

Directories

We have seen that after all of the overhead of superblocks and cylinder information, the actual information stored on the disk is in files. Files consist of two parts: an inode and one or more data blocks. Of course, users do not refer to file via an inode number, they use file names. The purpose of a directory is to store entries that associate a filename with an inode number.

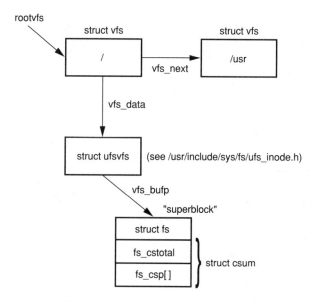

Figure 16.1 Incore file system structures

A directory file is created with the **mkdir** command and is initially allocated 512 bytes (a disk sector) to store its data. As more and more files are added to the directory, the directory file itself will grow in 512 byte increments. An optimization has been added with SunOS 5.x. Normally, the size of the directory file could only grow. If files were deleted, the directory file would stay the same size and would contain many unused entries. Under the current implementation, the size of the directory file will get *smaller* (also in 512 byte decrements) when new files are *added*! By making the directory file smaller when files are added, many files could be deleted, then added, and the file would not have to shrink and then grow. This change has been made to clean up directory files so they would not use unnecessary space.

The filename/inode pairs are stored in a directory file that consists of structures of type struct direct. There are exactly four fields in a struct direct (from **/usr/include/sys/fs/ufs_fsdir.h**):

- Inode number
- File name length
- Directory record length
- File name

When a file is created (via **open( )**, **creat( )**, **pipe( )**, or **mkdir( )**), an inode will be assigned to represent that object. The inode number and the name of the file will be stored in a directory structure and placed in the directory file. The record length will be the length of this particular directory record. If a file is deleted, the hole in the directory file will be accounted for by updating the size of the previous record to al-

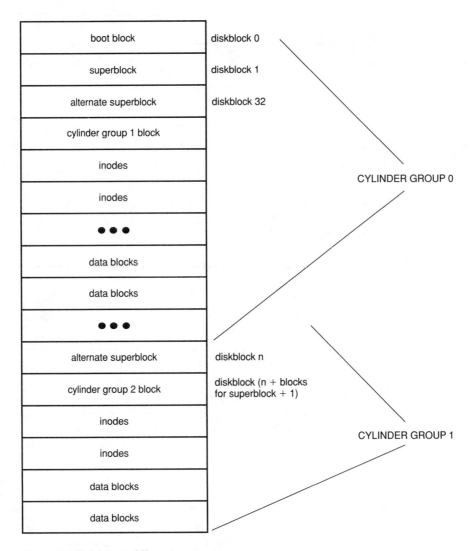

Figure 16.2 Disk layout of file system structures

low for the hole in the file. If the first entry in the directory file is deleted, the inode number will be set to 0. Directory files can be examined with the usual calls **read(2)** and **write(2)**, however, more convenient calls **opendir(3C), readdir(3C), seekdir(3C)**, and **telldir(3C)**, can be used to read the contents of a directory file.

Inodes

The fundamental data structure used to describe a file is an inode. We have been using the term informally so far and now we will examine in more the detail the structure and use of an inode. As was noted earlier, inode is short for *index node*. The obvious question is, "An index to what?" The inode number is an index into the table of inodes for that file system and that number along with the file system information is the fundamental means of identification for a file, not the file name. The following summarizes the contents of an inode (see **/usr/include/sys/fs/ufs_inode.h**):

- Type of file and access permission.
- File ownership (UID and GID).
- Number of links to this file.
- Time stamps for time last accessed, last changed, and the time the inode was changed.
- Size of the file in bytes.
- Number of physical blocks used by this file (reported in multiples of 512 bytes).
- Pointer to the vnode for this file.
- Pointer to the superblock for the file system this file lives in.
- Some locks to protect access to the inode (not necessarily the file itself).
- Pointer to blocks where the actual data for the file is stored.

A very important piece of information that is not in the inode is the file name. Since a name can be very long (**MAXNAMLEN** = 255), and a file may be known by many names (via links), the name is stored only in the directory file, rather than the inode itself. This means that each time a link is made to the file (using the **ln** command) the field <inode>**.i_ic.ic_nlink** is incremented and an entry in the directory will enter the new name and use the same inode number.

The inode also contains pointers to the data blocks where the data for the file stored. There are fifteen four-byte pointers in the inode for that purpose. The first twelve pointers are called *direct pointers* because they will contain the addresses of data blocks. If a data block being used is 4K (4,096) bytes, the direct pointers can access up to 48K (12 × 4K) bytes of data.

The three remaining pointers are called *indirect pointers* and will be used as needed to find data for larger files. If a file grows larger than 48K (still using 4K blocks), the first indirect pointer will be used. Instead of a data block, the indirect pointer will point to a block that has addresses of data blocks. Each address is four bytes so a 4K block can hold up to 1K (4K/4) data block addresses. This will provide access for files up to 4Mb plus 48K in length [(12 * 4K) + (1024 * 4K)].

If a file grows even larger, the second indirect pointer will be used in a fashion similar to the first. The pointer will point to a block of addresses, each in turn point to another block of addresses, which in turn point to data blocks. This will allow access to 4Gb of data (1K * 1K * 4K).

There is a triple indirect pointer that is not used and not needed by SunOS. It is not needed because 4K is the smallest data block allowed and 4Gb is the largest file allowed. On some older AT&T disk layouts, the data block sizes were 1K or 2K so the third indirect pointer may have been needed. Figure 16.3 summarizes the inode block pointer scheme.

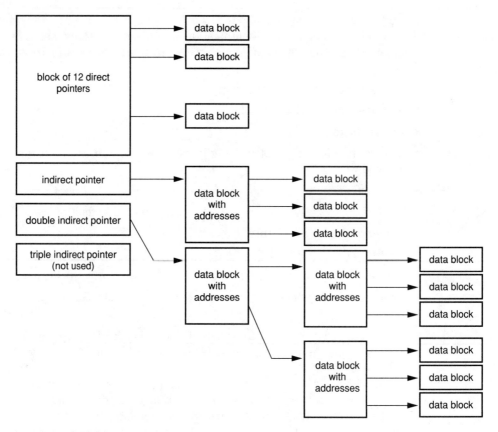

Figure 16.3 Inode block pointers

Filename Lookup

In the last section of Chapter 15, we looked at what happens when a file is opened and how the various file systems are searched to locate a file. Now with the directory structure in place, we can show a complete picture that ties together the following structure to show a file open:

- vfs
- vnode
- dirent (in the directory file)
- VOP_LOOKUP (using v_op from the vnode)
- inode
- file structure
- file system chunks (from the user area inside the proc structure)

The only remaining piece not previously explained is how the directory file is used to look up a file name. When the lookup routine is invoked (through the **vnode->**

v_op->vop_lookup pointer) for a UFS file, the routine **ufs_lookup( )** is entered, which will call **ufs_dirlook( )**.

After **usf_dirlook( )** has checked permissions on the file to be searched, the directory name lookup cache (DNLC) is searched. The DNLC is an optimization that has been added to speed up the search for file name. As each file is found, the file name and vnode pointer is added to the DNLC cached list of names. The contents of the DNLC is a hash chain that places filenames by hashing on the address of the vnode that represents the file and the file name. The first thing that a directory lookup will do is check the DNLC and if the file is currently in the list, the **ufs_dirlook( )** will return the vnode pointer and the search is done. Otherwise, each entry in the directory file is searched using the following algorithm:

```
IF ( the inode for this record is 0 (deleted)
 AND the length of the name searched for is the same as
     d_namlen
 AND the first character of the name is the same as this
     record's first character (d_name[0]
 AND a byte by byte comparison is the same )
THEN
 ( use the inode number to fetch the inode and put the
 name in the DNLC)
ELSE
 (skip to the next record [use d_reclen] )
```

Remember, in the C language, if any part of a logical *and* is false, the remaining components of the expression are not checked. So the reason for the complex *if* expression is to avoid the time consuming byte-by-byte comparison.

By adding the lookup portion to the open, the complete picture after an **open(2)** call can be shown. Figure 16.4 shows an example after opening the file **/usr/openwin/foo**.

Read and Write System Calls

In order to get a clear understanding of how the **read(2)** and **write(2)** system calls work, we are going to combine the two concepts of virtual memory (VM) and virtual file system (VFS) as shown in earlier chapters. The steps to perform a read or write are summarized here:

1. Using the VFS architecture the read/write calls will work their way down to the vnode for the file to be used and through the **v_op** pointer to find the **vop_read** or **vop_write** routine. In either case, for a UFS file, the call sequence will lead to **ufs_rdwr( )**.

2. **Ufs_rdwr( )** will perform a read by mapping the logical blocks of the file to kernel address space in a fashion exactly parallel to the way **mmap(3)** maps file space to user address space.

3. **Ufs_rdwr( )** will break up large requests (larger than a memory page), and map each portion of the file to a page.

4. Once the map is created, which may or may not have resulted in a page fault, the data is copied to the address space of the process requesting the I/O for a read. If

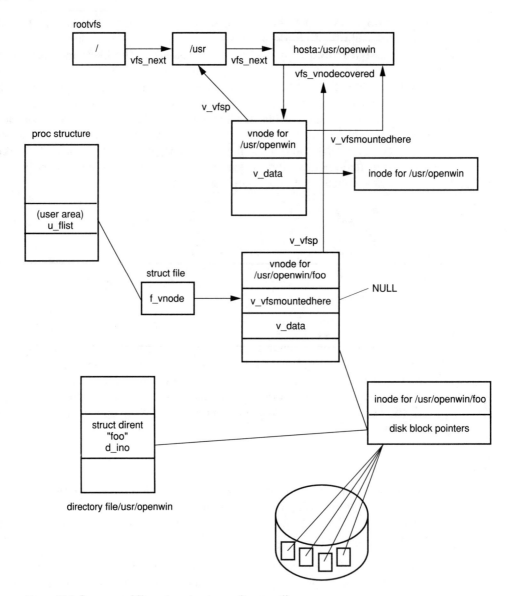

Figure 16.4 Summary of file system structures after open()

the pages requested are not currently in memory, **ufs_getpage( )** is called to
fault in the pages.

5. If the request is a write, the page to be written are copied from user address space
to kernel address space where **ufs_putpage( )** is called to start the writing of the
data to the device.

Figure 16.5 summarizes the memory mapping that occurs during a read or write.
Figure 16.5 illustrates several things of note. First, this is a good example of a seg-

ment mapping other than of type **segvn**. The use of **segmap** type segments is restricted to kernel use for transient mappings such as occur during a read or write. Next, notice the kernel executes a memory map in a fashion exactly analogous to the way a user process does. Last, notice use of anonymous memory to allocate the local pages for the user space.

In the absence of any direction, **ufs_getpage( )** will perform some optimization. Direction to **ufs_putpage** would come in the form of **madvise(3)** library call, which would set flags to direct behavior of the **ufs_getpage( )** activity. **Ufs_getpage( )** will analyze the pattern of multiple block read requests and if two consecutive pages of the file have been accessed, the routine will assume all pages are being accessed

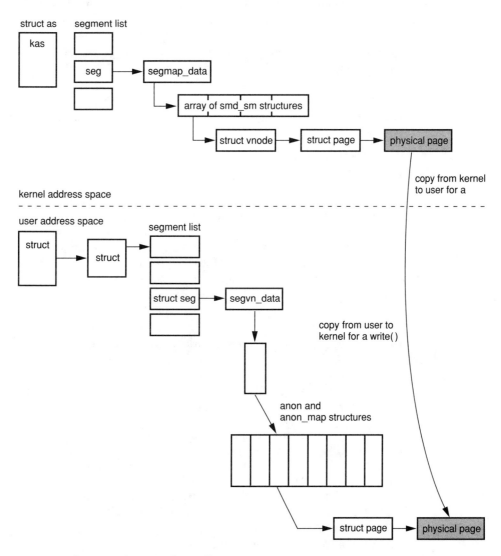

Figure 16.5 Summary of mapping for read/write

sequentially and perform *read-ahead*. Read-ahead means that pages may be faulted into memory with the original I/O request that have not yet been requested. Read ahead may be turned off by making the **madvise(3)** using the **MADV_RANDOM** flag (see manual page for **madvise(3)**). On the other side, there is no *read-behind*. A simple benchmark will show that it is faster to access a file from first byte to last than in the reverse order.

Tuning Read Ahead with maxcontig

In a further optimization for reading and writing, SunOS has implemented *clustered* I/O. Clustered I/O means attempting to improve file system performance by grouping sequential smaller I/O requests into a single larger request. In SunOS, the clustering is performed during both reads and writes. To implement clustered I/O only, the two routines **ufs_putpage( )** (for writing) and **ufs_getpage( )** need to be modified. These routines still work the same way as always.

- Read a block of data.
- Predict where the next read will occur (usually the next page or as dictated by **madvise( )**).
- If the prediction is correct, start read ahead.

The only change required is that instead of a single page being read and predicting the next page, read in a *cluster* of data and predict the next cluster. If the clusters are sequential, turn on read ahead.

The only question left is, "How big is a cluster?" The size of a cluster is determined by the **maxcontig** field of the superblock that is assigned at the time the file system is built (using **mkfs(1M)** or **newfs(1M)**), or by tuning the maxcontig field of the file system using **tunefs(1M)**. **Maxcontig** is the size (in bdisk blocks) that can be allocated contiguously on the disk without waiting. By default, the cluster size will be 7 disk blocks (7 * 8K = 56K) on most file systems. To use I/O clustering in an optimal fashion, the cluster must be set to the maximum value that the I/O subsystem can handle. That value is stored in a kernel variable named **maxphys**. The value of **maxphys** is the number of bytes the kernel is able to transfer in one I/O request. **Maxphys** is a read only (not tunable) value whose value can be retrieved by using **adb**. Once the value of **maxphys** is known, the value of **maxcontig** for a file system should be set according to the following calculation:

$$\text{<file system block size>} \times \text{maxcontig} <= \text{maxphys}$$

For example, if the block size of a file system is 8K (8,192) and **maxphys** is 63,488, then **maxcontig** should be set to 7 (63,488/8,192 = 7.75). Use the **tunefs** command to change the value of **maxcontig**. If there is a question about the disk block size for a file system, use the command **fstyp(1M)** to determine the correct value. The following summarizes these steps.

(Must be root to execute these commands)

```
#adb -k /kernel/unix /dev/mem
maxphys/D
maxphys:    126976
$q
#
```

(126,976 /8192 = 15.5)

```
# tunefs -a 15 /dev/dsk/c0t3d0s0
maximum contiguous block count changes from 7 to 15
#
#
```

Summary

This chapter has examined the data structures and architecture of superblocks, cylinder groups structures, inodes, and directories, as well as the algorithms for important tasks such as directory name lookup, **read(2)** and **write(2)**. Finally, we looked at a means to take advantage of the I/O clustering feature using **maxcontig** and **tunefs**.

There is an excellent discussion of I/O clustering in [13].

Part

6

Solaris Network Architecture

17

Network Implementation

Solaris 2.x still uses the basic networking model provided by Sun and is based on the OSI/ISO 7-layer architecture. However, there have been many changes to the underlying implementation of the networking model. Some of the changes include:

- Streams-based network device drivers
- TLI programmatic interface to transport layer programming
- Transport independent RPC
- IP multicasting
- Kerberos authentication
- Network parameter tuning

This chapter will explore these changes within SunOS 5.x.

Networking Technology

The basic architecture used by SunOS for networking is the OpenSystems Interconnect (OSI)/International Standard Organization (ISO) seven-layer model. This model is well described in [22], as well as many others, and the discussion here will focus on how the model was implemented by Sun, instead of the functionality of the model.

- Layer 1—Physical layer: This layer is concerned with the actual media for transfer of information such as twisted pair, fiber optic, fddi, token ring, and ethernet.
- Layer 2—Data link layer: In Sun implementations, the data link and the physical layers are included on the ethernet card. Sun uses ARP and ICMP protocols at this layer.
- Layer 3—Network layer: This layer deals with the routing of network messages to

the networks or deciding if a message is addressed to this particular host. Protocols used to perform this function at this layer are IP (Internet Protocol), IGMP, and RIP.

- Layer 4—Transport layer: The transport layer is concerned with the transport mechanism of the network traffic. The basic choices for ethernet are connection-oriented protocols, such as TCP, or connectionless protocols, such as UDP. X.25 is a connection-oriented protocol that may also be used at this layer.

- Layer 5—Session layer: The session layer deals with things such as waiting for responses to messages and network acknowledgments (ACK). This is generally taken care of by a programmatic interface. In the case of SunOS, the interface is Remote Procedure Calls (RPC).

- Layer 6—Presentation layer: The function of the presentation layer is to present the data to the network interfaces in a machine independent fashion. We do not want to have to deal with big-endian or little-endian issues at the lower levels of networking. Both ends of a networking conversation must agree on the format of the data. SunOS provides External Data representation (XDR) as both a set of library calls and a standard for network data representation.

- Layer 7—Application layer: The application layer is the interface to the user. Tools such as **mountd, lockd,** and **statd** are implemented on top of the other six layers of the network model.

Figure 17.1 shows a model depicting the relationships of these seven layers.

The most important thing to note about Figure 17.1 is that it is exactly that, a model. Not all applications are built using the model. Programs such as **ftp, telnet,** and **smtp** do not use the model in a strict layered fashion. Rather, the functionality of the layers is built into the program. Some programs do not start directly at the top layer. Many programmers choose to interface directly with the transport layer, for example, by using the Transport Layer Interface (TLI) on System V machines or the sockets interface on BSD machines. The notion is that the more a program sticks to the layered approach the more portable it will be across network implementations.

Another notion, that the layered approach may be more efficient, is probably not the case. As a network message passes through each layer, there is more work to be done and skipping some of the layers may actually improve performance.

Network Driver Implementation

The discussion of the SunOS implementation of networking will begin at the device driver level. In SunOS 5.x, the network device driver has been changed and is implemented as a STREAMS based, device driver. STREAMS based drivers were supported under SunOS 4.x, but not widely used, and in particular were not used to implement the network device driver. Before examining the network driver, the next section will examine the STREAMS interface in general.

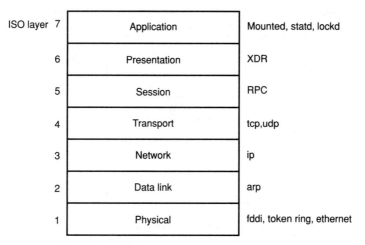

ISO layer 7	Application	Mounted, statd, lockd
6	Presentation	XDR
5	Session	RPC
4	Transport	tcp,udp
3	Network	ip
2	Data link	arp
1	Physical	fddi, token ring, ethernet

Figure 17.1 SunOS network implementation

What Is a Stream?

The UNIX STREAMS interface is a set of tools used primarily in the development of UNIX communications services. Historically, STREAMS was used to aid development of terminal interfaces. The original idea was that instead of developing a new driver for every type of terminal being made, there would be a standard raw interface. A user (or programmer) could connect to this raw device via a *stream*, and then modify the flow of information into the stream by using streams modules that were *pushed* into the stream flow. The original idea of using a stream based driver to work with terminals has been expanded now to include any communication service, most notably network interfaces.

The STREAMS package provided with System V compliant operating systems, consists of a set of system calls, kernel routines, and kernel resources. A STREAMS device driver is a special case of a character based device driver. A stream is constructed by linking a stream head and a stream driver with zero or more modules between the stream head and the stream driver. The stream head is the end of the stream closest to the user process.

All system calls made by the user that interface with the stream are processed by the stream head. The initial construction of the stream between the stream head and the driver occurs when the **open( )** system call is made. Figure 17.2 illustrates the construction of a stream.

Between the stream head and the raw device is a two-way flow of information, an *upstream* path and a *downstream* path, if you will. Into this flow of data, a user may *push* modules, which can manipulate the flow of data received by the raw device.

A stream module represents a black box that may modify the data as it travels upstream or downstream. A stream module is user written and contains a set of well-defined routines and stands alone from other stream modules. One module may be part of more than one stream at a time and one stream may have many modules inserted in its data path. Modules are pushed into the stream with the **ioctl( )** system call.

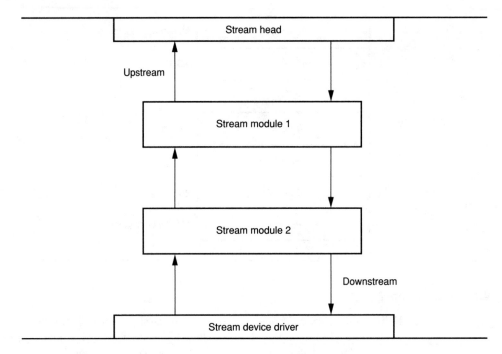

Figure 17.2 Construction of stream

Communication among modules pushed onto the stream is handled by the kernel and is transparent to the user. By using the **ioctl( )** system call, a programmer may send information to a particular module such as a signal. Again, such delivery of messages and message handling is taken care of by the kernel STREAMS package.

Streams and the Network Interface

The advantages of using a stream based driver for the network interface can now be shown. By default, TCP and IP protocols are used with Sun network equipment. In the STREAMS based driver, this configuration would appear as illustrated in Figure 17.3.

The action of configuring the network interface could be made to occur at boot time by using a utility called **autopush**. **Autopush** reads a configuration file that defines the modules to be pushed onto a particular stream device. Default network modules and devices are listed in the file **/etc/netconfig**. By using this scheme, it is easy to see how the basic network architecture can be changed simply by pushing a different protocol module onto the network stream, X.25 for example.

Transport Independent RPC

In order to achieve the modularity that is required by the STREAMS protocol, it was necessary to make the other layers of the network model more modular as well. The modules discussed in the previous sections were Transport Layer (Layer 4) modules, TCP, UDP, and Network Layer (Layer 3) module, IP. Since it is not known before-hand which transport modules will be pushed onto the network stream, the Session Layer module (Layer 5) must pass messages to the transport layer without regard to the type of transport.

This concept is the basis for Transport Independent Remote Procedure Calls(TI-RPC). RPC calls no longer specify the specific type of transport to be used, but rather specify the characteristics of the transport to be used. Characteristics such as connection-oriented protocol, connectionless protocol, or connection oriented with orderly release are used in lieu of TCP or UDP.

These properties of network transport are then passed to an intermediate layer whose function is to perform network or transport selection and then pass the message to the transport protocol module. For this mechanism to work, any and all transport modules must be prepared to accept a standard format message. This standard format message is specified by the Transport Provider Interface (TPI). The TPI specification is a standard part of SVR4 and all transport providers must adhere to this specification. At the other end of the transport module, there is a similar situation. There must be a standard way to pass the transport data to the network layers. This standard format is specified by the Data Link Provider Interface (DLPI). The DLPI defines how a user of the data link services interacts with the provider using STREAMS messages.

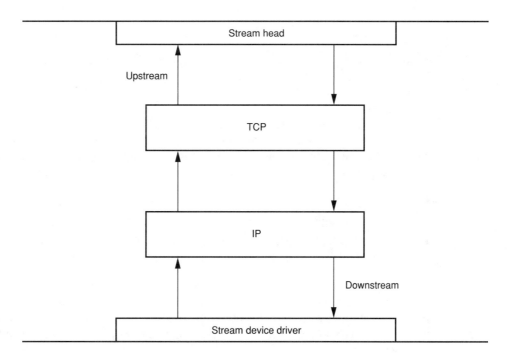

Figure 17.3 Network stream model

Transport Layer Interface (TLI) Programming

The Transport Layer Interface (TLI) is the preferred way to establish communications endpoints across the network in System V UNIX. TLI was first used in System V release 3 as an alternative to the sockets interface provided by Berkeley UNIX implementations.

TLI is functionally equivalent to sockets, but TLI attempts to more closely align with the ISO 7 layer networking model. The TLI functions are included in the network services library and programs must be linked with the -lnsl option when compiling network programs. This means the TLI functions are library calls and not system calls. These functions are written to be the interface between the transport user and the transport provider, or in ISO terminology, Layer 5 and Layer 4.

Using TLI is very similar to socket programming in that it uses the client-server architecture and each endpoint must know and understand its particular role in the architecture. The following is a list of basic socket system calls and the equivalent TLI library call to perform the same role.

```
Sockets      TLI
-------      ---
socket()     t_open()       to create an endpoint
bind()       t_bind()       to bind an address to the endpoint
accept()     t_listen()     to wait for connection request
             t_accept()     and make the connection
read()       t_rcv()        to receive data
write()      t_snd()        to send data
connect()    t_connect()    to make connection request
```

IP Multicasting

Solaris 2.0 is the first release of SunOS to support IP Multicasting. Multicasting is a feature that allows messages to be sent to more than one, but not all, hosts on the network. Sending to all hosts is the traditional broadcast that has been supported at all previous releases of SunOS.

The benefits of Multicasting fall into two general areas. The first is performance. It is more efficient to send a message to a group of receivers than to have to repeat the same unicast message to a list of hosts. Second, messages can be sent to a service or a program instead of to a system. Some examples where multicasting might be useful:

- A radio transmitter may send audio packets to subscribing systems.

- Database programs could send updates to a list of servers.

- Use multicast to find the location of the nearest service provider. This would eliminate the need to provide the service on each and every subnet.

Multicast addressing is implemented using a well-known class D internet address. For SunOS, the default multicast address is 244.0.0.0. SunOS provides the means to implement multicast routing. From the perspective of the sending application, this means the TLI or socket layer is passed the multicast address and all relevant parties will receive the message.

Kerberos Authentication

Kerberos is a network authentication scheme developed at MIT as part of Project Athena. The intent is to provide a public domain secure networking option for systems. In Solaris 2.x, a subset of the Kerberos Version 4 software is included, so that Solaris systems may use the services of a Kerberos Domain. The entire Kerberos software package from MIT includes:

- Applications Library
- Encryption Library
- Database Library
- Database Administration Utilities
- Authentication server
- Database Propagation Software
- User programs
- Applications based on Kerberos Authentication

The Solaris Distribution provides the Applications Library and one application, NFS, which allow use of Kerberos Authentication. The Kerberos applications library (**/usr/lib/libkrb.so**) takes the form of an option to the RPC programming interface. Solaris 2.x also provides the client side utilities to administer the client side of a Kerberos application.

The most common use of Kerberos authentication will be as an option to mounting and sharing file systems. For example,

```
# mount -F nfs -o kerberos station1:/usr/secure /usr/secure
# share -F nfs -o kerberos /usr/secure
```

To use the Kerberos Library, use the **–lkrb** option on the command line when compiling. In order to use the Kerberos option for sharing and mounting, the **kerbd** daemon must be running.

Network Parameter Tuning

With the advent of the streams model for network implementation, there are a number of modules available that may have parameters that can be changed to enhance performance. Some of these modules are listed below:

- /dev/arp
- /dev/icmp
- /dev/tcp
- /dev/udp
- /dev/ip

- /dev/le

- /dev/ie

In the past, specific values and variables have been available for changing through the **adb** utility. With Solaris 2.x, there is a new utility designed for use with network driver modules, **ndd(1M)**. **ndd(1M)** is a get and set utility used to change a particular value for a network protocol. This section is not intended to define the hundreds of variables used by the drivers, but to show how the **ndd** utility is used and to provide some examples. **ndd** gets and sets selected parameters from the selected driver. The basic form of the command is

```
ndd [-set] [network module] [parameter] [value]
# ndd -set /dev/ip ip_forwarding 0
```

If no module name is given, the user will be prompted for a module to work with. The user can then view the list of values by entering a @Code: ?. The output will show the values and which are writable.

```
# ndd
module to query ? /dev/ip
name to get/set ? ?
?                                   (read only)
ip_ill_status                       (read only)
ip_ipif_status                      (read only)
ip_ire_status                       (read only)
ip_rput_pullups                     (read and write)
ip_forwarding                       (read and write)
ip_respond_to_address_mask          (read and write)
ip_respond_to_echo_broadcast        (read and write)
ip_respond_to_timestamp             (read and write)
ip_respond_to_timestamp_broadcast   (read and write)
ip_send_redirects                   (read and write)
ip_forward_directed_broadcasts      (read and write)
ip_debug                            (read and write)
ip_mrtdebug                         (read and write)
ip_ire_cleanup_interval             (read and write)
ip_ire_flush_interval               (read and write)
ip_ire_redirect_interval            (read and write)
ip_def_ttl                          (read and write)
ip_forward_src_routed               (read and write)
ip_wroff_extra                      (read and write)
ip_cksum_choice                     (read and write)
ip_local_cksum                      (read and write)
ip_ire_pathmtu_interval             (read and write)
ip_icmp_return_data_bytes           (read and write)
ip_send_source_quench               (read and write)
ip_path_mtu_discovery               (read and write)
ip_ignore_delete_time               (read and write)
name to get/set ? ip_forwarding
value ? 0
name to get/set ?
```

Another method for tuning a network variable is to use the **/etc/system** file. An entry in the **/etc/system** file such as:

```
set ip:ip_forwarding=0
```

will accomplish the same as the above ndd session. Since the list of values and modules that are available for tuning in this fashion are likely to change from release to release, care should be taken not to depend on this tool too much.

Summary

This section of the book is short because in the strictest terms, networking is not part of the *internals* of the operating system. The use of the streams mechanism, however, is essential to many operations and overall system performance, and thus should be considered in the overall scheme of things. There are many excellent books on network theory and implementation. [3] is the best book I have seen for network programming topics including TLI, sockets, and RPC. [22] covers more the theory of operation for TCP/IP, which is the backbone of Sun implementations.

A

Tutorial for Using adb

The purpose of this tutorial is to provide guidance on how to use the debugger **adb**. **Adb** is the standard debugger that is provided with the Solaris 2.x distribution and can be used as any other debugger. **Adb** is a general purpose debugger that can set breakpoints, step through code, examine variables, and patch code in a manner similar to most debuggers. Although **adb** does not have the most convenient user interface, it can be used to debug any code without any special compiler flags or the need to have access to the source code. **Adb** is also the only debugger that is capable of debugging and examining the kernel and, through the **kadb** interface, breakpoints can be set in the kernel. **Adb** will be used primarily for two major functions. First, after reading the other parts of this book, you will be able to step through the major data structures and understand their interaction. Second, armed with the *roadmap* to the kernel you will be able to examine system crash files and get a glance at exactly why a system crashed.

The format of this appendix is to provide a tutorial introduction to the major features of **adb**. As it turns out the actual command syntax for **adb** is fairly straightforward, even though somewhat cryptic! It is not an objective of this section to provide an in-depth set of techniques for crash analysis. Ideally, the user will be able to look at crash files in enough detail to pinpoint a bug or fault and get faster results from Sun or other vendors' products that may have caused the problem.

Getting Started with adb

Starting **adb** is straightforward. The command syntax is as follows:

```
adb  [-k]  [-w]  [-I directory]  [ objectfile [corefile] ]
```

The -w option means *writable*. Normally, when **adb** is started it is used in a read-only mode. This means core files and executable can be examined, but not changed. To make changes to corefiles, **adb** must be started with the -w option.

The -k option means *kernel*. This option should be used when examining a kernel mapping or anytime **/dev/mem** is used for the *corefile* option. This will be used in this tutorial to examine kernel maps. (NOTE: You must have super-user permission use open **/dev/mem**.)

The -I option stands for *include*. This is used in a fashion similar to the -I option for the C compiler. Some commands to **adb** require that files be read (the **$<** and **$<<** commands). By default, the files are located in **/usr/lib/adb**. If you desire other files to be included in the search, use the -I option to specify a directory. (NOTE: Depending on the release you are working with, look for the files in **/usr/lib/adb** *or* **/usr/kvm/lib/adb**.)

The *objectfile* option is a binary image of the executable file that is being debugged. This binary image can be in memory or in a file. By default, the objectfile that will be used is **a.out**, the default output of the compilers. For the kernel, the file **/kernel/unix** or **/dev/ksyms** can be used. **/dev/ksyms** is a driver that uses the kernel symbol table to examine the kernel contents currently in memory. **Adb** will use the symbol table of an objectfile for some of its features. If an objectfile has been *stripped* (see **strip(1)**), **adb** can be used, but variable cannot be accessed by symbol, only by address.

The *corefile* option is a file that contains core or crash information about a process (or system) that has died. The default for this option is the file *core*. The core file is examined and will point directly to the cause of the crash.

Notice that no options are required for **adb**. Simply typing adb on the command line is the equivalent of typing adb a.out core. Since most people do not use the default output file from the compiler, a more typical sequence may look as follows:

```
% cc -o fubar fubar.c
% fubar
Segmentation Violation (core dumped)
% adb fubar core
physmem 17ab
```

In this case, the use of the core option was not needed, but is shown for illustration.

Creating and Using a Crash File

The above steps are used to gain access to an individual file and its core. Again, most often individual processes are more easily debugged with more *user friendly* debuggers such as **dbxtool** or **debugger**[22]. More typically, **adb** is used to analyze *crash* files. Crash files are created anytime the system panics. When the panic occurs, the system will take a snapshot of the kernel and of the contents of memory. These images are stored in the swap partition and are retrieved by using the **savecore(1M)** command.

The **savecore** command can be automatically invoked by uncommenting the appropriate lines in the file **/etc/rc2.d/S20sysetup** (there is a copy of this file in **/etc/init.d/sysetup**). The lines should look like this:

---

[22] **dbxtool** is provided as part of the SunOS 4.x distribution and as part of the SPARCworks_ Version 2 (a product of Sun Microsystems). **debugger** is part of the SPARCworks Version 3 toolset.

```
if [ ! -d /var/crash/'uname -n' ]
then mkdir /var/crash/'uname -n'
fi
echo 'checking for crash dump... \c'
savecore /var/crash/'uname -n'
echo ' '
```

Make a note of the directory used (**/var/crash/???**). There is no compelling reason to use a particular directory, so choose a directory on a file system with enough space. When the **savecore** command is encountered, two files will be created in the specified directory, **unix.0** and **vmcore.0** (the numbered suffix will be automatically incremented for each crash). The **unix.0** file will be as large as the kernel, about 1.5 to 2Mb. The **vmcore** file will be a dump of all of the pages of *interesting* processes that were running when the system crashed. Interesting in this sense means pages that were in use at the time of the crash. (Pages attached to sleeping processes are not *interesting*, for example.) The **vmcore** file can grow to be very large (I have personally seen core files of 100Mb), but are normally on the order of 8 to 10Mb. The actual size of the file will depend on the size of your physical memory and what was happening at the time of the crash, but will not be, under any circumstances, larger than physical memory. This fact should lead you to allow a swap partition at least the size of physical memory *if* you expect to save crash files intact.

If the system has crashed and the **savecore** command was not uncommented from the boot scripts, you can still retrieve the crash dump. As soon as the system reboots, log in as *root* and issue the **savecore** command. This needs to be the first thing that happens. If you let the system restart and processes start using the swap area, the crash images will be corrupt.

Once the crash files are saved, **adb** can be used to analyze the problems, by using the commands:

```
# cd /var/crash/'uname -n'  /* directory with the crash files */
# adb -k unix.0 vmcore.0
physmem 17ab
```

Using adb

Once **adb** has been invoked there is no user interface to speak of. There is no prompt, almost no error messages, and no feedback when things are okay. **Adb** simply uses a starting address and dumps out data and it is up to the user to decide whether the output makes sense. To examine data with **adb**, the basic command syntax is as follows:

```
<address> <,count> <command>
```

Address is either a virtual address, an expression that results in an address, or a symbol that is referenced in the symbol table. *Count* is a number or expression that evaluates to an integer (default is 1). *Command* is a *verb* followed by a modifier or list of modifiers (/ , ? and $ are the most common). Following are some examples:

```
The example uses the following program. The program was compiled into the
executable file named 'm':
```

```
int             x[10] = {9, 6, 3, 12, 5, 15, 10, 2, 4, 6};
main()
{
        while (1);                      /* this is put here so the */
                                        /* process can be terminated */
                                        /* by a signal to create a */
                                        /* core file   */
}
springboks% m
springboks% m &
[1] 325
springboks% kill -SEGV 325
springboks%
[1]  Segmentation Fault   m (core dumped)
```

Following is a sample abd session:

```
springboks% adb m core
core file = core - program "m"
SIGSEGV: Segmentation Fault
x,0t10/X
x:
x:              9           6           3           c
                5           f           a           2
                4           6
x,0t10/D
x:
x:              9           6           3           12
                5           15          10          2
                4           6
x/D
x:              9
x+8/D
x+8:            3
x+0t12,4/D
x+0xc:          12          5           15          10
$q
springboks%
```

In the example above, the address portion of the **adb** command is x or an expression using x. X is in the symbol table for the objectfile m and its address is known by **adb**. The other expressions, $x+8$ and $x+0t12$, are evaluated as offsets from x by **adb**. The default input radix for **adb** is hex, so the prefix $0t$ is used on the second expression to indicate 12(decimal) bytes from the starting address of x. If the count portion of the expression is missing, the default is 1. So x/D means dump one word, starting at x in decimal format. To dump the entire array, use an appropriate count, such as $x,0t10/X$ or $x,0t10/D$. These expressions mean dump 10 words, starting at x, in decimal format (D) or in hex (X) format.

The last field is the format. There are many choices for the format of the dump:

- o—2 byte octal
- O—4 byte octal
- x—2 byte hex
- X—4 byte hex

- d—2 byte decimal

- D—4 byte Decimal

- s—string format

- i—print assembly language instructions

- c—print characters

These are the most commonly used formats. See the manual page for some other formats.

More User Friendly Formats

Although the commands shown above are useful, they are tedious if the data or data structure you need to examine are very long. For example, if you wanted to see what the proc structure for a particular process looked like, you could use **adb** and dump the 400+ bytes starting at the appropriate address[23] to examine the structure. Then, you would have to examine the header file to determine the offset in bytes where the address space (struct as) pointer is located and trace it from there.

There is an easier way—*adb macros*. Listed in the directory **/usr/kvm/lib/adb** is a group of files that are used to dump structure in a more readable format. These files are in ASCII and can be viewed or modified as needed. These macros were generated by a command **adbgen**. **Adbgen** is used to generate macros for any generic data structure. The **/usr/kvm/lib/adb** directory is a set of files that are the macros for most of the kernel data structures. To use one of these files, use the name of the file instead of any count or formatting commands in your **adb** command line as follows:

```
ffabcd12$<proc
```

The *$<* syntax is an indication to **adb** to use the file name that follows to dump the data. By default, **adb** will look in the **/usr/lib/adb** or **/usr/kvm/lib/adb** directories for macro files. If you have a directory with other files, **adb** will search in that directory if it was invoked with the -I (include) option.

Armed with this new formatting tool, examine the following output from **adb** (the proc address was determined from 'ps').

```
#
# Output formatted by the macro
#

f010f4dc$<page
0xf010f4dc:     flags   nrm     cv      mapping         selock
                0       2       0       ff54afc0        0
0xf010f4e8:     vnode           offset          hash            vpnext
                ff452e08        0               f0111480        f010f554
0xf010f4f8:     vpprev          iolock.type     iolock.waiters
                f010f5cc        0               0
0xf010f500:     iolock.count    next            prev
```

---

[23] To get the address of a proc structure for a particular process, use ps -elf. The number shown under **ADDR** field is the address of the proc structure for that process.

```
                  1             f010f4dc              f010f4dc
0xf010f50c:    lckcnt  cowcnt    pagenum
                  0    0       edd
#
# this is the raw output
#
f010f4dc,3C/X
0xf010f4dc:    20000      ff54afc0    0           ff452e08
               0          f0111480    010f554     f010f5cc
               0          1           f010f4dc    f010f4dc
               0          edd         0           20000
               ff084ee8   ffffffff    f00d432c    ff492000
               0          f01244b8    f00f1e3c    0
               1          f010f518    f010f518    0
               ede        0           20000       ff54afcc
               0          ff452e08    1000        f00da214
               f010f590   f010f4dc    0           1
               f010f554   f010f554    0           edf
               0          20000       0           0
               ff452e08   2000        f00da340    f010f5cc
               f010f554   0           1           f010f590
               f010f590   0           ee0         0
```

As you can see, the macros help a lot with readability. There is a macro for most of the popular data structures. When in **kadb**, this list can be found with the command **"$M"**. There is no such command in **adb**, but a quick listing of the directory **/usr/kvm/lib/adb** will show what you need.

A Few More Basic Commands

There are some basic **adb** commands that will turn out to be useful for analyzing crashes and core files. These commands all start with '**$**' or use a '**:**'.

- **$c**   shows a stack trace
- **$r**   shows contents of registers
- **$s**   single-steps through program
- **addr:b** sets a breakpoint at **addr**
- **addr:d** deletes a breakpoint
- **$b**   lists all set breakpoints
- **:c**   continues a program

An Actual Example

Using only the basic commands shown, some macros, and the knowledge of how things are related, we can show an actual example of a system crash and use **adb** to identify the problem. The sequence of things will be as follows:

1. Use the **savecore** command to save the system crash and memory image files (or set up the boot scripts).

2. Enter **adb** using the saved crash files (**unix.0** and **vmcore.0**.

3. Starting with the cpu structure, find the actual instruction that caused the problem (**cpus** or **cpu0**).

4. Use the cpu structure to find the thread the instruction was running in.

5. Use the thread structure to find the process that was running the thread.

Inside each of these structures will be valuable information about what was happening at the time of the crash: the priority, any locks that were held, resource usage (page faults, system calls . . .), the last system call made, or the memory usage. We will also be able to tell if the system died because of a bug in a device driver, system call, or other kernel code.

The following example uses the crash file that was caused by the following program:

```
main() {
          syscall(180,12,34);
}
```

You will notice that this program is very simple. This is for a reason. The objective here is to show *kernel* crash analysis. Any manner of user code will not cause the kernel to crash. You can reasonably assume system calls do not cause problems, so the typical problem is caused by a locally developed device driver or as in this case a locally installed system call. This one is pretty obvious, because we know it is system call 180. Knowing this the problem can be easily tracked because you will know the exact instruction within the code that caused the problem. More reasonably there will be a wrapper to hide the system call or there may be many local system calls. In that case, an examination of the thread structure will show the system call number that was in progress at the time of the crash.

The following output shows these steps:

1. Dump the stack trace. The second argument to the trap instruction will give the address of the registers.

2. Dump the registers to show the pc (program counter), which is the actual instruction that failed.

3. Find out which process caused the problem by searching the cpu structure.

   The cpu structure will point to the thread structure that in turn points to the proc structure of the problem process. If this were a multiple cpu system, this step may have to be repeated.

4. Use the **proc2u** macro to find the command that started the process. From the proc structure, you can then find all of the files that were open, the signals that were pending, and other threads that may have been executing.

Note: The following is an actual adb session:

```
adb -k unix.0 vmcore.0

physmem       1b0d

$c
```

Dump the registers.

```
complete_panic(0x1,0xf00b2400,0xff300624,0xf00d013c,0xf000aeb8,0x900000e3) + 108
do_panic(0xf00bbb50,0xf03626d8,0x20,0xffff6000,0x1f,0xf00c4800) + 1c
panic(0xf00bbb50,0xf03627fc,0xf00000c8,0x13,0x13,0xf00b2800) + 1c
die(0x9,0xf03627fc,0xf00000c8,0x80,0x2,0xf00bbb50) + 60
trap(0xf00d4284,0xf03627fc,0xf00000c8,0x80,0x2,0x6) + 6b4
```

> Use the second argument of the trap call to dump registers.

```
0xf03627fc$<regs
0xf03627fc:    psr            pc              npc
               904000c0       ff306620        ff306624
0xf0362808:    y              g1              g2              g3
               0              ff21491c        8000000         ffffff00
0xf0362818:    g4             g5              g6              g7
               0              f03629e0        1               ff300600
0xf0362828:    o0             o1              o2              o3
               fff1           f0362994        0               ffffffff
0xf0362838:    o4             o5              o6              o7
               ffffffff 1               f0362848       0
```

> Find the instruction that caused the problem.

```
ff306620/i
snafu_sys+0xc0:       stb      %l1, [%l0]
```

> Examine the CPU structure

```
cpu0$<cpu
cpu0:
```

```
cpu0:           id              flags           thread          idle_t
                0               1b              ff300600        f0141ec0
cpu0+0x10:      lwp             callo           fpu
                f03629e0        0               f034ad18
cpu0+0x1c:      next            prev            next on         prev on
                f00cf654f00cf6540               0
cpu0+0x2c:      lock    npri    queue           limit           actmap
                0       110     ff003000        ff003528        ff032250
cpu0+0x3c:      maxrunpri       max unb pri     nrunnable
                60              0               1
cpu0+0x4c:      runrun kprnrn   chsnlevel       dispthread      thread lock
                1       0       0               ff300600        0
cpu0+0x58:      intr_stack      on_intr         intr_thread     intr_actv
                f015ffa0 0                   f015cec0          0
cpu0+0x68:      base_spl
                0
```

> **Use the thread pointer to get back to the proc structure.**

ff300600$<thread
Use the thread pointer to get back to the proc structure.
adb
```
0xff300600:
                link            stk             stksize
                0               f0362938        1938
0xff30060c:
                bound           affcnt          bind_cpu
                0               0               -1
0xff300614:
                flag            procflag        schedflag       state
                0               0               91              4
0xff300620:     pri             epri            pc              sp
                49              0               f000aeb8        f0362568
0xff30062c:     wchan0          wchan           cid             clfuncs
                0               0               1               ff0cfb3c
0xff30063c:
                cldata          ctx             lofault         onfault
                ff4b0300        0               0               0
0xff30064c:
                nofault         swap            lock            cpu
                0               f0361000        ff              f00cf654
0xff30065c:
                intr            delay_cv        tid             alarmid
                0               0               1               0
                realitimer
0xff30066c:     interval.sec    interval.usec   value.sec       value.usec
                0               0               0               0
0xff30067c:
                itimerid        sigqueue        sig
                0               0               0               0
0xff30068c:
                hold            forw            back
                0               0               ff300600        ff300600
0xff30069c:
                lwp             procp           next            prev
                f03629e0        ff30b000        ff493600        ff416800
```

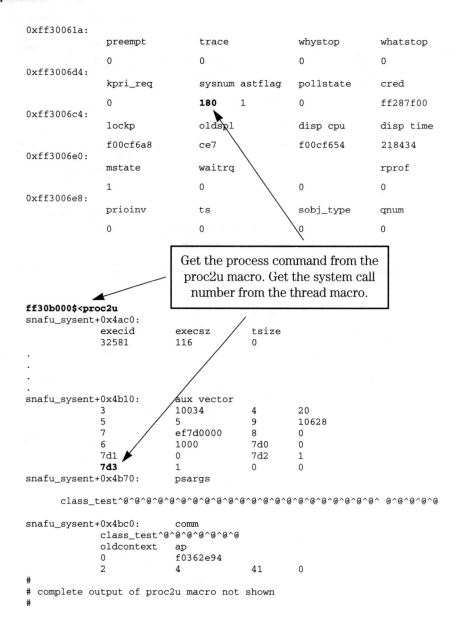

```
0xff30061a:
          preempt         trace            whystop         whatstop

          0               0                0               0
0xff3006d4:
          kpri_req        sysnum astflag   pollstate       cred

          0               180    1         0               ff287f00
0xff3006c4:
          lockp           oldspl           disp cpu        disp time

          f00cf6a8        ce7              f00cf654        218434
0xff3006e0:
          mstate          waitrq                           rprof

          1               0                0               0
0xff3006e8:
          prioinv         ts               sobj_type       qnum

          0               0                0               0
```

> Get the process command from the proc2u macro. Get the system call number from the thread macro.

```
ff30b000$<proc2u
snafu_sysent+0x4ac0:
          execid          execsz           tsize
          32581           116              0
.
.
.
.
snafu_sysent+0x4b10:      aux vector
          3               10034            4        20
          5               5                9        10628
          7               ef7d0000         8        0
          6               1000             7d0      0
          7d1             0                7d2      1
          7d3             1                0        0
snafu_sysent+0x4b70:      psargs

    class_test^@^@^@^@^@^@^@^@^@^@^@^@^@^@^@^@^@^@^@^@^@^@^@ @^@^@^@^@^@

snafu_sysent+0x4bc0:      comm
          class_test^@^@^@^@^@^@^@
          oldcontext      ap
          0               f0362e94
          2               4                41       0
#
# complete output of proc2u macro not shown
#
```

Code and Shell Script Examples

The programs presented in this section are offered as examples to illustrate many of the points made in the text. They are not offered as necessarily useful in themselves, but should be viewed as tools for a larger sense. Following is the list of programs shown here:

Thread examples

- file1.c
- matrix1.c
- thr_sell.c
- thr_sig.c

Kernel examples

- kernel.sh
- tune.sh
- mycall.c
- sizes.c
- ts_table (text file)

Miscellaneous Demos

- fast.c
- get_class_info.c
- procfs.c

Rather than explain each program here, there is an introduction to each program before the listing. All of the programs shown here were compiled and run on a SPARCstation 2 using SPARCworks version 3.0.1. Any time or benchmarks shown are from the same machine. The code shown is original code developed by the author that has been derived from many (public domain) sources.

Program 1: Fast.c

This program is a demonstration of using **mmap** to map a large file into the user space. To run this program, create a file using **mkfile**. The file should be large (> 3Mb). Time the results using **/bin/time**. There is a section commented out at the end of the loop that makes the **msync(2)** system call. This will force the pages to be marked invalid and will cause this program to run much slower. This will also exercise the pager and thus can be used to measure some of the paging performance.

```
#include "mem.h"
/*
 * This Program will mmap a file and access the pages
 * randomly ( madvise()). Each page is accessed and made
 * dirty by writing a byte (char) on that page.
 * Uncomment the last section and each time through the
 * main loop will result in re-reading the pages which
 * will exercise the page and swapper. This program can then
 * be used to compare performance after changing paging
 * parameters. Compile with the -DDEBUG option to see
 * more descriptive output.
 */

main(int argc, char **argvp, char **envp)
{
        int         fd, len, pg, i, j, f_loop;
        struct stat   stat_buf;
        char          *paddr;
        char          c;
        f_loop = 10;
        if ((fd = open(DPATH, O_RDWR)) == -1)
                error("open");
        /* Get the size of the file to be mapped. */
        if (fstat(fd, &stat_buf) == -1)
              error("fstat");
        len = stat_buf.st_size;
#ifdef DEBUG
        printf("The size in bytes is %d\n", len);
#endif                            /* DEBUG */
        /*
         * get the system page size and round the file length up to the
         * nearest page size.
         */
        if ((pg = sysconf(_SC_PAGESIZE)) == -1)
                error("sysconf");
        len += pg - (len % pg);
#ifdef DEBUG
        printf("The page size is %d\n", pg);
        printf("The rounded up length is %d\n", len);
#endif                            /* DEBUG */
        paddr = mmap((char *) 0, len, PROT_READ | PROT_WRITE, MAP_SHARED, fd, 0);
        if (paddr == (caddr_t) - 1)
                error("mmap");
#ifdef DEBUG
```

```
            printf("paddr is %x\n", paddr);
#endif                              /* DEBUG */
            /* use madvise() to set the access to random */
            madvise(paddr, len, MADV_RANDOM);
#ifdef DEBUG
            printf("Random access advice set...\n");
#endif                              /* DEBUG */
            /*
             * loop through the file sequentially, first the
             * odd pages then the even pages.
             */
            for (j = 0; j < f_loop; j++) {
                    printf("loop %d\n", j);
                    for (i = 0; i < len - pg; i += (2 * pg)) {
                            c = *(paddr + i);
                            /* write a couple of characters to ea pg */
                            /* to make the page 'dirty' */
                            *(paddr + i) = 'Y';
                            *(paddr + i + 1) = 'Y';
                    }
                    for (i = pg; i < len - pg; i += (2 * pg)) {
                            c = *(paddr + i);
                            *(paddr + i) = 'Y';
                            *(paddr + i + 1) = 'Y';
                    }
                    /*
                     * Invalidate any pages that might still be in memory, if
                     * it's the last time through the file leave the pages in
                     * memory and make the page daemon free them up. Uncomment
                     * this section to exercise the pager.
                     */
                    /*
                    if (j < f_loop - 1)
                            if (msync(paddr, len, MS_INVALIDATE) == -1)
                                    error("msync");
                    }
                    */
            }
}
void
error(char *string)
{
        perror(string);
        exit(1);
}
```

Program 2: procfs.c

This program uses the **ioctl(2)** interface to the **procfs** file system to show the various segments in a process. The program takes a process id (PID) as an argument. The PID is then converted to a filename, which is located in /proc. The program will print out the beginning address of each segment, the size of each segment, and the protections of each segment. To examine process outside of the timeshare class, this program will have to be run as root. This program is useful to show how a tool such as **proctool** or a debugger could be built.

```
#include <sys/types.h>
#include <sys/signal.h>
#include <sys/fault.h>
#include <sys/syscall.h>
#include <sys/procfs.h>
```

```
#include <sys/stat.h>
#include <fcntl.h>
#include <stdlib.h>

void        *p;
int         retval;
int         convert_file_name(char *, char *);
main(argc, argv)
        char        *argv[];
        int         argc;
{
        char        filename[6];     /* proc filename are five chars plus
                                      * NULL byte */
        char        fullname[12];
        int         i, length;
        int         n_mappings;
        int         fd;
        prmap_t     *prmaps;
        memset(filename, '0', 5);
        memset(fullname, 0, 12);
        filename[6] = '\0';
        strcpy(fullname, "/proc/");
        if (argc != 2) {
                printf("Usage: procfs <PID>");
                exit(2);
        } else {            /* convert argument to filename */
                convert_file_name(argv[1], filename);
        }
        strcat(fullname, filename);
        printf("Opening - %s\n", fullname);
        fd = open(fullname, O_RDWR);
        if (fd < 0) {
                perror("bad file open\n");
                exit(4);
        }
        ioctl(fd, PIOCNMAP, &n_mappings);
        printf("Number of mappings for this proc - %d\n", n_mappings);
        prmaps = (prmap_t *) malloc((n_mappings * sizeof(prmap_t)));
        ioctl(fd, PIOCMAP, prmaps);
        for (i = 0; i < n_mappings; prmaps++, i++) {
                printf("%10x\t", prmaps->pr_vaddr);
                printf("%10dK\t", prmaps->pr_size / 1024);
                /* check the segment flags */
                if (prmaps->pr_mflags & MA_READ)
                        printf("read ");
                if (prmaps->pr_mflags & MA_WRITE)
                        printf("write ");
                if (prmaps->pr_mflags & MA_EXEC)
                        printf("exec ");
                if (prmaps->pr_mflags & MA_SHARED)
                        printf("shared");
                printf("\n");
        }
}
/*
 * this routine will build an appropriate filename entry
 * for the /proc filesystem
 */
int
convert_file_name(char *argv, char *filename)
{
        int         length;
        length = strlen(argv);
        switch (length) {
```

```
        case 5:
                strcpy(filename, argv);
                break;
        case 4:
                filename[1] = argv[0];
                filename[2] = argv[1];
                filename[3] = argv[2];
                filename[4] = argv[3];
                break;
        case 3:
                filename[2] = argv[0];
                filename[3] = argv[1];
                filename[4] = argv[2];
                break;
        case 2:
                filename[3] = argv[0];
                filename[4] = argv[1];
                break;
        case 1:
                filename[4] = argv[0];
                break;
        default:
                 printf("Not a valid filename for /proc\n");
                 exit(3);
         }
    }
```

Program 3: get_class_info.c

This following program will demonstrate use of the **priocntl** system call to gather information (**getclassID( )** routine) about the scheduling class of a process and
change the class and class parameters for a PID (**setclassID( )** routine). The argument to the program is a process ID. If the PID is in a different class than the current
class (TS by default), you will have to be super-user to run the program. **Prioc-
ntl(2)** will not process request for information on system class (SYS) processes.
The error message will say permission denied if a PID in the SYS class is used.

```
/*
 * get_class_info() uses the priocntl(2) interface to get the scheduling
 * class name of a given process id. It uses the PC_GETCLINFO
 * and PC_GETPARMS arguments for class specific information and process
 * specific scheduling information, respectively.
 *
 */

#include <stdio.h>
#include <sys/priocntl.h>
#include <sys/rtpriocntl.h>
#include <sys/tspriocntl.h>

main(int argc, char *argv[])
{
        pcinfo_t     pcinfo;
        id_t         pid, classID;
        pcparms_t    process_parms;
        id_t         getclassID(id_t, pcparms_t *);
        id_t         setclassID(id_t);
        void         print_rt_params(rtparms_t *);
        void         print_ts_params(tsparms_t *);
```

```
        if (argc != 2) {
                perror("Usage: get_class_info <pid>");
                exit(1);
        } else
                pid = atoi(argv[1]);
        pid = getpid();
        /*
         * change the indicated PID to the RT class
         */
        setclassID(pid);

        /* Retrieve the scheduling class id of the given pid */
        if ((classID = getclassID(pid, &process_parms)) == -1) {
                perror("unknown class ID");
                exit(1);
        }
        /*
         * Place the scheduling class id in the pcinfo struct. struct
         * is documented in priocntl(2) man page and sys/priocntl.h.
         * Use this structure and PC_GETCLINFO argument to retrieve the
         * class specific information for the scheduling class that pid
         * resides in—this includes the name of the scheduling class.
         *
         * Note: the first two arguments may be NULL . priocntl disregards
         * them for PC_GETCLINFO.
         */
        pcinfo.pc_cid = classID;
        if (priocntl(0L, 0L, PC_GETCLINFO, (caddr_t) & pcinfo) == -1L) {
                perror("PC_GETCLINFO failed");
                exit(1);
        }
        printf("Process ID: %d, Class: %s \n", pid, pcinfo.pc_clname);
        /*
         * Print out the class specific info. For a realtime process
         * pc_clparms will point to an rtparms_t struct. For a time share
         * process, pc_clparms will point to a tsparms_t struct.
         */
        if (strcmp(pcinfo.pc_clname, "RT") == 0)
                print_rt_params((rtparms_t *) process_parms.pc_clparms);
        else if (strcmp(pcinfo.pc_clname, "TS") == 0)
                print_ts_params((tsparms_t *) process_parms.pc_clparms);
}
/*
 * This routine will change the class of the specified process to the RT
 * class.
 */
id_t
setclassID(id_t pid)
{
        rtparms_t       *rt_arg;
        pcparms_t        arg;
        pcinfo_t         info;

        /* get class id type */

        strcpy(info.pc_clname, "RT");
        if (priocntl(0L, 0L, PC_GETCID, &info) == -1) {
                perror("PC_GETCID Failed");
                exit(2);
        }
        arg.pc_cid = info.pc_cid;
        rt_arg = (rtparms_t *) arg.pc_clparms;
        /* set the basic RT class parameters */
```

```
                rt_arg->rt_pri = 0;
                rt_arg->rt_tqsecs = RT_TQDEF;          /* use the default */
                rt_arg->rt_tqnsecs = 0;

                if (priocntl(P_PID, pid, PC_SETPARMS, &arg) == -1) {
                        perror("PC_SETPARMS Failed");
                        exit(3);
                }
        }

        /*
         * Given a pid, getclassID() will retrieve the scheduling class specific
         * parameters for the process. This is returned in a pcparms struct.
         * documented in priocntl(2) man page and sys/priocntl.h
         */
        id_t
        getclassID(id_t pid, pcparms_t * pcparms)
        {
                pcparms->pc_cid = PC_CLNULL;
                if (priocntl(P_PID, pid, PC_GETPARMS, (caddr_t) pcparms) == -1)
                        return (-1);

                return (pcparms->pc_cid);
        }

        void
        print_rt_params(rtparms_t * rtparms)
        {
                printf("Priority: %d\nTime quantum: %d\n",
                        rtparms->rt_pri, rtparms->rt_tqsecs);
        }

        void
        print_ts_params(tsparms_t * tsparms)
        {
                printf("User priority limit: %d\n", tsparms->ts_uprilim);
                printf("User priority: %d\n", tsparms->ts_upri);
        }
```

The following programs are examples of code using threads. Mostly they have been gathered from the AnswerBook and other source material and been updated to reflect the current interface with the threads library so they will compile. They have also been debugged so they actually work!

Program 4: file1.c

This program creates two threads. The one thread will read data from a buffer, the other will write into the buffer. The problem is that both threads cannot run at the same time. The reader cannot read until the buffer is full and the writer cannot write until the buffer is empty. These conditions are indicated by the use of semaphores. This problem is fairly easy because there are only two buffers and the read/write will always be in sequence (buffer0, buffer1, buffer0, buffer1...). The more general problem is random access to many buffers. (left as an exercise for the reader).

```
#include <stdio.h>
#include <synch.h>
#include <thread.h>
#include "t.h"
```

```
#define SIZE 9
typedef struct {
        char            data[SIZE];
        int             size;
}               Buffer;
Buffer          buffer[2];
sema_t          emptybuf, fullbuf;
void            *reader(void);
void            *writer(void);
main()
{
        thread_t        treader, twriter;
        sema_init(&emptybuf, 2, 0, NULL);
        sema_init(&fullbuf, 0, 0, NULL);
        thr_create(NULL, NULL, (VPTR) reader, (void *) NULL, THR_NEW_LWP, &treader);
        thr_create(NULL, NULL, (VPTR) writer, (void *) NULL, THR_NEW_LWP, &twriter);
        thr_join(twriter, NULL, (void **) NULL);
}
void        *
reader(void)
{
        int             i = 0;
        printf("Reader started\n");
        while (1) {
                sema_wait(&emptybuf);
                buffer[i].size = read(0, buffer[i].data, SIZE);
                sema_post(&fullbuf);
                if (buffer[i].size <= 0)
                        break;
                i ^= 1;
                printf("Reader Buffer is %d\n", i);
        }
}
void        *
writer(void)
{
        int         i = 0;
        printf("Writer started\n");
        while (1) {
                sema_wait(&fullbuf);
                if (buffer[i].size <= 0)
                        break;
                write(1, buffer[i].data, buffer[i].size);
                sema_post(&emptybuf);
                i ^= 1;
                printf("Writer Buffer is %d\n", i);
        }
}
```

Program 5: matrix1.c

Matrix operations are classic examples of the types of operations that can be run in parallel. To compute an entry in the result matrix (for a matrix multiply), sum the products of the entries in a row and column from each operand. The beauty is that each result entry can be computed completely independently from all of the other results, which means no mutexes or semaphores are needed to protect (or delay) the operations. The following algorithm will create a separate thread for each calculation and each thread will be passed a unique (uniqueness guaranteed by the lock mechanisms) row and column number to work on. The main loop will then wait for all of the thread to complete. This is small matrix (4 × 4) and only 16 threads are created. This could get to be a lot of threads for a larger matrix (100 × 100 = 10,000 threads). A better solution would be to pass as an argument the number of CPUs in the system and create only that number of threads.

```c
#include <stdio.h>
#include <synch.h>
#include <sys/t_lock.h>
#include <thread.h>
#include "t.h"

#define SIZE 4 /* for now the rows and columns will be the same */

typedef int     Matrix[SIZE][SIZE];

struct row_col {
        int             row;
        int             col;
};
void            *worker(struct row_col *);

static Matrix   first = {{1, 2, 3, 4},
{2, 3, 4, 5},
{3, 4, 5, 6},
{4, 5, 6, 7}};

static Matrix   second = {{7, 6, 5, 4},
{6, 5, 4, 3},
{5, 4, 3, 2},
{4, 3, 2, 1}};
Matrix          result;
main()
{
        PrintMatrix(first, "First");
        PrintMatrix(second, "Second");
        multiply(first, second, result);

        PrintMatrix(result, "Result");
}

PrintMatrix(matrix, mesg)
        Matrix          *matrix;
        char            *mesg;
{
        int             row, col;

        printf("\n%s Matrix\n", mesg);
        for (row = 0; row < SIZE; row++) {
                printf("\n");
                for (col = 0; col < SIZE; col++) {
                        printf("%d   ", (*matrix)[row][col]);
                }
        }
}

multiply(m1, m2, m3)
        Matrix     *m1, *m2, *m3;
{
        int        j, i;
        thread_t            t_list[SIZE][SIZE];
        struct row_col  data;

        for (i = 0; i < SIZE; i++)
                for (j = 0; j < SIZE; j++) {
```

```
                                        data.row = i;
                                        data.col = j;
                                        thr_create(NULL, NULL, (VPTR) worker, &data,
                                        THR_NEW_LWP, &t_list[i][j]);
                                        while (thr_join(0, 0, 0) == 0);
                        }
}
void              *
worker(struct row_col * data)
{
        int          row, col, i;
        row = data->row;
        col = data->col;
        result[row][col] = 0;
        for (i = 0; i < SIZE; i++)
                result[row][col] += first[row][i] * second[i][col];
}
```

Program 6: thr_sell.c

This program simulates multiple vendors selling seats for the same event (in this case
seats in a C programming class). This would normally be done by having separate
processes running and accessing a piece of shared memory. This method uses
fork( ), exec( ), shmget( ), semget( ) . . . in other words, a large number of system
calls. The problem to be solved is selling the same seat more than once. The program
below presents a solution using almost no system calls. There are a group of threads
that sell the seats and the seat *database* is in global memory. The results are the
same, but with much better performance. The fork/exec version is not listed here, but
is distributed in the disk in **shmp.c** and **shmc.c**. The number of threads/processes
(NCHILD) and the number of seats (NUM_SEATS) should be increased (try 50 and
1,000 respectively) and then the two methods compared for performance.

```
#include <stdio.h>
#include <sys/types.h>
#include <memory.h>
#include <thread.h>
#include "t.h"

#define NCHILD 3
#define NUM_SEATS 15
struct CLASS {
        char          class_number[5];
        char          start_date[7];
        char          title[50];
        int           seats_left;
        mutex_t       lock;
};

key_t           key;
char            *shm_ptr;
void            *shmat();
int             shmid;
thread_t        t_id[NCHILD];
char            pname[14];
void            *sell_seats(void);
struct CLASS    class;

main(argc, argv)
```

```
            int        argc;
            char       *argv[];
    {
            int        i;
            strcpy(pname, argv[0]);
            key = getpid();
            printf("Parent process id - %d\n", key);
            shm_init();
            for (i = 0; i < NCHILD; i++) {
                    thr_create(0, 0, (VPTR) sell_seats, NULL, THR_NEW_LWP, &t_id[i]);
                    printf("Making the threads - %d\n", t_id[i]);
            }
            wait_and_wrap_up();
    }

    shm_init()
    {
        strcpy(class.class_number, "1001");
        strcpy(class.title, "C Programming");
        strcpy(class.start_date, "122594");
        class.seats_left = NUM_SEATS;
        mutex_init(&class.lock, 0, 0);
    }

    wait_and_wrap_up()
    {
            int            ch_active = NCHILD;
            thread_t       wait_rtn;
            while (ch_active > 0) {
                    thr_join(0, &wait_rtn, 0);
                    printf("Thread %d is complete\n", wait_rtn);
                    ch_active--;
            }
            printf("Cleaning up\n");
            exit(7);
    }

    void        *
    sell_seats(void)
    {
            int        all_out = 0;
            srand((unsigned) getpid());
            while (!all_out) {
                    if (class.seats_left > 0) {
                            mutex_lock(&class.lock);
                            class.seats_left--;
                            mutex_unlock(&class.lock);
                            printf("Thread %d Sold Seat - %2d left\n", thr_self(),
                            class.seats_left);
                    } else {
                            all_out++;
                            printf("Thread %d sees no seats left\n", thr_self());
                    }
                    sleep((unsigned) rand() % 10 + 1);
            }
    }
```

Program 7: thr_sig.c

This program demonstrates one method of handling signals when using threads. The call to **thr_sigsetmask( )** blocks **SIGINT** from the main thread. The behavior to observe here occurs when **SIGINT** is sent. If **thr_sigsetmask** is used, the signal handler will not be invoked. The line is commented out, **SIGINT** will go through the handler.

```
#include <sys/types.h>
#include <signal.h>
#include <thread.h>
#include <sys/ksynch.h>
#include <stdio.h>

mutex_t        lock;
int            flag;
int            count = 0;
void           *simulate_process();
void           handler(int);
main()
{
        thread_t    t_id;
        sigset_t    set;

        sigemptyset(&set);
        sigaddset(&set, SIGINT);
        thr_sigsetmask(SIG_BLOCK, &set, NULL);
        thr_create(NULL, NULL, simulate_process, NULL, THR_NEW_LWP, &t_id);
        sigset(SIGINT, handler);
        while (!flag) {
                sigwait(&set);
                printf("Count %d\n", count);
        }
        thr_join(0, 0, 0);
}

void
handler(int signal)
{
        printf("Handling Signal in handler\n");
        mutex_lock(&lock);
        count++;
        if (count == 3)
            flag = 1;
        mutex_unlock(&lock);
}

void            *
simulate_process()
{
        while (1) {
                printf("Processing...\n");
                count++;
                sleep(2);
        }
}
```

The following programs (shell scripts) are used to find the values for various kernel variables. In order to use the scripts that run **adb** with the -k option, you must be super-user.

Program (shell script) 8: kernel.sh

There is no great mystery in the following shell script except that it is a list for the most common variable discussed in the book. This script must be invoked with root privileges because of the -k option to **adb**. NOTE: Any **adb** commands can be used in a script in this fashion. If you want to write to a variable, use the -w option and the correct **adb** syntax.

```
#!/bin/csh
adb -k /dev/ksyms /dev/mem < EOF
tune_t_fsflushr/D
maxusers/D
max_nprocs/D
maxphys/D
ufs_ninode/D
maxuprc/D
nsegkp/D
ncsize/D
lotsfree/D
tune_t_gpgslo/D
desfree /D
handspread/D
slowscan/D
fastscan/D
minfree/D
physmem/D
pagesize /D
EOF
```

Program (shell script) 9: tune.sh

The following script was actually lifted from the manual page for **tunefs** under SunOS 4.x. The concept is still valid. By setting **maxcontig** with **tunefs**, you will get the optimal amount or read-ahead for a file system. The optimal amount is normally computed by dividing **maxphys** (see previous script) by the system page size (normally 4K—see previous script). The following script must be invoked as root (because of the **mount** and **umount**). Make sure to choose a file system not currently in use that has enough space for a large file (**fubar** in this case). The larger the file (count) the easier it will be to see the changes, but it will take a while. This script took 2–3 minutes on a SPARCstation 2.

```
#!/bin/sh
for i in 5 10 15 20 25 30 35 40
do    umount /usr/share/src
      tunefs -a $i /usr/share
      mount /usr/share
      dd if=/dev/zero of=/usr/share/fubar bs=4k count=8000
      umount /usr/share/src; mount /usr/share# to clear the cache
      time dd of=/dev/null if=/usr/share/fubar bs=4k
done
```

Program 10: mycall.c

One of the more useful things you can do without hacking the kernel directly is to add your own system call. The loadable interface is provided in various header files but is not really documented anywhere (notably absent in the AnswerBook!). The method is very similar to creating a loadable device driver. This code should be compiled with -c and **-DKERNEL** flags (need to super-user) and then linked as mentioned in the comment. The key is to make an entry in the file **/etc/name_to_sysnum**. The entry must be the same name as the object module and a number not already in use. It is not necessarily a good idea to use the next largest number, I have experienced problems with that plan. The number in the file are not consecutive, choose one not in use from the list (I picked 180). The number will be the index to use when making the **syscall( )** call in your application to use the system call.

Notice also how arguments are passed to the system call. Create a structure that embeds the arguments inside and pass a pointer to the call.

```
/* * These routines are responsible for constructing the downloadable syscall
 * module
 */

#include <sys/types.h>
#include <sys/vnode.h>
#include <sys/file.h>
#include <sys/cred.h>
#include <sys/stropts.h>
#include <sys/systm.h>
#include <sys/pathname.h>
#include <sys/exec.h>
#include <sys/thread.h>
#include <errno.h>

/*
 * This is the loadable module wrapper.
 */

/*
 * To compile this code use the -D_KERNEL flag to the
 * compiler. Also use the -c option to create the object module. create  * loadable module
   'ld -r -o <module> <.o file> make an entry in the
 * /etc/name_to_sysnum file. Copy the object module to /kernel/sys.
 * reboot the system (init 6). This will re-read sysnum file and make an * entry in the
   system call entry table.
 *
 */

#include <sys/modctl.h>
#include <sys/syscall.h>

struct call_args {
        int arg1;
        int arg2;
        };

static int      snafu_sys(struct call_args *);

static struct sysent snafu_sysent = {
        2,                      /* number of argument */
        0,                      /* flags */
        snafu_sys,              /* the function itself */
        (krwlock_t *) NULL      /* kernel lock */
};

/*
 * Module linkage information for the kernel.
 */
extern struct mod_ops mod_syscallops;
static struct modlsys modlsys = {
        &mod_syscallops,        /* define loader routines */
        "SNAFU system call",    /* descriptive string */
        &snafu_sysent           /* sysent structure */
};

static struct modlinkage modlinkage = {
        MODREV_1,               /* loader revision number */
```

```
                (void *) &modlsys,     /* start of list of things to load here */
                0                      /* end of list */
};

/* ok to unload */
static int    module_keepcnt = 0;

_init()
{
        printf("SNAFU LOAD SYSTEM CALL\n");
        return (mod_install(&modlinkage));
}

_fini()
{
        if (module_keepcnt != 0)
                return (EBUSY);

        printf("SNAFU REMOVE SYSTEM CALL\n");
        return (mod_remove(&modlinkage));
}

_info(modinfop)
        struct modinfo *modinfop;
{
        printf("SNAFU INFO SYSTEM CALL\n");
        return (mod_info(&modlinkage, modinfop));
}

snafu_sys(struct call_args *snafu)
{
        printf("Passed arg1 - %d\n",snafu->arg1);
        printf("Passed arg2 - %d\n",snafu->arg2);
        printf("SNAFU SYSTEM CALL\n");
}
```

Program 11: sizes.c

Again, this program contains no great insight or mystery, but it is useful for finding
the header files and the specific data structures in the kernel. The results of this program are shown in the table in Appendix C. It is noted there, but it is worth noting
here also that some of these results are machine specific and the program should be
run on your particular platform to guarantee accurate results.

```
#include <sys/mutex.h>
#include <sys/thread.h>
#include <sys/modctl.h>
#include <sys/t_lock.h>
#include <sys/proc.h>
#include <sys/class.h>
#include <sys/vnode.h>
#include <sys/vfs.h>
#include <sys/fs/ufs_fs.h>
#include <sys/fs/ufs_inode.h>
#include <vm/as.h>
#include <vm/page.h>
#include <vm/seg.h>
#include <sys/cpuvar.h>
#include <vm/seg_vn.h>

main()
```

```
{
        printf("Sizeof mutex %d\n", (sizeof(kmutex_t)));
        printf("Sizeof cv %d\n", (sizeof(kcondvar_t)));
        printf("Sizeof sema %d\n", (sizeof(ksema_t)));
        printf("Sizeof vnode %d\n", (sizeof(vnode_t)));
        printf("Sizeof vnodeops %d\n", (sizeof(vnodeops_t)));
        printf("Sizeof vfs %d\n", (sizeof(vfs_t)));
        printf("Sizeof rw %d\n", (sizeof(krwlock_t)));
        printf("Sizeof lwp %d\n", (sizeof(klwp_t)));
        printf("Sizeof thread %d\n", (sizeof(kthread_t)));
        printf("Sizeof longlong %d\n", (sizeof(longlong_t)));
        printf("Sizeof stack_t %d\n", (sizeof(stack_t)));
        printf("Sizeof label_t %d\n", (sizeof(label_t)));
        printf("Sizeof pcb %d\n", (sizeof(struct pcb)));
        printf("Sizeof clock_t %d\n", (sizeof(clock_t)));
        printf("Sizeof ucontext %d\n", (sizeof(struct ucontext)));
        printf("Sizeof k_siginfo_t %d\n", (sizeof(k_siginfo_t)));
        printf("Sizeof k_sigset_t %d\n", (sizeof(k_sigset_t)));
        printf("Sizeof Proc structure %d\n", (sizeof(struct proc)));
        printf("Sizeof lrusage structure %d\n", (sizeof(struct lrusage)));
        printf("Sizeof user structure %d\n", (sizeof(struct user)));
        printf("Sizeof turnstile_id_t %d\n", (sizeof(turnstile_id_t)));
        printf("Sizeof sclass_t %d\n", (sizeof(sclass_t)));
        printf("Sizeof superblock %d\n", (sizeof(struct fs)));
        printf("Sizeof csum %d\n", (sizeof(struct csum)));
        printf("Sizeof cg %d\n", (sizeof(struct cg)));
        printf("Sizeof inode %d\n", (sizeof(struct inode)));
        printf("Sizeof as %d\n", (sizeof(struct as)));
        printf("Sizeof page %d\n", (sizeof(struct page)));
        printf("Sizeof seg %d\n", (sizeof(struct seg)));
        printf("Sizeof segvn_data %d\n", (sizeof(struct segvn_data)));
        printf("Sizeof icommon %d\n", (sizeof(struct icommon)));
        printf("Sizeof cpu_t %d\n", (sizeof(struct cpu)));
}
```

Program 12: ts-table (timeshare dispatch table)

Adjusting the dispatch parameter table is one of the most powerful things you can do to affect system wide performance. As a demonstration, try running two benchmarks, one that is CPU intensive and one that is I/O intensive. (assume the timeshare class). If the table is working correctly, the time to run each benchmark separately should be the very close (±10%) when they are run concurrently. This would be true since the I/O bound process sleeps most of the time and the CPU bound process will run as needed.

To show how the table can change this, try installing the following table using **dispadmin( )**. The table shown reverses the usual philosophy by allowing CPU bound processes to generally rise in priority and I/O bound process to receive lower priority. To install the table, use the following commands (assume new table is in a file **table.new**) (must be root):

```
#
#dispadmin -c TS -g > table.orig  /* save the original table */
# dispadmin -c TS -s table.new
#
```

The new table:

```
# Timesharing Dispatcher Configuration
RES=100
```

```
# ts_quantum ts_tqexp ts_slpret ts_maxwait ts_lwait PRIORITY LEVEL
        100      10       1          5       10     #    0
        100      11       1          5       11     #    1
        100      12       1          5       12     #    2
        100      13       1          5       13     #    3
        100      14       1          5       14     #    4
        100      15       1          5       15     #    5
        100      16       1          5       16     #    6
        100      17       2          5       17     #    7
        100      18       2          5       18     #    8
        100      19       2          5       19     #    9
         80      20       2          5       20     #   10
         80      21       2          5       21     #   11
         80      22       2          5       22     #   12
         80      23       3          5       23     #   13
         80      24       4          5       24     #   14
         80      25       5          5       25     #   15
         80      26       6          5       26     #   16
         80      27       7          5       27     #   17
         80      28       8          5       28     #   18
         80      29       9          5       29     #   19
         60      30      10          5       30     #   20
         60      31      11          5       31     #   21
         60      32      12          5       32     #   22
         60      33      13          5       33     #   23
         60      34      14          5       34     #   24
         60      35      15          5       35     #   25
         60      36      16          5       36     #   26
         60      37      17          5       37     #   27
         60      38      18          5       38     #   28
         60      39      19          5       39     #   29
         40      40      20          5       40     #   30
         40      41      21          5       41     #   31
         40      42      22          5       42     #   32
         40      43      23          5       43     #   33
         40      44      24          5       44     #   34
         40      45      25          5       45     #   35
         40      46      26          5       46     #   36
         40      47      27          5       47     #   37
         40      48      28          5       48     #   38
         40      49      29          5       49     #   39
         20      50      30          5       50     #   40
         20      50      31          5       50     #   41
         20      50      32          5       51     #   42
         20      51      33          5       51     #   43
         20      51      34          5       52     #   44
         20      51      35          5       52     #   45
         20      52      36          5       53     #   46
         20      52      37          5       53     #   47
         20      52      38          5       54     #   48
         20      53      39          5       54     #   49
         10      53      40          5       55     #   50
         10      54      41          5       55     #   51
         10      54      42          5       56     #   52
         10      55      43          5       56     #   53
         10      55      44          5       57     #   54
         10      56      45          5       57     #   55
         10      57      46          5       58     #   56
         10      58      47          5       58     #   57
         10      58      48          5       59     #   58
         10      59      49          5       59     #   59
```

Data Structure Summary

Structure	Size in bytes	File
as	48	\<vm/as.h\>
cg	172	\<sys/fs/ufs_fs.h\>
clock_t	4 (typedef'd to long)	\<sys/types.h\>
cpu_t	580	\<sys/cpuvar.h\>
csum	16	\<sys/fs/ufs_fs.h\>
fs	1380	\<sys/fs/ufs_fs.h\>
icommon	128	\<sys/fs/ufs_inode.h\>
inode	304	\<sys/fs/ufs_inode.h\>
k_siginfo_t	28	\<sys/signal.h\>
k_sigset_t	8	\<sys/signal.h\>
kcondvar_t	2	\<sys/t_lock.h\>
klwp_t	1568	\<sys/klwp.h\>
kmutex_t	8	\<sys/t_lock.h\>
ksema_t	12	\<sys/t_lock.h\>
krwlock_t	8	\<sys/t_lock.h\>
kthread_t	264	\<sys/thread.h\>
label_t	8 (array of 2 ints)	\<sys/machtypes.h\>
longlong_t	8	\<sys/types.h\>
lrusage	48	\<klwp.h\>
page	60	\<vm/page.h\>
pcb	1192	\<sys/pcb.h\>
proc	776	\<sys/proc.h\>

Structure	Size in bytes	File
sclass_t	16	<sys/class.h>
seg	28	<vm/seg.h>
segvn_data	52	<vm/seg_vn.h>
stack_t	12	<sys/ucontext.h>
turnstile_id_t	2	<sys/turnstile.h>
ucontext	448	<sys/ucontext.h>
user	340	<sys/user.h>
vfs_t	52	<sys/vfs.h>
vnode_t	56	<sys/vnode.h>
vnodeops_t	156	<sys/vnode.h>

These sizes were found by running the **sizes** program (listed in Appendix B) on a SPARCstation2 running SunOS 5.3 (patch level 101674-01). The sizes program should be run on your configuration to determine any differences.

Glossary

/etc/system A file used to control system boot-time activities, such as kernel modules to load, variables to change, or where to search for kernel variables.

address space Normally refers to the virtual address space of a process. In SunOS, this is a 4Gb range of address that is a collection of mapping to physical objects.

anonymous memory Anonymous memory is used to map any object in the virtual memory system that does not have identity in the file system. Such objects include Copy-on-write (COW) pages, uninitialized data segments, and stack segments. Anonymous memory objects are typically backed up by swap space.

bounded dispatch latency See real-time.

cache A place in hardware or software to hold critical data that can be accessed very rapidly. Typically, caches are used to keep lists that are referenced a great deal and the overhead of a lookup is too great. SunOS has a hardware cache and software caches to hold inodes, directory names, super blocks, and other data structures.

callout queue A list of functions to be run some period of time in the future. Time is measured in clock ticks.

condition variable A synchronization primitive that allows a thread to block and wait for any arbitrary condition to be true. Basic operations are **cond_wait( )** and **cond_signal( )**.

copy-on-write (COW) COW is a policy that dictates when a copy of a page is required by two or more processes, the page will not actually be copied until one on the process writes on the page. This will prevent pages from being created that are never changed.

deadlock Deadlock occurs when a process or a group of processes are stopped because they cannot acquire the resources needed to continue.

dispatch parameter table Depending on the particular scheduling class, there may be a table that determines the priority of a thread within the class. Such table are provided for the TS and RT classes. These tables can be changed using **dispadmin(1M)**.

dispatch queue(s) A list of runable threads. There is a set of dispatch queues for each CPU in the system.

inode The fundamental data structure used to keep track of information about an individual file. Such information includes the file type, pointers to data blocks, time stamps, and more. An inode does not contain the file name.

interrupt An event that will stop the current activity until the interrupt has been serviced. After an interrupt, the current activity will continue where it was stopped.

kernel stack A portion of the user address space used to hold a copy of the kernel program, copies of system call parameters, and I/O buffers.

library call A piece of pre-written user code that may or may not result in a system call. Libraries are typically found in **/usr/lib** and are documented in section 3 of the standard UNIX documentation.

lightweight process (LWP) A data structure that is used to define the interface between user and kernel address space. One LWP will map to exactly one kernel thread.

memory management unit (MMU) A piece of hardware that translates virtual addresses into physical addresses.

mutex The most commonly used synchronization primitive. Basic operations are **mutex_lock( )** and **mutex_unlock( )**. A mutex can be held by one thread only.

page A page is a contiguous collection of bytes in the hardware or software. The size of a page is chosen to be convenient for the hardware. In SunOS, a page is typically 4K. A page is the fundamental unit of memory transfer.

pageout, pagein Paging, as managed by the pageout process, is the management of the amount of available physical memory by performing pageout and pagein activities.

preempt An event that will take over the CPU from the current activity. The original activity will not return.

process state In general, a process can be in one of four states: runable, running, sleeping, or exited. Each of these states is reflected by the **ps** command. During the lifetime, a process will migrate between these states until it exits.

quantum The amount of time a thread is given to run before a context switch must occur, also known as the time-slice.

reader/writer lock A synchronization primitive used primarily with database applications that will allow any number of threads to read a field, but only one thread to write to the same field. Basic operations are **rw_rdlock( )**, **rw_wrlock( )**, and **rw_unlock( )**.

real-time The idea of real-time programming is the concept of being able to take control of the CPU within a bounded period of time. Typically, this period of time is on the order of 1–2 milliseconds in SunOS.

scheduling class SunOS is delivered with three scheduling classes (RT,TS, and SYS) each with its own calls and characteristics. The system also provides the means to add any new scheduling classes as needed.

segment A collection of pages with contiguous addresses and of the same type.

semaphore A synchronization primitive very similar to a mutex except that more than one thread can hold a semaphore at once. Basic operations on a semaphore are **sema_post( )** and **sema_wait( )**.

signal A software interrupt. If a signal is received, the thread will stop to service the signal and then return to the original sequence of steps.

stream A stream is a flow of information in the form of messages from a stream head and the stream device. The stream is created when a program open( )'s a STREAMS type device, normally a tty or a serial port.

superblock A large data structure that keeps all of the relevant information needed to manage a file system. Such information includes, the data block size, number of free inodes, number of files, and so on.

swapping When paging activities cannot keep up with the demand for physical memory, entire processes must be swapped out, which means all of the pages of a particular process are paged out.

synchronization primitives The four basic types of controlling access between threads: mutex, semaphore, reader/writer lock, and condition variable. The basic operations on such primitives are acquire and release.

system call A system call is kernel code that allows controlled access to system resources. Found in section 2 of standard UNIX documentation (compare to *library calls*).

thread A thread of control, specifically, an executable sequence of instructions with one entry point and one exit point.

tick The basic unit of measure for time in SunOS systems. One tick is 1/100th of a second. This means the system will receive a clock interrupt 100 times per second.

turnstile A turnstile is a pointer to a set of sleep queues. When a thread is blocked for any reason, it will be attached to the list of threads on a particular sleep queue.

vfs A vfs (virtual file system) structure is used for filesystems in much the same way and inode is used for individual files. A vfs structure contains the data and pointers to the routines to manage a filesystem.

virtual memory Virtual memory (VM) is a concept that allows programmers to transparently access more memory than is physically available. In SunOS, the virtual address space is 4Gb.

vnode A data structure that is used as an abstract for various file system objects. A vnode is used in an object oriented way so the kernel does not need to have knowledge of a particular filesystem type, only how to access it through the vnode.

zombie A zombie process is process that has exited, but has not yet had its status reaped by the wait call (either from the parent or the init process).

Bibliography

[1] Leffler, Samuel, Marshall McCusick, Michael Karels, and John Quaterman, *The Design and Implementation of the 4.3 BSD UNIX Operating System*. Reading, Mass: Addison-Wesley, 1988

[2] Bach, Maurice J., *Design of the UNIX Operating System*. Englewood Cliffs, N.J.: Prentice-Hall, 1986

[3] Stevens, Richard, *UNIX Network Programming*. Englewood Cliffs, N.J.: Prentice-Hall, 1990

[4] Eykholt, J. R., S. R. Kleiman, R. Faulkner, A. Shivalingiah, M, Smith, D. Stein, J. Voll, M. Weeks, D. Williams, "Beyond Multi-processing...Multithreading the SunOS Kernel." SunSoft, Inc. (1992)

[5] Sun Microsystems, "Solaris SunOS 5.0, Multithreading and Real-time, A White Paper." 1991

[6] Stein, D. and D. Shah, "Implementing Lightweight Threads." SunSoft, Inc. (1992)

[7] Kleiman, Steven, Jim Voll, Anil Shivalingiah, Dock Williams, Mark Smith, Steve Barton, Glenn Skinner, "Symmetric Multiprocessing in Solaris 2.0." Sun Microsystems, Inc. (1991)

[8] Steve Kleiman, Bart Smaalders, Dan Stein, Devang Shah, "Writing Multithreaded Code in Solaris." SunSoft, Inc. (1991)

[9] Khanna, Sandeep, Michael Sebree, John Zolnowsky, "Realtime Scheduling in SunOS 5.0." SunSoft, Inc. (1992)

[10] McKusick, Joy, Leffler, Fabray, "A Fast File System for UNIX." Computer Systems Research Group, University of California, Berkeley (1984)

[11] Moran, Joseph P., "SunOS Virtual Memory Implementation." Sun Microsystems, Inc. (1987)

[12] Chartock, Howard, and Peter Snyder, "Virtual Swap Space in SunOS." Sun Microsystems, Inc. (1990)

[13] McVoy, L. W., and S.R. Kleiman, "Extent-like Performance from a UNIX File System." Sun Microsystems, Inc. (1991)

[14] Snyder, Peter, "tmpfs: A Virtual Memory File System." Sun Microsystems, Inc. (1991)

[15] Sheehan, Kevin, "MMAP as an Alternative to Traditional I/O." Sun Microsystems, Inc. (1987)

[16] Gomes, Ron, "The Process File System and Process Model in UNIX System V," 1991, Roger Faulkner - Sun Microsystems Inc., AT&T Bell Laboratories

[17] Rosenthal, David S. H., "Evolving the Vnode Interface." Sun Microsystems, Inc. (1990)

[18] Hsieh, Michael M., Tek C. Wei, William Van Loo, "A Cache System Architecture Dedicated for the System I/O Activity on a CPU Board." Sun Microsystems, Inc. (1989)

[19] Gingell, Bob and Joseph Moran, "SunOS Virtual Memory Architecture." Sun Microsystems, Inc. (1987)

[20] Goodheart, Berney, and James Cox, *The Magic Garden Explained*, Sydney, Australia: Prentice-Hall, 1994.

[21] Henry, S. Lee, and John R. Graham, *Solaris 2.x System Administrators Guide*, New York: McGraw-Hill, Inc., 1995

[22] Comer, Douglas, *Internetworking with TCP/IP*, 3 vols., Englewood Cliffs, N.J.: Prentice-Hall, 1990–1992.

Index

A

a.out, 149
abbreviations, xvii
access time, 13
acquire operation, 42
adb, xv, 21, 22, 23, 83, 176, 179-188, 200
  command syntax, 181-183
  commands and options for adb, 179-180, 184
  crash files, 83, 180-181
  dump format, 182-183
  macros, 183-184
  sample session, 182, 184-188
  sequence of adb debugging session, 184-185
  starting adb, 179-180
  using adb, 181-183
address space, 64, **65**, 74, 75, 76, **77**, 108
addresses
  allocating stacks, 7-8
  application binary interface (ABI), 10
  child processes, 36
  contexts, 66
  data segment, 6-7
  extensible linking format (ELF), 5-6
  fastscan rate, 88
  frames, 64
  handspreadpages, 87
  hardware address translation (HAT), 76, **77**, 83
  hash table for pages, 80-81
  heap, 7
  holes, 8
  initialization of data, 6
  kernel address space, 76, **77**
  kernel mode, 9-10, 12
  kernel stack, 8, **9**
  least recently used (LRU) algorithm in pages, 80
  memory management unit (MMU), 64, 66
  page replacement, 86
  pages, 64, 66, 75, 80-81, **81**, 85-86
  private data, 6-7
  process address space, 5
  public vs. private pages, 80
  scanrate, 87
  segmentation violation (SIGSEGV), 6
  segments, 5, 66, 75, 77-79, **79**
  slowscan rate, 88
  swapping control in global memory management, 88-90
  swapping out stacks, 7
  text segment, 6
  uninitialized data, 7
  user context, 7
  user mode, 8-9, 11, 12
  user stack, 7-8
  virtual address space, 4-6, **5**
add_drv( ), 18
aging of lightweight processes (LWP), 40
allocating kernel memory, lifetime of processes, 111
allocating library space in thread programming, 37
allocating stacks, 7-8
American National Standards Institute (ANSI), xvii
anonmap_alloc( ), 83
anonymous memory or swap space, 73, 79, 82, 152
anon_map, 82
application binary interface (ABI), 10
application layer, 170
architecture of Solaris kernel (*see also* architectures), 15-23
/kernel directory, 18-21, **19**
/kernel/unix, 16, 18
/vmunix, 15
adb debugger, 22, 23
block structure, 19-20, **19**
data structures, 20-21
device drivers, 16, 18, 20
dynamic linking, 16
file system management, 20
forceload command, 18, 23
high water mark, 22
interprocess communication (IPC), 20, 21
loadable modules, 16, **17**, 18, 36
mapping objects, 20
mmap( ), 20
process creation, 20
pseudo-devices, 20
pseudo-file systems, 20
scheduling, 20
semaphores, 21
shared library model, 16, **17**
signal handling, 20
static core kernel program, 16, **17**, 18
static linking, 16
structure of kernel, 15-18
system calls, 19-20
system configuration file (/etc/system), 18, 21-23
tuning the kernel, 21
variables, 21
virtual memory (VM), 20
architectures (*see also* architecture of Solaris kernel)
CPU selection, multiprocessor architecture, 121
master/slave multiprocessing, 94-95, **95**
multiprocessor architecture, 68-69
Solaris network architecture, 167-177
system architecture, 67-68, **67**
thread (*see* thread architecture)
argc, 7
arguments, stack allocation, 7-8
argv, 7
as, 207
asymmetric multiprocessing (ASMP), 93, 94-95
asynchronous kernel functions, 10-11, **11**
as_alloc, 76
as_checkprot( ), 83
as_dup( ), 76, 111
as_fault, 83
as_free( ), 76
as_map( ), 76
as_swapout, 76
AT&T file system, 145-148, **146**, **147**
atexit( ), 113
atomic operations, 42-43
autopush, 172
a_contents, 76
a_cv, 76
a_hat, 76
a_lock, 76
a_seglast, 76
a_segs, 76

B

backing store memory, 67
Berkeley Software Distribution (*see* BSD disk-based)
bound and unbound threads, 39-40, 41, 50, 58

bounded dispatch latency, 93, 97, 129-130
Bourne shell, xiii, 8
BSD disk-based file system, 145-148, **146**, **147**
buffers, 20, 195

C

C shell, xiii, 8
cache, 66
  cache snooping, 68-69
  performance levels, 69-70
  virtual memory cache (VAC), 85
  write-through vs. write-back, 68
cache snooping, 68-69
callout queue, 28-29, **29**
callout_t, 28, 29
calls (*see* system calls)
cat, 12
central processing unit (CPU), xvii, 3, 67
  CPU data structure, 50-51
  CPU selection, multiprocessor architecture, 121
  loose affinity and CPU selection, 121
  time-slice, 11, 98
cfork, 111
cg, 207
child processes, 36, 110, 113, 115
chunks, file descriptors, 113, 140-141, **142**, 160
classes for scheduling, 93, 100-101, 105-106, **106**
cleanup of processes, 113-114
clock, 27
  callout queue, 28-29, **29**
  clock handler, 28-29
  two-handed clock algorithm, 86
clock( ), 28
clock_t, 47, 207
close( ), 113, 141, 149
clustered I/O, 164
code locking, 56
common operating system environment (COSE), xiii, xvii
companion disk, 225-226
condition variables, 42, 44-45, 46, 50, 52
cond_broadcast( ), 119
connectivity, xiii
contexts, 66
  machine contexts, 27
  user context, 7
copy-on-write (COW), xvii, 79, 80, 110
core kernel program, static, 16, **17**, 18
COREDUMP, 108
counting semaphores (*see* semaphores)
cpu data structure, 50-51
cpu_dispthread, 51
cpu_idle_thread, 51
cpu_intr_thread, 51, 122
cpu_kprunrun, 51, 120
cpu_next, 51, 52
cpu_prev, 51
cpu_runrun, 51, 120
cpu_t, 122, 207
cpu_t->cpu_intr_thread, 122
cpu_thread, 51
crash files, 83, 180-181
create( ), 157
csum, 207
cs_nbfree, 156
cs_ndir, 156
cs_nffree, 156

cs_nifree, 156
cv_, 52
cv_broadcast( ), 119
cv_signal( ), 44-45, 86, 103
cv_wait( ), 44-45, 103
cylinder group structures, 156

D

data link provider interface (DLPI), 173
data locking, 57
data segment, 6-7
  heap, 7
  initialization of data, 6
  private data, 6-7
  uninitialized data, 7
data structures, 207-208
  cpu data structure, 50-51
  file system data structures, 155-159
  kernel data structures, 20-21
  lightweight processes (LWP), 47-48, **48**
  proc data structure, 51-52, **52**, 107-108
  roadmap of thread data structures, 51-52,
    52
  semaphores, 21
  synchronization of data structures, 52-53,
    53
  thread data structure, 48-50, **49**
  virtual memory (VM), 81-83, **82**
dbxtool, SunOS4.x, 180
ddi_add_intr( ), 122
dead (deathrow) threads, 101-102, 103
deadlock, 55-56
debugging
  adb tutorial, 179-188
  dbxtool, SunOS4.x, 180
  proc structure, 107-108
  SPARCworks 3, 180
desperation swap, 89
deterministic scheduling, 98
device drivers, 16, 18, 20
  add_drv( ), 18
  modload( ), 18
  pseudo-file systems, pseudo-devices, 20
  STREAMS-based, 169, 170
direct virtual memory access (DVMA), 8,
    74
directories, 156-158, **158**
  /kernel directory, 18-21, **19**
disk drive management, 3
dispadmin( ), 98, 100, 123-127, 204
dispatch latency, 97, 129-130
dispatch queues, 98, **99**, 102, 117-118, **118**,
    121
dispq_t, 118
distributed file systems, 143-144
DKERNEL, 201
dup( ) and dup2( ), 141
dynamic linking, 16
dynamic RAM (DRAM), 66

E

echo$, 8
electronic mail, xiii
envp, 7
error checking, lifetime of processes, 111
event handler, 12
exec( ), 41, 76, 105, 108, 114, 115, 117, 198
execle( ), 114
execv, 9
execve( ), 114
exit( ), 8, 33, 34, 58, 76, 86, 101, 105, 108,
    112, 113, 117
EXITLWPS, 108
extended fundamental types (EFT), 148-149,
    149, 154
extensible linking format (ELF), 5-6
external data representation (XDR), 170

F

family tree for processes, 107-108, 113
fast file systems, 148
fast.c, 189, 190-191
fastscan rate, 88
fat fast file system (FFFS), 145
fat file systems, 148
faulting into virtual memory, 83
file descriptor file system (FDFS), 145
file descriptors, 113, 140-141, **142**, 160
file system management, 20, 133-162
  /proc, 143, 149-152
  architecture, 135-142
  AT&T, 145-148, **146**, **147**
  Berkeley Software Distribution (see BSD
    disk-based)
  BSD disk-based, 145-148, **146**, **147**
  chunks, file descriptors, 113, 140-141, **142**,
    160
  close( ), 141, 149
  clustered I/O, 164
  create( ), 157
  creating files, 157
  cylinder group structures, 156
  data structures, 155-159
  directories, 156-158, **158**
  distributed file systems, 143-144
  extended fundamental types (EFT), 148-
    149, **149**, 154
  fast file systems, 148
  fat fast file system (fffs), 145
  fat file systems, 148
  file descriptor file system (fdfs), 145
  file descriptors, 113, 140-141, **142**, 160
  filename lookup, 160-161
  first in first out (fifo) file system, 144
  fopen( ), 140
  High Sierra file system (hsfs), 143
  index nodes (see inodes)
  inodes, 135, 145, 157, 158-159, 160,
    160
  ioctl( ), 149
  links, 140
  local structures, 140
  looking up files, 139-140, 160-161
  loopback file system (lofs), 144
  lseek( ), 149
  maxcontig, 164-165
  name file system (namefs), 145
  name length, 157
  name of file, 157
  network file system (nfs), 144
  open( ), 135, 136, 139, 140, 141-142, 149,
    157, **162**
  opendir( ), 158
  personal computer file system (pcfs), 143
  pipe( ), 157
  pipes, 135
  pointers, direct and indirect, 159
  proc structure, 107-108
  process file system (proc), 144
  process identification (PID), 149-150
  pseudo-devices, 135
  pseudo-file system, 143, 144, 149
  read( ), 149, 155, 158, 161-164, **163**, 165
  read-ahead functions, 164-165
  read-behind functions, 164
  readdir( ), 158
  record length, 157
  remote file system (rfs), 144
  seekdir( ), 158
  superblocks, 135, 145, 155-156
  swap partitions, 153-154
  swapping, 144, 149, 152-153, 153-154,
    153
  system open file table (SOFT), 141
  System V enhancements, 148-149
  telldir( ), 158

temporary file system (tmpfs), 144
translucent file system, 143
transparency of, 135
tunefs( ), 164, 165
types, 143-145
UNIX file system (ufs), 143
vfs (virtual file system) structures, 135, 137-
    139, **138**, **139**, 140, 160
virtual memory (VM), 135
virtual swap, 143, 149, 152-153, **153**
vnodes (virtual node), 135-137, **136**, 160
volume table of contents (VTOC), 148-149,
    154
write( ), 149, 155, 158, 161-164, **163**, 165
file1.c, 189, 195-196
filenames, 157
file_t, 141
first in first out file system, 144
fopen( ), 140
forceload, 18, 23
fork( ), 4, 9, 33, 35-36, 41, 42, 59, 76, 80, 101,
    105, 108, 110, 111, 114, 115, 117, 119, 198
forkall( ), 110
format, 154
frames, 64
free( ), 7, 114
fs, 207
fstyp( ), 164
fs_bsize, 155
fs_cgsize, 156
fs_csp, 156
fs_cstotal, 156
fs_flags, 156
fs_fsize, 155
fs_minfree, 156
fs_ncg, 155
fs_optim, 156
fs_rotdelay, 156
fs_rps, 156
fs_state, 156
ftp, 170
fubar, 201
functions
  stack allocation, 7-8
  synchronous vs. asynchronous kernel func-
    tions, 10-11
  thread architecture, 56
f_count, 141
f_next, 141
f_offset, 141
f_prev, 141
f_vnode, 141

G

getclassID( ), 193
get_class_info.c, 189, 193-195
global memory management, 85-90
  desperation swap, 89
  fastscan rate, 88
  handspreadpages, 87
  iostat( ), 90
  lotsfree variable in global memory manage-
    ment, 86-88
  memory management unit (MMU), 85
  minfree variable in global memory manage-
    ment, 86-88
  page in and page out, 85-86
  page replacement, 86
  pages, 85-86
  sar( ), 90
  scanrate, 87
  slowscan rate, 88
  swapping control in global memory manage-
    ment, 88-90
  system paging strategy, 86-88, **87**
  two-handed clock algorithm, 86
  vmstat( ), 90
group identification (GID), xvii

H

hand-crafted processes, 108
handspreadpages, 87
hardware address translation (HAT), 76, **77**, 83
hardware architecture, 27-29, 63-71
  address space, 64, **65**
  backing store memory, 67
  cache, 66, 68
  cache snooping, 68-69
  central processing unit (CPU), 67
  contexts, 66
  dynamic RAM (DRAM), 66
  frames, 64
  hardware address translation (HAT), 76, **77**, 83
  memory management unit (MMU), 64, 66, 67
  multiprocessor architecture, 68-69
  multiprocessors and thread architecture, 35
  overlay managers, 64
  page fault, 68
  pages, 64, 66
  performance levels, 69-70
  segments, 66
  static RAM (SRAM), 66
  system architecture, 67-68, **67**
  system calls, 64
  virtual address cache (VAC), 67
  write-back cache, 68
  write-through cache, 68
hash table, pages, 80-81
hat_memload( ), 83
heap, 7
hierarchical deadlock, 55, 56
High Sierra file system (HSFS), 143
high water mark, 22
HOLDLWPS, 108
holes, 8

I

icommon, 207
identity of threads, 34, 37, 39
IGMP protocol, 170
independence of threads, 34, 37, 39
index nodes (*see* inodes)
inheritance, priority inheritance, 123-124, 129
init( ), 108, 112
initialization of data, 6
initialization of process, 111
inodes, 135, 145, 157, 158-159, 160, **160**, 207
interactive scheduling class, 103
interesting processes, 114
internet protocol (IP), 169, 170, 174
interprocess communication (IPC), 3, 10, 20, 21, 41, 74
interrupts, 12, 13, 27, **28**, 95-97, 101, 102, 122-123
inversion, priority inversion, 123-124
invisibility of threads, 34, 37, 39
ioctl( ), 149, 150, 151, 152, 171, 172, 191
iostat( ), 28, 90
isfork, 111
isvfork, 111
i_ic.ic_nlink, 159

K

kadb( ), 86, 131
kas, 76
kcondvar_t, 207
kerbd, 175
Kerberos authentication, 169, 175
kernel address space, 76, **77**
kernel coding examples, 189
  kernel.sh, 189
  mycall.c, 189
  sizes.c, 189
  ts_table (text file), 189
  tune.sh, 189
kernel data structures, 20-21
kernel mode, 4, 9-10, 12
kernel overview, 1-30
  /kernel directory, 18-21, **19**, 36
  /kernel/unix, 16, 18, 36
  /vmunix, 15, 36
  access time, 13
  adb debugger, 22, 23
  allocating stacks, 7-8
  application binary interface (ABI), 10
  architecture of Solaris kernel, 15-23
  block structure of kernel, 19-20, **19**
  callout queue, 28-29, **29**
  central processing unit (CPU) management, 3
  clock, 27
  clock handler, 28-29
  data segment, 6-7
  data structures of kernel, 20-21
  device drivers, 16, 18, 20
  disk drive management, 3
  dynamic linking, 16
  event handler, 12
  extensible linking format (ELF), 5-6
  file system management, 20
  forceload command, 18, 23
  hardware, 27-29
  heap, 7
  high water mark, 22
  holes, 8
  initialization of data, 6
  interprocess communication (IPC), 3, 20, 21
  interrupts, 12, 13, 27, **28**, 95-97
  kernel address space, 76, **77**
  kernel data structures, 20-21
  kernel mode, 4, 9-10, 12
  kernel stack, 8, **9**
  lightweight processes (LWP), 38, **38**, 39-41
  loadable modules in kernel, 16, **17**, 18, 36
  machine context, 27
  mapping objects, 20
  memory management, 3
  mmap( ), 20
  multiple access resource management, 3
  network management, 3
  preempts, 93, 95-97, 102, 120, 121
  private data, 6-7
  process address space, 5
  process creation, 20
  process status register (PSR), 27
  processes, 4
  profiling timer management, 3
  program counter, 27
  pseudo-devices, 20
  pseudo-file systems, 20
  registers, 27
  resource management, 3-13, **4**
  scheduling, 20
  segmentation violation (SIGSEGV), 6
  segments, 5
  semaphores, 21
  shared library model, 16, **17**
  shared resource management, 3
  signal handling, 20
  sleep mode, 13
  stack allocation, 7-8
  static core kernel program, 16, **17**, 18
  static linking, 16
  structure of kernel, 15-18
  swapping out stacks, 7
  synchronous vs. asynchronous kernel functions, 10-11
  syscall( ), 26-27
  system calls, 12-13, 19-20, 25-27
  system configuration file (/etc/system), 18, 21-23
  text segment, 6
  thread architecture, 36-37
  time-of-day clock management, 3
  traps, 25, 27
  tuning the kernel, 21
  uninitialized data, 7
  user context, 7
  user mode, 8-9, 11, 12
  user stack, 7-8
  variables, 21
  virtual address space, 4-6, **5**
  virtual memory (VM), 20
  wrappers, 25-26
kernel stack, 8, **9**
kernel.sh, 189, 200-201
KERNEL_BASE_DEBUG, 10
kill( ), 58
kilobyte (K), xvii
klwp_t, 47, 48-49, 50, 51, 108, 207
kmem_alloc( ), 114
kmem_free( ), 114
kmutex_t, 57, 207
Korn shell, xiii
krwlock_t, 207
ksema_t, 207
kthread_t, 47, 48-49, 50, 51, 52, 106, 108, 207
k_siginfo_t, 207
k_sigset_t, 47, 207

L

L1, 131
label_t, 207
latency concepts, 97, 129-130
ldstub, 43
LDSTVD, 53
LD_BIND_NOW, 131
least recently used (LRU) algorithm in pages, 80
libraries
  /usr/lib/libc.so, 19-20
  /usr/lib/libnsl.so, 19-20
  allocation of library space in thread programming, 37
  dynamic linking, 16
  library calls and thread architecture, 34
  MT-safe functions, 56
  shared library model, 16, **17**
  static linking, 16
  thread library, /usr/lib/libthread.so, 38, **38**, 39
library calls, 34, 38, 39
  deadlock, 55-56
lifetime of processes, 105-115
  allocation of kernel memory, 111
  atexit( ), 113
  cfork, 111
  child processes, 110, 113, 115
  chunks, file descriptors, 113, 140-141, **142**, 160
  classes for scheduling, 105-106, **106**
  cleanup of processes, 113-114
  close( ), 113
  copy-on-write (COW), 110
  creating a process, 110-112, **111**, 113-114, **114**
  error checking, 111
  exec( ), 105, 108, 114, 115
  execle( ), 114
  execve( ), 114
  exit( ), 105, 108, 112, 113
  family tree for processes, 113
  fork( ), 105, 108, 110, 111, 114, 115
  hand-crafted processes, 108
  init( ), 112
  initialization of process, 111
  interesting processes, 114
  lightweight processes (LWP), 111
  parent processes, 110, 113, 115
  pointers, 112

lifetime of processes, *continued*
  proc structure, 107-108
  process identification (PID), 111
  termination of processes, 112-113
  user area, 108
  vfork( ), 111
  virtual forks, 110
  wait( ), 105, 108, 112, 113-114, 115
  zombie processes, 113
lightweight processes (LWP), xvii, 38, **38**, 39-
  41, 108, 111
  aging, 40
  binding a thread, THR_BOUND, 41
  bound and unbound threads, 39-40, 41, 50
  creating LWPs, thr_create( ) and thr_setcon-
    currency( ), 41
  data structures, 47-48, **48**
  fields in the LWP data structure, 48
  lwp_ prefix, 47
  managing lightweight process (LWP) pool,
    40-41
  pointers, 48
  proc structure, 107-108
  signal handling, 40, 48
  SIGWAITING, 40, 41
  system calls, 47-48
  virtual CPU and lightweight processes
    (LWP), 39-40
links, 140
  dynamic linking, 16
  shared library model, 16, **17**
  static linking, 16
loadable modules in kernel, 16, **17**, 18, 36
local structures, 140
lockd, 170
locks, 118
  acquire operation, 42
  atomic operations, 42-43
  code locking, 56
  condition variables, 42, 44-45, 46, 50, 52
  cooperation of threads using locsk, 42
  data locking, 57
  deadlock, 55-56
  interruption of locks, 42-43
  ldstub used to prevent lock breakage, 43
  mutex locks, 42, 43, 46, 50, 52, 123
  mutex_tryenter( ) lock breaker, 42
  reader-writer locks, 42, 44, 46, 50, 52
  release operation, 42
  semaphores, 42, 43-44, 46, 50, 52
longjmp( ), 48
longlong_t, 207
looking up files, 139-140, 160-161
loopback file system (lofs), 144
loose affinity and CPU selection, 121
loosely coupled operating systems, 93-94
lotsfree variable in global memory management, 86-88, **87**
lrusage, 207
ls, 74
lseek( ), 141, 149
lwait, 125-126
lwp_ prefix, 47
lwp_curinfo, 48
lwp_cursig, 48
lwp_cv, 48
lwp_procp, 48
lwp_sigholdmask, 48
lwp_thread, 48

M

machine context, 27
macros, adb macros, 183-184
madvise( ), 84, 163, 164
MADV_RANDOM, 164
main( ), 7, 8, 33, 51, 117
malloc( ), 7, 21, 77, 114
mapping, 20, 74, 75, **75**, 84, 150, 151-152

master-slave multiprocessing, 94-95, **95**
matrix operations, 196-197
matrix1.c, 189, 196-198
maxcontig, 165, 201
MAXNAMLEN, 159
maxphys, 164, 201
MAXPID, 111
maxusers, 21
maxwait field, 125
max_nprocs, 21, 22
memctl( ), 64, 84, 97, 130
memory management, 3, 61-90
  address space, 64, **65**, 74, 75, 76, **77**, 108
  backing store memory, 67
  cache, 66, 68
  cache snooping, 68-69
  central processing unit (CPU), 67
  contexts, 66
  copy-on-write (COW), 79, 80, 110
  crash files, 83
  desperation swap, 89
  direct virtual memory access (DVMA), 74
  dynamic RAM (DRAM), 66
  fastscan rate, 88
  faulting into virtual memory, 83
  frames, 64
  global memory management, 85-90
  handspreadpages, 87
  hardware address translation (HAT), 76, **77**,
    83
  hardware architecture, 63-71
  hash table for pages, 80-81
  iostat( ), 90
  kernel address space, 76, **77**
  least recently used (LRU) algorithm in
    pages, 80
  lotsfree variable in global memory manage-
    ment, 86-88, **87**
  mapping, 74, 75, **75**, 84, 150, 151-152
  memory management unit (MMU), xvii, 50,
    64, 66, 67, 85
  minfree variable in global memory manage-
    ment, 86-88, **87**
  multiprocessor architecture, 68-69
  named objects, 74
  overlay managers, 64, 73
  overlays, 73
  page fault, 68
  page in and page out, 85-86
  page replacement, 86
  pages, 64, 66, 75, 80-81, **81**, 85-86
  performance levels, 69-70
  proc structure, 107-108
  public vs. private pages, 80
  random access memory (RAM), 73
  sar( ), 90
  scanrate, 87
  segments, 66, 75, 77-79, **79**
  shared memory, 36
  slowscan rate, 88
  static RAM (SRAM), 66
  swap space or anonymous memory, 73, 79,
    82, 152
  swapping control in global memory manage-
    ment, 88-90
  system architecture, 67-68, **67**
  system calls, 64
  system paging strategy in global memory
    management, 86-88, **87**
  two-handed clock algorithm, 86
  unnamed objects, 74
  virtual address cache (VAC), 67
  virtual memory (VM), 63-64, 73-84, 108,
    109
  vmstat( ), 90
  write-back cache, 68
  write-through cache, 68
memory management unit (MMU), xvii, 50,
  64, 66, 67, 85

minfree variable in memory management, 86-
  88, **87**
mixed-mode scheduling, 98
mkdir, 157
mkfiel, 190
mkfs( ), 147, 148, 164
mmap( ), xv, 20, 41, 64, 76, 84, 152, 161, 190
modes
  event handler, 12
  interrupts, 12, 13
  kernel mode, 9-10, 12
  mixed-mode scheduling, 98
  sleep mode, 13
  time-slice, 11, 98
  user mode, 8-9, 11, 12
modinfo, 23
modload( ), 18, 23
modules, loadable modules in kernel, 16, **17**,
  18, 36
modunload, 23
mount, 201
mountd, 170
msync( ), 64, 190
MT-safe functions, 56
multicasting, IP multicasting, 174
multiple access resource management, 3
multiprocessor architecture, xvii, 58-59, 68-69
multithreaded programming (*see also* thread
  architecture), xvii, 33-34
mutex locks, 42, 43, 46, 50, 52, 107-108, 123
mutex_enter( ), 43, 45
mutex_exit( ), 43, 45
mutex_lock( ), 43, 123
mutex_tryenter( ) lock breaker, 42
mutex_unlock( ), 43
mycall.c, 189, 201-203
m_, 52

N

name file system (namefs), 145
named objects, 74
ncallout, 29
ndd( ), 176, 177
network architecture, 3, 167-177
  application layer, 170
  autopush, 172
  data link layer, 169
  data link provider interface (DLPI), 173
  external data representation (XDR), 170
  ftp, 170
  IGMP protocol, 170
  international standard organization (ISO),
    169
  internet protocol (IP), 169, 170, 174
  Kerberos authentication, 169, 175
  layers of network, OSI/ISO, 169, **171**
  lockd, 170
  mountd, 170
  multicasting, IP multicasting, 174
  network layer, 169-170
  network parameter tuning, 169, 175-177
  open systems interconnect (OSI), 169
  physical layer, 169
  presentation layer, 170
  protocols, 170
  remote procedure calls (RPC), 169, 170, 172
  RIP protocol, 170
  session layer, 170
  smtp, 170
  statd, 170
  STREAMS, 171-172, **172**, **173**
  STREAMS-based device drivers, 169, 170
  telnet, 170
  transport independent remote procedure
    calls (TI-RPC), 173
  transport layer, 170
  transport layer interface (TLI), 169, 170, 174
  transport provider interface (TPI), 173

UDP.X.25 protocol, 170
upstream vs. downstream path of informa-
    tion, 171-172
network file system (nfs), xvii, 144
network layer, 169-170
newfs( ), 148, 164
NFPCHUNK, 140
nprocs, 21, 22
nroff, xiii
nswapped, 89, 90
NTSILE_SQ, 118
number of threads in multithread program-
    ming, 34, 37, 39

O
object oriented programming (OOP), xvii
Open Windows release 3 (OW3), xvii
open( ), 4, 36, 74, 135, 136, 139, 140, 141-142,
    149, 157, 161, **162**, 171
opendir( ), 158
operating systems, loosely and tightly cou-
    pled, 93-94
order of execution in multithread program-
    ming, 34, 37, 38, 39
overlay managers, 64, 73
overlays, 73

P
page fault, 68
pager, 108
pages, 64, 66, 75, 80-81, **81**, 85-86, 207
    fastscan rate, 88
    handspreadpages, 87
    hash table, 80-81
    least recently used (LRU) algorithm in
        pages, 80
    page replacement, 86
    public vs. private pages, 80
    scanrate, 87
    slowscan rate, 88
    swapping control in global memory manage-
        ment, 88-90
page_freelist, 80
page_hash, 81
param.c, 21
parent PID (PPID), xvii
parent processes, 110, 113, 115
pcb, 207
personal computer file system (pcfs), 143
pinning threads, 122
pipe( ), 36, 157
pipes, 36, 41, 135
pirec_t, 47
pointers
    direct and indirect, to inodes, 159
    lifetime of processes, 112
    lightweight processes (LWP), 48
    thread architecture, 49, 50
popen( ), 36
portable operating system interface (POSIX),
    xiii, xvii
preempt( ), 120, 121
preempts, 93, 95-97, 102, 120, 121
presentation layer, 170
priocntl( ), 98, 100, 117, 119, 127, 193
priority field, 125
priority of execution in thread architecture,
    50, 99, **101**, 102, 119-120, 121, 123-124
private data, 6-7
pri_t, 47
proc data structure, 51-52, **52**, 107-108, 207
proc( ), 152
process address space, 5
process file system (proc), 144
process identfication (PID), xvii, 111, 149-
    150, 191, 193
process management, 4, 12, 91-131

access time, 13
allocating kernel memory, 111
allocating stacks, 7-8
application binary interface (ABI), 10
asymmetric multiprocessing (ASMP), 93, 94-
    95
atexit( ), 113
blocking processes and threads, 38
bounded dispatch latency, 93, 97, 129-130
cfork, 111
child processes, 36, 110, 113, 115
chunks, file descriptors, 113, 140-141, **142**,
    160
classes for scheduling, 93, 100-101, 105-106,
    106
cleanup of processes, 113-114
close( ), 113
contexts, 66
copy-on-write (COW), 110
CPU selection in multiprocessor architec-
    ture, 121
creating a process, 110-112, **111**, 113-114,
    114
data segment, 6-7
dead (deathrow) threads, 101-102, 103
deterministic scheduling, 98
dispadmin( ), 123-127
dispatch latency, 97, 129-130
dispatch queues, 98, **99**, 102, 117-118, **118**,
    121
error checking, 111
event handler, 12
exec( ), 105, 108, 114, 115
execle( ), 114
execve( ), 114
exit( ), 105, 108, 112, 113
extensible linking format (ELF), 5-6
family tree for processes, 113
fork( ), 105, 108, 110, 111, 114, 115, 119
hand-crafted processes, 108
heap, 7
high water mark, 22
holes, 8
inheritance, priority inheritance, 123-124,
    129
init( ), 112
initialization of process, 6, 111
interactive scheduling class, 103
interesting processes, 114
interprocess communication (IPC), 10, 20,
    21, 41
interrupts, 12, 13, 95-97, 101, 102, 122-
    123
inversion, priority inversion, 123-124
kernel mode, 9-10, 12
kernel stack, 8, **9**
latency concepts, 97, 129-130
lifetime of processes, 105-115
lightweight processes (LWP), 38, **38**, 39-41,
    111
loose affinity and CPU selection, 121
loosely coupled operating systems, 93-94
lwait, 125-126
mapping, 41
mmap( ), 41
master-slave multiprocessing, 94-95, **95**
maxwait field, 125
mixed-mode scheduling, 98
mutex locks, 123
parent processes, 110, 113, 115
pinning threads, 122
pipes, 41
pointers, 112
preempts, 93, 95-97, 102, 120, 121
priocntl( ), 127
priority field, 125
priority of execution in thread architecture,
    50, 99, **101**, 102, 119-120, 121, 123-124
private data, 6-7

proc data structure, 51-52, **52**, 107-108
process address space, 5
process identification (PID), 111
process states, 101-102, **102**, 103, 117
processor affinity, 99
processor_bind( ), 127
p_online( ), 127
quantum field, 125
real-time processes, 93, 97, 129-131
real-time scheduling class, 100
runaway real-time processes, 131
scheduling concepts, 93-103, 117-127
segments, 5
sleep queues, 13, 99, 102, 103, 118-119
slpret field, 125
STREAMS requests, 98
swapping out stacks, 7
symmetric multiprocessing (SMP), 93, 94,
    95, **96**
synchronization of processes, 41
synchronous vs. asynchronous kernel func-
    tions, 10-11
system calls, 12-13, 36, 98
system scheduling class, 100
table-driven scheduling, 93
termination of processes, 112-113
text segment, 6
thread scheduling, 98-99, 119-120
threads vs., 34-35, 36-37, **37**
tightly coupled operating systems, 93-94
time-share scheduling class, 100, 103
time-slice, 98, 102, 120, 124
timeshare class dispatch tables, 125-127,
    204-205
tqexp field, 125
turnstiles, 99, 118-119
uninitialized data, 7
user area, 108
user context, 7
user mode, 8-9, 11, 12
user stack, 7-8
variables, 21
vfork( ), 111
virtual address space, 4-6, **5**
virtual forks, 110
wait( ), 105, 108, 112, 113-114, 115
zombie processes, 113
process states, 101-102, **102**, 103, 117
process status register (PSR), 27
processor affinity, 99
processor_bind( ), 50, 127
procfs.c, 189, 191-193
proc_t, 107
profiling timer management, 3
program counter, 27
protocols, 170
ps( ), 150
pseudo-devices, 20, 135
pseudo-file system, 20, 143, 144, 149
ptrace( ), 149
public vs. private pages, 80
p_as, 107, 111
p_brkbase, 107
p_brksize, 107
p_child, 107, 113
p_cred, 107
p_cstime, 107
p_cutime, 107
p_flag, 107
p_fltmask, 107
p_hash, 81
p_ignore, 107
p_link, 107
p_lock, 57
p_lwpblocked, 107
p_lwpcnt, 107
p_lwprcnt, 107
p_lwptotal, 107

p_mapping, 81
p_next, 81
p_nextofkin, 107
p_offset, 81
p_online( ), 127
p_parent, 107
p_ppid, 113
p_prev, 81
p_rpof_timerid, 107
p_ru, 112
p_sibling, 107, 113
p_sig, 107
p_siginfo, 107
p_sigmask, 107
p_stat, 107, 111, 113, 117
p_stime, 107
p_stksize, 107
p_tlist, 51
p_utime, 107
p_vnode, 81
p_vpnext, 81
p_vpprev, 81
p_zombcnt, 107

Q

quantum field, 125

R

random access memory (RAM), 73
read( ), 4, 12, 35, 36, 68, 149, 155, 158, 161-
    164, **163**, 165
read-ahead functions, 164-165
read-behind functions, 164
readdir( ), 158
reader-writer locks, 42, 44, 46, 50, 52
real-time processes, 93, 97, 129-131
  bounded dispatch latency, 129-130
  dispatch latency, 129-130
  latency concepts, 129-130
  runaway real-time processes, 131
  running, 130-131
real-time scheduling class, 100
recursive deadlock, 55
registers, 27
release operation, 42
remote file system (rfs), xvii, 144
remote procedure calls (RPC), xvii, 169, 170,
    173
resource management, 3-13, **4**
  access time, 13
  allocating stacks, 7-8
  application binary interface (ABI), 10
  central processing unit (CPU) management,
    3
  data segment, 6-7
  disk drive management, 3
  event handler, 12
  extensible linking format (ELF), 5-6
  heap, 7
  holes, 8
  initialization of data, 6
  interprocess communication management, 3
  interrupts, 12, 13
  kernel or system mode, 4, 9-10, 12
  kernel stack, 8, **9**
  memory management, 3
  multiple access, 3
  network management, 3
  private data, 6-7
  process address space, 5
  processes, 4
  profiling timer management, 3
  segmentation violation (SIGSEGV), 6
  segments, 5
  shared, 3
  sleep mode, 13
  stack allocation, 7-8

swapping out stacks, 7
synchronous vs. asynchronous kernel func-
    tions, 10-11
system calls, 12-13
text segment, 6
time-of-day clock, 3
uninitialized data, 7
user context, 7
user mode, 8-9, 11, 12
user stack, 7-8
virtual address space, 4-6, **5**
RIP protocol, 170
rootvfs, 138
rtproc_t, 106
rt_cput_choose( ), 121
rt_dptbl( ), 124
rt_preempt( ), 120
runaway real-time processes, 131
runin, 89, 90
runout, 89, 90
rw_, 52
rw_lock, 119
rw_rdlock( ), 44
rw_unlock( ), 44
rw_wrlock( ), 44

S

sar( ), 90
scanrate, 87
sched, 89, 108
scheduling concepts, 20, 93-103, 117-127
  asymmetric multiprocessing (ASMP), 93, 94-
    95
  bounded dispatch latency, 93, 97, 129-130
  classes for scheduling, 93, 100-101, 105-106,
    106
  CPU selection in multiprocessor architec-
    ture, 121
  dead (deathrow) threads, 101-102, 103
  deterministic scheduling, 98
  dispadmin( ), 123-127
  dispatch latency, 97, 129-130
  dispatch queues, 98, **99**, 102, 117-118, **118**,
    121
  fork( ), 119
  inheritance, priority, 123-124, 129
  interactive scheduling class, 103
  interrupts, 95-97, 101, 102, 122-123
  inversion, priority, 123-124
  latency concepts, 97, 129-130
  loose affinity and CPU selection, 121
  loosely coupled operating systems, 93-94
  lwait, 125-126
  master-slave multiprocessing, 94-95, **95**
  maxwait field, 125
  mixed-mode scheduling, 98
  mutex locks, 123
  pinning threads, 122
  preempts, 93, 95-97, 102, 120, 121
  priocntl( ), 127
  priority field, 125
  priority of execution, 50, 99, **101**, 102, 119-
    120, 121, 123-124
  process states, 101-102, **102**, 103, 117
  processor affinity, 99
  processor_bind( ), 127
  p_online( ), 127
  quantum field, 125
  real-time processes, 93, 97, 129-131
  real-time scheduling class, 100
  runaway real-time processes, 131
  sleep queues, 99, 102, 103, 118-119
  slpret field, 125
  STREAMS requests, 98
  symmetric multiprocessing (SMP), 93, 94,
    95, **96**
  system calls, 98
  system scheduling class, 100

table-driven scheduling, 93
thread scheduling, 98-99, 119-120
tightly coupled operating systems, 93-94
time-share scheduling class, 100, 103
time-slice, 98, 102, 120, 124
timeshare class dispatch tables, 125-127,
    204-205
tqexp field, 125
turnstiles, 99, 118-119
sclass_t, 105, 208
seekdir( ), 158
seg, 208
seg->s_ops->fault( ), 83
seg->s_ops->getprot( ), 83
segdev, 78
segdev_data, 78
segkmem, 78
segkmem_data, 78
segkp, 78
segkp_data, 78
segmap, 78, 163
segmap_data, 78
segmentation violation (SIGSEGV), 6
segments, 5, 66, 75, 77-79, **79**
  data segment, 6-7
  extensible linking formt (ELF), 5-6
  heap, 7
  initialization of data, 6
  private data, 6-7
  segmentation violation (SIGSEGV), 6
  text segment, 6
  types of segments, 78-79
  uninitialized data, 7
segvn, 78, 83, 163
segvn_data, 78, 208
semaphores, 21, 42, 43-44, 46, 50, 52
sema_, 52
sema_p( ), 43, 52
sema_post( ), 44
sema_v( ), 43, 52
sema_wait( ), 44
semctl( ), 44
semget( ), 44, 198
semop( ), 44
session layer, 170
setclassID( ), 193
SEXECED, 108
shared library model, 16, **17**
shared resource management, 3
  thread architecture, 34, 56-57
shells, xiii
shmc.c, 198
shmget( ), 198
shmp.c, 198
shm_at( ), 4, 36
shm_get( ), 36
SIDL, 107
sigaction( ), 58
sigaltstack( ), 58
SIGBUS, 57
SIGCLD, 113
SIGFPE, 57
SIGINT, 11, 58, 199
SIGIO, 58
SIGKILL, 11, 131
signal handling, 20
  lightweight processes (LWP), 40
  signal masks, 58
  thread architecture, 33, 40, 48, 50, 57-58
SIGSEGV, 6, 57
sigwait( ), 58
SIGWAITING, 40, 41
SIG_DFL, 58
SIG_IGN, 58
sizes program, 208
sizes.c, 189, 203-204
SJCTL, 108
SKILLCL, 107, 108
SKILLED, 108

sleep mode, 13
sleep queues, 99, 102, 103, 118-119
sleep( ), 44-45, 103
sleepq_t, 118
SLOAD, 107, 108
SLOCK, 108
slowscan rate, 88
slpret field, 125
smtp, 170
SNOWAIT, 108
SNWAKE, 108
socket( ), 4
Solaris network architecture (*see* network architecture)
SONPROC, 107
SOWEUPC, 108
SPARCstation2, 208
SPARCworks 3, 180, 190
SPASYNC, 108
spl( ), 59
splr( ), 59
SPREXEC, 107, 108
SPRFORK, 107, 108
SPROCTR, 107, 108
SRUN, 107, 117
SRUNLCL, 108
SSLEEP, 107
SSTOP, 107
SSYS, 107
stacks
  allocating stacks, 7-8
  holes, 8
  kernel mode, 9-10, 12
  kernel stack, 8, **9**
  loadable modules in kernel, 16, **17**, 18, 36
  static core kernel program, 16, **17**, 18
  swapping out stacks, 7
  trace, stack trace, xv
  user context, 7
  user mode, 8-9, 11, 12
  user stack, 7-8
stack_t, 208
statd, 170
states, process states, 101-102, **102**, 103, 117
static core kernel program, 16, **17**, 18
static linking, 16
static RAM (SRAM), 66
STRC, 107
STREAMS, 98, 169, 170, 171-172, **172**, **173**
struct csum, cg, 156
struct proc, 21
struct seg, 77
ST_OSYSCALL, 26
ST_SYSCALL, 26
SULOAD, 108
Suninstall program, 154
superblocks, 135, 145, 155-156
SVFDONE, 108
SVFORK, 108
SWAITSIG, 108
swap space or anonymous memory, 73, 79, 82, 152
swapping, 7, 28, 144
  desperation swap, 89
  global memory management, 88-90
  swap partitions, 153-154
  virtual swap, 149, 152-153, **153**
swap_l, 82
symmetric multiprocessing (SMP), 93, 94, 95, **96**
synchronization
  data structures, 52-53, **53**
  processes, 41
  threads, 41-46, 50, 56
synchronous kernel functions, 10-11, **11**
synchronous vs. asynchronous signals or threads, 57-58
syscall( ), 26-27, 202
sysent, 26

system architecture, 67-68, **67**
system calls, 12-13, 19-20, 25-27, 36, 47-48, 56
  deadlock, 55-56
  scheduling concepts, 98
  syscall( ), 26-27
  system call numbers, 26-27
  traps, 25
  virtual memory (VM), 64
  wrappers, 25-26
system configuration file (/etc/system), 18, 21-23
system open file table (SOFT), 141
system or kernel mode, 4
system scheduling class, 100
System V interface description (SVID), xiii, xvii
sys_preempt( ), 120
SZOMB, 107
s_as, 77
s_base, 77
s_data, 78
s_next, 77
s_ops, 78, 83
s_prev, 77
s_size, 77

T

table-driven scheduling, 93
table.new, 204
telldir( ), 158
telnet, 170
temporary file system (tmpfs), 144
text formatting, xiii
text segment, 6
thread architecture, 31-59, 108
  acquire operation, 42
  aging of lightweight processes (LWP), 40
  allocation of library space, 37
  atomic operations, 42-43
  binding a thread, THR_BOUND, 41
  blocking processes and threads, 38
  bound and unbound threads, 39-40, 41, 50, 58
  child processes, 36
  code locking, 56
  communication between threads, library calls, 34
  concepts of thread architecture, 33-46
  condition variables, 42, 44-45, 46, 50, 52
  cooperation of threads using locsk, 42
  cpu structure, 50-51
  creating lightweight processes (LWP), 41
  creation of threads, thr_create( ), 37-38, 51, 58
  data structures, lightweight processes (LWP), 47-48, **48**
  data structures, thread data structure, 48-50, **49**
  dead (deathrow) threads, 101-102, 103
  deadlock, 55-56
  dispatch queues, 49
  efficiency of thread programming, 35
  exec( ), 41
  exit( ), 33, 34, 58
  fork( ), 33, 35-36, 41, 42, 59
  freelists, 49
  functions, 56
  hardware, multiprocessors, 35
  identity of threads in multithread programming, 34, 37, 39
  implementation of thread architecture, 47-54
  incorrect use of threads, 35
  independence of threads in multithread programming, 34, 37, 39
  inheritance, priority inheritance, 123-124, 129
  interruption of locks, 42-43

interrupts, 101, 102
inversion, priority inversion, 123-124
invisibility of threads in multithread programming, 34, 37, 39
kernel operation and design, 36-37
ldstub used to prevent lock breakage, 43
LDSTVD, 53
library calls, 34, 38, 39
lightweight processes (LWP), 38, **38**, 39-41, 108
lightweight-process (LWP) pool management, 40-41
locking data, 42, 43, 44, 46, 50, 52, 56-57, 123
lwp_ prefix, 47
main( ), 33, 51
memory management unit (MMU), 50
MT-safe functions, 56
multiprocessor use, 58-59
multithreaded programming, 33-34, 55-59
mutex locks, 42, 43, 46, 50, 52, 123
mutex_tryenter( ) lock breaker, 42
number of threads, 34, 37, 39
order of execution, 34, 37, 38, 39
pinning threads, 122
pointers, 49, 50
preempts, 97
priority of execution, 50, 99, **101**, 102, 119-120, 121, 123-124
proc data structure, 51-52, **52**, 107-108
process management and scheduling concepts, 98-99
processes vs. threads, 34-35, 36-37, **37**
program structure, 35
read( ), 35
reader-writer locks, 42, 44, 46, 50, 52
release operation, 42
roadmap of thread data structures, 51-52, **52**
scheduling classes, 49
scheduling concepts, 119-120
semaphores, 42, 43-44, 46, 50, 52
sharing data, 34, 56-57
signal handling, 33, 40, 48, 50, 57-58
signal masks, 58
SIGWAITING, 40, 41
sleep queues, 99, 102, 103, 118-119
STREAMS requests, 98
synchronization of data structures, 52-53, **53**
synchronization of threads, 41-46, 50, 56
synchronous vs. asynchronous signals or threads, 57-58
system calls, 47-48, 56
theory of operation, 33-46
thread library, /usr/lib/libthread.so, 38, **38**, 39
throughput efficiency, 35
time-slice, 98, 102, 120, 124
turnstiles, 49, 99, 118-119
t_ prefix, 47
t_link, 49
use of threads, 34-35
virtual CPU and lightweight processes (LWP), 39-40
write( ), 35
writing threaded code, 56-57
thread coding examples
  file1.c, 189
  matrix1.c, 189
  thr_sell.c, 189
  thr_sig.c, 189
thread library, /usr/lib/libthread.so, 38, **38**, 39
thread_deathrow, 101-102
throughput efficiency in thread architecture, 35
THR_BOUND, 41, 58
thr_create( ), 37-38, 51, 58, 117
thr_kill( ), 58
thr_sell.c, 189, 198
thr_setsigmask( ), 58
thr_sig.c, 189, 199
thr_sigsetmask( ), 199

tightly coupled operating systems, 93-94
time-of-day clock management, 3
time-share scheduling class, 100, 103
time-slice, 11, 98, 102, 120, 124
timeout( ), 28
timeshare class dispatch tables, 125-127, 204-205
timing management, proc structure, 107-108
tqexp field, 125
trace( ), 150
translucent file system, 143
transmission control protocol (TCP), xvii
transparency of file system management, 135
transport independent remote procedure calls (TI-RPC), xvii, 173
transport layer, 170
transport layer interface (TLI), 169, 170, 174
transport provider interface (TPI), 173
traps, 25, 27
troff, xiii
truss( ), 150
tsproc_t, 106
ts_cpu_choose( ), 121
ts_dptbl( ), 124
ts_init( ), 106
ts_maxwait, 121
TS_ONPROC, 117
ts_preempt( ), 120
TS_RUN, 117
TS_SLEEP, 117
ts_table (text file), 189
ts_timeleft, 119
tune.sh, 189, 201
tunefs( ), 164, 165, 201
tune_t_gpgslo, 89, 90
tuning the kernel, 21
turnstiles, 99, 118-119
turnstile_id_t, 52, 119, 208
two-handed clock algorithm, 86
typedef, 107
t_ prefix, 47
t_back, 50
t_bind_cpu, 50
t_bound_cpu, 50
t_cldata, 49, 112
t_epri, 50, 123
t_forw, 50
t_hold, 50
t_link, 49, 118
t_lwp, 50
t_mmuctx, 50
t_next, 50
t_open( ), 4
t_prev, 50
t_pri, 50
t_prioinv, 50
t_sig, 50
t_sobj_type, 50
t_state, 117
t_ts, 50

U

ucontext, 208

UDP.X.25 protocol, 170
ufs_dirlook( ), 161
ufs_getpage( ), 162, 163, 164
ufs_lookup( ), 161
ufs_ninode, 21
ufs_putpage( ), 162, 163, 164
ufs_rdwr( ), 161
uf_next, 140
umount, 201
uninitialized data, 7
UNIX development, xiii
UNIX file system (ufs), xvii, 143
unmmap( ), 86
unnamed objects, 74
untimeout( ), 28
upstream vs. downstream path of information, 171-172
user, 208
user area, process management, 108
user context, 7
user datagram protocol (UDP), xvii
user identification (UID), xvii
user interface for UNIX, xiii
user mode, 8-9, 11, 12
user/include/sys, 21
uucp, xiii
u_file, 140

V

variables, 21
    condition variables, 42, 44-45
    lotsfree variable in global memory management, 86-88, **87**
    minfree variable in memory management, 86-88, **87**
    proc structure, 107-108
    stack allocation, 7-8
vfork( ), 110, 111
vfs (virtual file system) structures, 135, 137-139, **138**, **139**, 143, 160
vfs_data, 138
vfs_next, 138
vfs_op, 137
vfs_root( ), 139
vfs_t, 208
vfs_vnodecovered, 138
vi, 9, 80
virtual address cache (VAC), xvii, 67, 85
virtual CPU and lightweight processes (LWP), 39-40
virtual forks, 110
virtual memory (VM), xvii, 7, 20, 63-64, 73-84, **82**, 108, **109**, 135
    address space, 64, **65**, 74, 75, 76, **77**, 108
    cache, 66, 68
    cache snooping, 68-69
    concepts, terms, definitions, 73-75
    contexts, 66
    copy-on-write (COW), 79, 80, 110
    data structures, 81-83, **82**
    direct virtual memory access (DVMA), 8, 74
    dynamic RAM (DRAM), 66

faulting into virtual memory, 83
frames, 64
hardware address translation (HAT), 76, **77**, 83
hash table for pages, 80-81
kernel address space, 76, **77**
least recently used (LRU) algorithm in pages, 80
mapping, 74, 75, **75**, 84, 150, 151-152
memory management unit (MMU), 64, 66
named objects, 74
overlay managers, 64, 73
overlays, 73
page fault, 68
pages, 64, 66, 64, 75, 80-81, **81**
public vs. private pages, 80
random access memory (RAM), 73
roadmap of virtual memory, 81-83, **82**
segments, 66, 75, 77-79, **79**
static RAM (SRAM), 66
swap space or anonymous memory, 73, 79, 82, 152
system calls, 64
unnamed objects, 74
vfs (virtual file system) structures, 135, 137-139, **138**, **139**, 143, 160
vnodes (virtual node), 135-137, **136**, 160
write-back cache, 68
write-through cache, 68
virtual swap, 143, 149, 152-154, **153**
vmstat, 10, 28
virtual address space, 4-6, **5**
vmstat( ), 90
vnodes (virtual node), 135-137, **136**, 160
vnode_t, 208
volume table of contents (VTOC), 148-149, 154
vondeops_t, 208
VOP_ACCESS, 141
vop_lookup( ), 139
VOP_OPEN, 141
vop_read, 161
vop_write, 161
v_data, 136-137
v_op, 136, 161
v_vfsmountedhere, 139, 140
v_vfsp, 139, 140

W

wait( ), 101, 105, 108, 112, 113-114, 115
waiters field, 52
waitid( ), 113
wakeup( ), 44-45, 103
warranty for companion disk, 225
wrappers, 25-26
write( ), 35, 36, 68, 149, 155, 158, 161-164, **163**, 165
write-back cache, 68
write-through cache, 68

Z

zombie processes, 113